Living Hope

Living Hope

*A Practical Theology of Hope
for the Dying*

Russell G. Herbert

✚ EPWORTH

British Library Cataloguing in Publication data

A catalogue record for this book is available
from the British Library

0 7162 0613 7/978 0 7162 0613 2

First published in 2006
by Epworth Press
4 John Wesley Road
Werrington
Peterborough PE4 6ZP

Printed and bound in Great Britain by
William Clowes Ltd, Beccles, Suffolk

Contents

To Tamara, Charlie, Rosalie and Eleanor

Preface

Primarily, I have not set out to write a book about dying or caring for the dying – volumes that deal with such subjects are plentiful already. Rather, this book looks at hope: what it is, what it means, how it develops and how we might cultivate such development. Palliative care provides the context for this discussion here, and that is largely because it was through the experience of being a Christian minister in situations of death and dying that I initially became acutely aware of the need to understand the nature of hope more fully. But if we can grasp hope in the face of death, we lay hold of the very life force of all authentically Christian ministry. Thus it is my hope that this book will not only inspire and enable those whose interest is in caring for the dying, but indeed anyone who longs to be better equipped for the task of nurturing hope in others. The concluding chapter seeks to make some of the wider implications of a 'ministry of hope' explicit, although I imagine that readers will naturally discern the broader significance of the discussion as it unfolds.

This book started out as a doctoral thesis. The rewritten version here aims to retain something of the depth of that work but in a way that engages a wider audience. I have thus left out some of the more detailed analysis of my original research, focusing instead on the sort of things that ministers and carers are likely to encounter as we strive to cultivate hope in pastoral practice. We will follow the stories of a number of men and women in their struggle to find hope. The intention is to offer a practical theology of hope that really is *practical*.

As I reflect on the whole process of writing a PhD and subsequently reworking a thesis into its present form for publication, I am reminded of the personal struggle to sustain hope. These things would never have happened were it not for those who have supported, encouraged and inspired me over these last few years. I wish to express my sincerest gratitude to the Reverend Professor Paul Ballard for his constant wisdom, support and encouragement from day one. Thanks must also go to the people of Dorothy House Hospice, Bradford-on-Avon, for the practical experience in which I was privileged to share. I am especially thankful to Karen Wilkinson for our conversations in the early stages of my encounters with palliative nursing. My friends in the Ringsash Methodist Church Circuit in Devon deserve a special acknowledgement. It has been an honour to serve among them in these early years of my ministry.

I wish to thank my family. Words cannot express my gratitude to Mum and Dad, and also Rod and Val, for their encouragement and support. Most of all, I thank Tamara, Charlie, Rosalie and Eleanor for putting up with a book-obsessed husband and father over these last few years. I thank God for them and for the source of hope they are to me. It is to them that this book is dedicated.

R.G.H.
Morchard Bishop, Devon,
March 2006

Introduction:
The Importance of Hope

Always be ready to make your defence to anyone who demands from you an accounting for the hope that is in you.

1 Peter 3.15

What is your hope?

Any Christian striving to give an 'accounting' of their hope needs first to reflect upon just what that hope is. Those who care for the dying would seek not only to 'explain' their hope, but to *give* it in some real way.

What, then, is our Christian hope, and how might it be expressed? How might we go about the task of *living hope*?

The need for hope: pastoral encounters

The Christian pastoral carer does not have to look far to be reminded of the need for hope. The following scenarios will probably strike more than one chord of familiarity. They illustrate the multi-layered concern for a hope that is real where the experience of dying can threaten to engulf people with utter despair.

Hope and helplessness: the need for confidence in pastoral care

Sarah, a young curate, is on her way to the local hospice to visit one of her parishioners. As she pulls into the car park she becomes acutely aware of her uncertainty over the situation she is about to enter. She feels nervous and insecure. She is visiting because she wants to be of help, but she has been told that the person she is visiting is probably in the final week of his life and she wonders just what sort of help she can provide. As she walks towards the building, each step takes her deeper into an indescribable sense of helplessness. What will she say when she arrives? What sort of prayer should she pray? How can her presence be of any value at all when death is so near? Sarah longs to be of real practical help to this dying person, yet in her search for the right things to say and do she feels an overwhelming sense of personal inadequacy.

Sarah is aware that pastoral care must never be driven simply by the urge to satisfy a personal desire to 'feel useful'. Such an approach would be seriously lacking in Christian integrity, and in any case it is usually only a matter of time before others sense whether an individual is expressing care that is motivated by genuine compassion or is just trying to feed an appetite for feeling good about themselves. But Sarah is not merely pursuing her own personal agenda. She just wants a deeper confidence in her choice of words and actions – some assurance that they could make a positive difference.

How might a pastoral carer like Sarah approach their ministry to the dying with confidence? Sarah identifies *hope* as the very thing that she longs to bring to others. But how might she be assured that she really is nurturing hope through the things she says and does? This book will explore both the nature of Christian hope and how it might be fostered. We will examine what we hope for and how we might share it as a *living hope*.

Despair in the Church: examining our hope

Tom, 63, is a lifelong member of his local church. In that time he has served as steward, organist, and taught in the Sunday school. He rarely misses a service or church meeting. Though he occasionally frustrates others through his obstinate resistance to change in church life, he is respected for his faithfulness and reliability.

A few weeks ago Tom felt acute chest pains. His wife Jenny persuaded him to go and see his GP. He was quickly sent to hospital for tests and following an electrocardiogram (ECG) Tom was informed that he has cardiovascular disease and is at risk of having a major heart attack. He was told that he must immediately take appropriate medication and radically review his diet. No mention has been made of his life expectancy, but since receiving his diagnosis Tom has become very withdrawn. Jenny is desperate to talk about it but every time she raises it with Tom he either changes the subject or goes silent. Furthermore, Tom has insisted that Jenny must not tell anyone else about his condition.

Eventually Jenny calls her minister and asks him to visit as soon as possible. Jenny tells Tom what she has done. He briefly loses his temper and then retreats into a sulk. When the minister arrives, Jenny tells him everything while Tom sits in silence. Attempting to draw Tom into the conversation, the minister asks a few open-ended questions about how Tom might be feeling. Each question is answered by Jenny, who before long ends up doing all the talking on Tom's behalf.

An opportunity for the minister to converse directly with Tom emerges when Jenny leaves the room to make tea. After a few moments of silence Tom bursts into tears. He shares with the minister how he feels completely shocked by his news and that he is terrified by the thought of dying. He explains that he has always had a Christian faith, but right now feels so totally alone, distanced from God and from other people. He describes himself as 'spiritually frozen' – unable to pray or even think about God without feeling utter despair. When Jenny eventually returns to the room she also is in tears. She puts her arm around Tom, turns to the minister and asks, 'We will see one another again in the next life, won't we?'

It is easy to assume that because a person has been immersed in church life for years, listened to thousands of sermons and familiarized themselves with all the language of worship and prayer, they must have grown to a spiritual maturity that is so robust and integrated that they can face anything. However, a lifetime of exposure to church culture is itself no guarantee that the Christian gospel of hope will have taken root in a person's being in any meaningful way at all. Tom is someone who knows very well that the Christian message is all about eternal life – indeed, he could quote many scripture verses to demonstrate this. But he has never appropriated these things personally – he has not 'owned' Christian hope. To Tom the biblical passages and verses from popular hymnody which express hope of life everlasting can sound hackneyed. For all his familiarity with them, they have not engaged with his personal struggle and as such appear to him as glib reassurances and pious clichés.

A major challenge facing pastoral carers is to find ways of enabling people like Tom to explore the hope that the Christian gospel presents so that it might become 'real' and meaningful to them. Both Tom and Jenny have a sense of what they *want* to hope for – namely eternal life and some kind of reunion beyond death. But the substance of the Christian hope has never really been unpacked and examined by them in a personal way. It has not become a *living hope*. That is the concern of this book.

Hope and healing

Jane is in her late fifties. She is a great believer in the power of prayer. Several years ago she experienced the healing of a benign but nevertheless painful tumour following prayer with the laying-on of hands. Subsequently Jane sought to develop a healing ministry within her local church. She helped to establish a group that meets weekly to pray specifically for the sick, as well as a monthly service in which, following the sharing of communion, prayer for healing and anointing with oil is offered. As a result of Jane's own experience of healing, and the vision and initiatives born out of it, healing has become an important theme in the congregation's understanding of its life and ministry.

Six months ago Jane discovered a lump under her breast. Tests revealed that it was cancer. A mastectomy and an aggressive course of chemotherapy followed, but it soon became apparent that cancer was present throughout her body.

Jane has gone forward for prayer with the laying-on of hands in several church healing services. The prayer group prays for her every week with tremendous fervour. She assures everyone she meets of her faith that God has healed her before and will do so again. Eventually Jane is admitted to a hospice. One day, the same friend who prayed for Jane when she experienced healing several years ago visits her. Quoting Mark 16.18, she tells Jane that Jesus promises that those who believe 'will lay their hands on the sick and they will recover'. With Jane's permission, she then prays for Jane, 'claiming healing' in the name of Jesus. Two hours after her friend leaves, Jane dies.

Was it appropriate for Jane's friend to pray for her in this way? On the one hand, Jane's previous experience of healing was a genuine source of hope for her. To pray for further healing reminded Jane of the power of prayer that had strengthened and sustained her in the past. Such prayer was the natural expression of a faith that was real, vibrant and alive. On the other hand, ought her friend to have given greater emphasis to preparing Jane for death? Was it in any way misleading to nurture a hope for physical recovery when death was so near?

If the ministry of healing is to be approached holistically, it must be able to embrace the reality of death and dying. This in no way undermines a commitment to praying for healing. Rather, it challenges approaches to prayer that would define healing exclusively in terms of *cure*. Such constrictive understandings need to be refocused on the gospel of *resurrection*. It is, after all, the cross and resurrection to which all of Jesus' miracles point in the New Testament.[1] Christian faith is resurrection faith. This should be the foundation of any prayer for healing, and it is the basis upon which pastoral carers can seek to enable death with dignity.

Resurrection will be a central theme in this book. We will explore the dynamics of what it means to hope for resurrection. How might someone like Jane be encouraged to hope in a way that builds on a confidence in God's power and promise to heal, without shying away from the reality that death comes to us all at some point? How might the ministries of healing and palliative care be united in the same *living hope*?

False hopes and denial? The quest for a 'realistic' hope

David, 47, has worked in banking since leaving school. For many years his ambition has been to set up his own business as an antiques dealer. Two months ago he tendered his resignation at the bank, having bought a small shop. His plan was to spend the next three months doing minor alterations to the premises before opening for business. However, just a few weeks before he embarks on this career change, David discovers that he has cancer.

Following a consultation at the hospital, David begins a course of radiotherapy. No sooner has he started this does David talk incessantly about his intention to 'get back to the shop when this is all sorted out'. Despite his determination, further scans at the end of David's course of therapy indicate that the cancer is still growing. More aggressive treatment follows. David remains insistent that he will soon be returning to work.

David's family has a rather different outlook. They feel sure that David has less than a year to live, but dare not challenge his thinking through fear of undermining what they describe as his 'positive attitude'. One day, during a conversation with his GP, David is told that it is unlikely that any further treatment will cure him. For the first time, he breaks down in tears. When he returns home he becomes very withdrawn and for the next few days says very little to anyone.

The silence is eventually broken when David announces to his wife that he wishes to make an appointment to see a local vicar. This surprises his wife, since David has not attended church in years. David explains that he wishes to get things in order for his funeral. Though a little perplexed by this, his wife feels some relief that David at least seems to be acknowledging the seriousness of his illness. However, it is not long before David seems to want to talk about nothing *other* than his funeral arrangements. His previous interest in the shop, as well as his longstanding fascination with reading about antiques on the internet and in books, is abandoned. By the time David and his wife go to see the vicar, David has convinced himself that he has only a couple of weeks left to live, and is panicking that there will be little time left to prepare for his funeral.

David's story illustrates how hoping can be the very thing that keeps a person going. As long as he was able to sustain his expectation of setting up his antiques business, David had an interest in life. Yet his family felt awkward about this. They sensed that David's hope lacked a reality base, that he was effectively denying his illness. In the event, they did not need to confront him over this concern, as it was of his own accord that he came to recognize that he was dying. But here is another 'unrealistic' response in David. If one form of denial is the non-acceptance that death is near, another is the refusal to see that there may still be living to be done. David displays a fatalistic resignation to death. This shows how hopelessness, as well as hope, can be unrealistic.

The experience of *living* hope is essentially a process. The person who hopes is one who is moving forward, living and growing, as well as dying. It is a process of discovery and negotiation, where some aspirations are attained as others are laid to rest. David illustrates this organic nature of hoping, which can be a painful struggle at times. An important question for pastoral carers is, *what sort of things should we look for when striving to discern what is 'realistic' in the hope we seek to nurture?* Our exploration of *living hope* will consider this concern for a reality base, as well as what might be meant by the term 'realistic' itself.

'I'm not a Christian but I know what I like' – living hope in a postmodern world

Sue serves as a part-time voluntary lay assistant on the chaplaincy team at her local hospital. One day, having just visited and prayed with a patient who requested to see her, Sue is beckoned over by a young woman on the other side of the ward. She introduces herself as Angela, and tells Sue that she overheard her praying. She asks if Sue could pray for her also.

It soon becomes apparent that Angela is very anxious. She is due to have surgery later on that day. Angela is deeply worried that she may not regain consciousness after the operation. Sue asks if she has a faith. Angela replies, 'Oh no, I'm not at all religious. I went to church as a kid, but it was all very boring.' A conversation develops in which Angela describes Christianity as 'irrelevant to today's world'. She tells Sue that she believes in 'something spiritual', but is not sure what that 'something' is. For all her apparent scepticism, Angela nevertheless wants Sue to pray for her. She grasps Sue's hand and with a look of desperation on her face says, 'I don't know what to ask you to pray for, but just say something for me will you?'

In some ways Angela reflects what might be described as the postmodern context of contemporary western culture. The term 'postmodern' is perhaps often used more readily than it is understood. Because of the breadth of its application, it has a tendency to lack analytical clarity at times. Indeed, it is a term that can be used to say 'something about everything', resulting in saying 'nothing about anything'. Nevertheless, the term does denote certain cultural trends that cannot be ignored by a book that seeks to identify ways in which pastoral carers can foster a *living hope* in people who find themselves in despair in today's world.

First, Angela is quite dismissive of Christianity as a

'religion'. A defining feature of postmodernity is its 'incredulity towards metanarratives'.[2] In other words, any kind of 'grand story' that is claimed as authoritative and ultimately true is regarded with suspicion. It is considered that metanarratives denote institutions, formalism, organized religion and authoritarianism, which all produce dominance, limit choice and restrict freedom. With this suspicion goes a predisposition towards individualism. The postmodern mind stresses the importance of personal choice from the plurality of options available. Special value is given to pragmatism in the making of choice: 'Does this work for me?' Something of this can be seen in Angela. Though she would discard Christianity as irrelevant, she knows that she desires 'something' from this person she has overheard praying, and that she wants her to 'do' some prayer 'for' her.

Angela's request for prayer from Sue highlights another important hallmark of postmodernity: personal spirituality. While church attendance statistics suggest a contemporary decline in commitment to 'organized Christianity', the surge of interest in New Age and varied forms of eastern mysticism evince an intrigue with the spiritual.[3] Again, this is commonly approached in a highly individualistic, privatized way. Postmodern culture regards spirituality, like everything else, through consumerist eyes: the individual must be free to pick and choose from the plurality of spiritual traditions that are out there to be 'had', and so tailor something that best accords with personal taste.

Many who we meet will be people like Angela – people reluctant to identify themselves with 'Christian' hope, but who long to find a way of hoping in and for 'something' that is transcendent. How might Christian pastoral carers go about the task of *living hope* in a spiritually thirsty world?

In search of a ministry of hope

The questions we are raising are utterly practical and profoundly theological. They can be summarized in the following
way: *what is Christian hope, and how might we nurture it in
others?*

It was not long after I began my training as a Christian
minister that I found myself focused on these questions. As I
reflected upon them with growing intensity I sensed a twofold
curiosity. On the one hand, what might those who work with
the dying say – the doctors, nurses and hospice workers? After
all, these are the palliative care 'professionals', whose insights
would come out of their own 'hands-on' experience of working
with life and death. Yet as a minister, or more fundamentally
as a Christian, I believe that life and death points us beyond
human science to something more ultimate: God. Thus I
resolved that whatever may be learned from nursing and palliative health care, whether anecdotal or research-based findings,
it must all be brought into a critical conversation with the voice
of Christian theology. Unless my practice is theologically
grounded, I am left wondering what makes my work *ministry*.
The quest then, is for a *practical theology of hope for the dying*.

The importance of this quest is highlighted by three practical
theologians in particular, who in different ways have each
wrestled with similar concerns as those raised here, drawing
from both psychology and theology. The first is Donald Capps,
whose *Agents of Hope: A Pastoral Psychology* takes up the
issue of confidence in pastoral care. This is the very concern of
Sarah, above, in her longing for some reassurance that her
ministry might make a positive difference to someone who is
dying. While Capps himself does not explore death and dying at
length, he does argue that it is in 'the role that pastors play as
agents of hope' that Christian pastoral care in general is distinguished from other 'helping professions'. He writes, 'Where
other professionals may offer hope as a byproduct of what they
do, the offer of hope is central to what pastors do. Oftentimes,
it is all that they can offer.'[4] Perhaps because hope is essentially

intangible it can be difficult to grasp some kind of concrete reassurance that it really has been offered and that a positive difference has been made in the lives of others who would otherwise be in despair.

A second book to highlight the importance of hope is Bruce Rumbold's *Helplessness and Hope: Pastoral Care in Terminal Illness*. This also engages with the feeling of inadequacy that threatens to engulf a pastoral carer in Sarah's position. Rumbold describes a desperate sense of 'nothing more to do' that can overwhelm those who care for the dying. He suggests that it is precisely out of this experience of helplessness that hope is born, for it is only when we behold the stark reality that makes us feel so helpless that we can properly engage with it, break out of denial and work towards a mature hope.[5]

The issue of denial and the concern for a 'realistic' hope reminds us of David, above. David's resolve to start an antiques business illustrates how vital it can be to sustain a meaningful sense of future if we are to carry on living in hope. Andrew Lester in his *Hope in Pastoral Care and Counseling* emphasizes just this point. Lester explores how hopelessness represents the loss or breakdown of a personal *future story*. Effective counselling, he argues, can restore hope by deconstructing stories of despair and creatively envisioning future narratives.[6] Like Capps and Rumbold, Lester stresses just how important hope is as a practical and theological concern. We will return to these writers later in the book, as they have each made a significant contribution towards the search for a ministry of hope.

As a student minister, my own quest for a practical theology of hope for the dying eventually became the basis of a doctoral research project.[7] It is upon the findings of the resultant study that this book is based. Two particular sources formed the core material in this research, and are foundational to the present book. The first source is a body of literature emerging from within the disciplines of psychology and nursing science over the last 40 years. This explores the nature and sources of hope as a psychological and clinical construct. The second source is what has come to be known as the *theology of hope movement*, especially the work of its pioneer, Jürgen Moltmann. This stresses the centrality of eschatology, that is, the doctrine of the last things, for all theology. The fundamental agenda of this movement focuses on the future that is promised by God, arguing that all authentically Christian theology is characterized by a forward-reaching, future-oriented bearing.

The structure and outline of this book

In this book a summary will be given of both the *psychology* and the *theology* of hope. These fundamental sources will then be drawn from in order to offer a *practical theology of hope for the dying*. Here *dying* refers to the pastoral context; *hope* itself is the topic.

A practical theology that is truly grounded in the experience of hope in a palliative context is one that takes seriously the research of those who have studied hope in the face of death as a fundamental human experience. For this reason we will begin by exploring the *psychology of hope*. Then we will turn to Moltmann and the *theology of hope*, in order to identify some of the key theological concerns that relate to the meaning of Christian hoping. The following chapter constitutes the core of the book, offering a definition of the dynamics of Christian hope and discussing its spirituality, drawing on the psychological and theological insights set before us. Practical suggestions for pastoral care will then be made as reflection is given to strategies for cultivating hope in others. Finally, consideration will be given to the wider implications of the practical theology of hope offered here for pastoral care in general.

This book thus takes an interdisciplinary approach. It expresses the conviction that a practical theology of hope for the dying must listen to the voices of both the *psychology* and the *theology* of hope. Priority of either one of these disciplines over the other is not intended. A practical theology that is truly adventurous is one that is conscious of the danger of getting the balance wrong but takes the risk nevertheless. The exact relationship between theology and the human sciences presents questions that lie beyond the scope of this book. Stephen Pattison has pointed out that on the one hand: 'Pastoral action, if it is to be effective, must pay close attention to people, the human situation and the world in which we live. To this end, pastoral care must obtain understandings from many different "secular" sources.'[8] At the same time, 'the theological tradition has been extensively ignored or forgotten about by those involved in pastoral care on both sides of the Atlantic'.[9] What is offered here is an attempt at a creative and critical dialogue between sources.

The core argument that will be presented is that the most profound experience of hope, according to psychology and nursing science, is a mysterious sense of anticipation that transcends specific goals. It will be argued that while hope is a basic human phenomenon, it finds its most complete, holistic expression in resurrection, which is the heart of Christian hope. Only such a hope is sufficiently all-encompassing and robust to engage with the reality of death.

The title *Living Hope* conveys something of the double-barrelled nature of the study. 'Living' expresses both an adjective and a verb. As an adjective, the meaning of the *content* of Christian hope will be explored – what makes it a *living* hope? But at least as important are the actual *dynamics* of hoping. In this respect something of an emphasis will be given to the verb – how might we *live* hope? We are concerned for the practicalities of ministering Christian hope to the dying, and so we will return to the issues raised by the pastoral encounters outlined in this introduction as we reflect upon how we may give 'an accounting for the hope' that is in us (1 Peter 3.15).

Notes

1 In his classic study of healing, Morris Maddocks writes, 'the concern of the biblical writers is more for the significance of the mighty works than for the works themselves'. Morris Maddocks, *The Christian Healing Ministry* (2nd edition), London: SPCK, 1990, p. 30.

2 Jean-François Lyotard, *The Postmodern Condition*, ET (trans. G. Bennington and B. Massumi), Minneapolis: University of Minnesota Press, 1984, p. xxiv.

3 Grace Davie, *Religion in Britain since 1945: Believing without Belonging*, Oxford: Blackwell, 1994, pp. 41–3, 83–4.

4 Donald Capps, *Agents of Hope: A Pastoral Psychology*, Minneapolis: Fortress Press, 1995, p. 1.

5 Bruce Rumbold, *Helplessness and Hope: Pastoral Care in Terminal Illness*, London: SCM Press, 1986.

6 Andrew Lester, *Hope in Pastoral Care and Counseling*, Louisville: Westminster John Knox Press, 1995.

7 Russell Herbert, *A Practical Theology of Hope for the Dying*, unpublished PhD thesis, University of Wales, Cardiff, 2003.

8 Stephen Pattison, *A Critique of Pastoral Care* (3rd edition), London: SCM Press, 2000, p. 16.

9 Pattison, *A Critique of Pastoral Care*, p. 31.

2

The Psychology of Hope

It is a peculiarity of man that he can only live by looking to the future –
sub specie aeternitatis. *And this is his salvation in the most difficult*
moments of his existence, although he sometimes has to force his mind
to the task.

Viktor Frankl, *Man's Search for Meaning*[1]

Viktor Frankl was a psychiatrist who survived the experience of
being imprisoned in a Nazi concentration camp. His book
Man's Search for Meaning describes the personal struggle to
sustain hope in the midst of such horror, where he and his
contemporaries found themselves in close proximity to death
every day. Though not a systematic study of the psychological
dynamics of hoping, it is a book that probes deeply into the
ambiguous experience of being poised to die while being kept
alive by hope. Its context of raw devastation and brokenness
serves to remind just how profoundly and practically relevant
the psychology of hope is to those who seek to care for the
dying.

Ever since the original publication of *Man's Search for
Meaning* in 1946, a growing fascination with the psychology of
hope has developed. As psychologists and nursing scientists
have come to understand hope as a vital dimension of human
existence, basic to both our survival and our development, a
vast body of research has accrued. Essentially this focuses on
two key questions. First, *what is hope?* This question seeks a
definition and description of the nature of hope. Second, *what
are the sources of hope?* This explores the factors that influence
hope, for better or for worse.

What is hope? How it might be described

Before moving towards a definition of hope, three important observations might be made about the way that psychologists and nursing scientists have described it.

Hope is a basic and essential human reality

Perhaps the most fundamental observation that psychologists and nursing scientists have made is that without hope there is no life. Having hope lies at the core of what it is to be human. Essential to being alive is to be animated by a basic sense of forward-moving thrust. Hope gives vitality, lifting men and women above and beyond the limits of present experience. With hope, 'Man acts, moves, achieves. Without hope, he is often dull, listless, moribund.'[2] Frankl's account of the concentration camps describes how hope, so closely intertwined with meaning, is essential for life, and that its absence may mean death.[3]

Hope is closely related to coping

An important research area within nursing science is the study of *coping*. This concerns the various strategies that people employ in coming to terms with illness and adapting to the changes that illness can present. Here hope has been identified as a major theme: those who are 'hopeful' are those who find ways of giving positive cognitive appraisal to situations of stress.[4]

One very significant work to relate hope with coping strategy is Elisabeth Kübler-Ross's *On Death and Dying*. This has become something of a classic textbook study of the dying trajectory. It presents a theory of five stages through which dying persons proceed, along with the psychiatric defence mechanisms deployed with each stage. Kübler-Ross identifies hope as 'the one thing that usually persists through all these stages'. While it can take different forms, including *denial* for example, hope is identified as a source of vitality in the dying person. Kübler-Ross reports, 'No matter what we call it, we found that all our patients maintained a little bit of it and were nourished by it in especially difficult times.'[5]

Hope has been identified as vital for coping because it is said to be an important *power resource*. Whereas powerlessness and a lack of control generally pervade the experience of chronic illness, hope can operate as a key to rediscovering a sense of personal power.[6] The problem here is the implication of a rather narrow understanding of coping. In a palliative context, it may be most unhelpful to define hope and coping in terms of mastery and control as prerequisites. As death approaches, it would seem more appropriate to talk of 'laying things down'. A psychology of hope that will be meaningful to the dying needs to offer the prospect of discovering a sense of empowerment but in a way that is not constricted to mastery and control. Our story of David illustrates this need. On the surface David may have the appearance of coping very well with illness as he maintains his determination to resume running his new antiques business as soon as he is able. But as things develop he is confronted with the reality of his deteriorating health. To David this represents an abrupt disempowerment. If hope is to be meaningful to David it must offer him some sense of being energized and enabled in a new way as he comes to terms with his limitations. Later we shall see that such an experience might be described as a feeling of *possibility*, even in the face of death, and is intrinsic to the very mystery of hope.

Hope can influence physical health

Some research claims that hope may have a positive effect on physical health by triggering certain responses in the body's immune system.[7] Frankl suggests a link between bodily health and a hopeful state of mind, attributing the rising death rate in the concentration camp to the disappointed hope of liberation. He writes, 'the sudden loss of hope and courage can have a deadly effect'.[8]

Three areas of concern should be raised. First, while there may be a certain plausibility about the link between mind and body, there is currently relatively little scientific evidence, beyond the anecdotal, to support the claim that hope in itself can bring physical cure. This represents an important challenge for medical research. Second, there is a danger of burdening patients with the responsibility to 'be positive' in order to be cured. The patient who tries to maintain a 'positive attitude' of hope but whose disease persists could be encumbered with feelings of guilt and inadequacy. This perhaps parallels the sort of pressure that can be placed on an individual when divine healing is prayed for and the suggestion is made that such healing depends upon the level of faith that he or she has. Our story of Jane gives us an idea of the kind of situation in which such pressure could be created, even though in her case it is to some extent Jane herself who is urging people to believe that God will miraculously cure her. Third, there is a danger that positive physical health outcomes could become the sole criteria for assessing the value and importance of hope. The search for hope in a palliative care context is after all chiefly concerned with finding ways of sustaining hope even in the certainty of death.

For all these concerns, there is nevertheless much to be said for the prospect that hoping may positively affect physical health. If the process of hoping may help to yield a better quality of life for those who are dying, that can only be a good thing. That is not to say that one hopes *in order* to be cured. But if a 'side effect' of the psychological experience of hope is a better state of bodily health than would otherwise be the case, the importance of hoping as a coping strategy is reinforced even more.

What is hope? How it might be defined

Hope and related concepts

As we begin to focus more on the specific question of how hope might be defined, it is important to point out that a number of similar yet distinct concepts exist with which hope could be confused. One of these is *wishing*. On the whole, psychologists and nursing scientists have tended to regard hope as more profound and complex than wishing, which is generally associated with simply 'desiring or longing for something'.[9] Because wishing is highly specific in what is desired, it is less flexible than hope in renegotiating goals, and thus less realistic.

Wishing is a term that has been used extensively in the psychoanalytic tradition. According to Sigmund Freud, wish denotes unconscious desires repressed from infanthood. He describes wishes as the 'capital' with which dreams are made, and religion as 'illusions, fulfillments of the strongest and most urgent wishes of humanity'.[10]

William Lynch, Jesuit and author of a major volume on the psychology of hope, argues that wishing is in fact an important ingredient in hoping, and in so doing poses a challenging response to the Freudian critique of religion. Lynch suggests that Freud got it the wrong way round: it is actually the *failure* to wish that produces anxiety. Wishing is the very opposite of apathy, for it ventures to imagine how things might be different. Thus it is basic to hope, and Lynch advocates 'absolute wishing', by which he means a healthy ability to devote oneself without inhibition to the pursuit of personal desires. This is to be sharply distinguished from 'the wishing of absolutes', which refers to the rigid striving after objects of desire with no sense of realistic limitation. Lynch warns of the danger of what he calls the 'absolutizing instinct', which can mislead wishing into such a state of 'black and white' fixation. Our stories of Jane's apparent certainty of a miraculous cure and David's insistence that he will return to work suggest two ways in which such 'absolutizing' might be encountered. This sort of wishing can be illusory, as Freudian psychoanalysis would suggest. But Lynch helps us to see how wishing might actually be a sign of psychological health. As such, hoping, and not least Christian hope, can be understood positively in terms of wishing, and not simply reduced to the fulfilment of repressed wishes as Freud does.[11]

Another concept related to yet distinct from hope is *optimism*. The word is derived from the Latin *optimus*, meaning 'the best'. Thus nursing scientists have defined it as 'a disposition that expects the best possible or emphasizes primarily the positive aspects of a situation'.[12] The psychologist Charles Snyder draws attention to Eleanor Porter's *Pollyanna*.[13] The central thrust of Porter's novel is that something positive can always be found in anything negative. Because optimism focuses more on circumstances than on personal desire, it tends to be slightly more rational and realistic than the kind of wishing that some nursing scientists try to distinguish from hope. Furthermore, in its striving to 'be positive', optimism may function as an early step in the hoping process.

Nevertheless, hope is more mysterious and sophisticated than the simple act of stressing the positive side of circumstance. In the face of death, optimism runs aground in its search for the best possible outcome. There something deeper is needed – something that is less rigid in its outlook, less cognitively constricted and more accepting of disappointment. In a sense, something of this 'clutching at straws' might be seen in our story of Tom's wife Jenny, who in her desperation to grasp at something positive cries, 'We will see one another again in the next life, won't we?' Such a vision of eternally restored relationships may well form a significant part of Christian hope. But in Jenny's context it possibly has more of the appearance of a vain attempt to relieve some of her acute anguish by clasping for the only positive thing she can find. Like optimism, hoping does involve envisioning something beyond the present, but not in a way that simply stresses the best possible outcome. Rather, to hope is to engage meaningfully with the very worst, most painful experiences of present brokenness, where in our search to 'be positive' we find ourselves at a loss.

Nevertheless, hoping often seems to be portrayed in terms of 'positive attitude', especially in the popular media. This attitude might be described as the *fighting spirit* – denoting courage, strength, determination and heroism. Its combatant nature is frequently extolled as a virtue. Two examples are the following comments, the first made by television sports presenter the late Helen Rollason, and the second by actor Geoffrey Hughes:

I love life and have no intention of giving it up without a very good fight.[14]

Sheer willpower and positive thinking kept me going.[15]

Confronting illness with courage and determination, seeing it as the enemy to be fought, may be a part of hope. Like optimism, it could be a valuable step in the process of hoping. In our story of David, his family feels awkward about challenging his resolve to return to work quickly, through concern that they might undermine the one thing that is keeping him going. However, the brittle nature of this approach eventually becomes apparent, when David breaks down in tears as he begins to take on board his prognosis.

Hope is more profound and complex than the fighting spirit alone. The militant language that characterizes the fighting spirit loses its appropriateness as death approaches. This is because it reflects an optimism that is closed to painful feelings and inflexible about outcomes, regarding death as defeat. The language of hope can express concepts of courage and strength, but in order to do so must align such virtues with an acceptance of death in a way that does not imply defeat. In coping terms (above) this will mean 'empowerment' but not conceived simply as 'control'.

One of the most important concepts related to hope is *expectation*. In 1969 Ezra Stotland's *The Psychology of Hope* was published. It became foundational, forming the predominant conceptual framework of hope as a psychological phenomenon for almost 20 years. Stotland defined hope as 'an expectation greater than zero of achieving a goal',[16] and described how we perceive goals, are motivated towards them, and encounter anxiety when goal attainment is threatened.

Clearly, expectation is an important part of the experience of hope. This is illustrated by Tom, who describes his feeling of hopelessness as something of a 'frozen' state. Without hope we lose the forward movement that is essential to life and become overwhelmed with futility; we find ourselves in a void, depleted of any sense of being animated. To live in hope is basic to what it means to live at all, for to live in hope is to be sustained by the expectation that what lies ahead is worth living for.

But is it appropriate to define hope in terms of expectation alone? Over the years nursing scientists have suggested that the hope they observe in patients seems more complex than that, especially in a palliative context. After all, how might hope, which involves a sense of looking forward to the future in expectation, be a reality for those whose future is acutely limited as death approaches sooner rather than later?

In 1985 Karin Dufault and Benita Martocchio put forward a model that became the new paradigm for understanding hope in nursing science, interpreting it as something that is multi-layered. They distinguished between two spheres of hope, namely the *particularized* and the *generalized*. Particularized hope is that which is concerned with specific objects, that is, the attainment of particular goals. This is close to Stotland's definition. Generalized hope, however, is hope that is not focused on any particular object or goal. This is a sort of intangible but very real and dynamic 'positive glow on life'. It is expressed by a dying patient as she attempts to describe what is perhaps rather difficult to articulate because of its mysterious profundity: 'I don't hope for anything in particular. I just hope . . . At this stage, you just hope; there is nothing left to do but hope. Hope is quite enough.'[17] In other words, as the philosopher Gabriel Marcel once put it, 'to hope' is different from 'to hope that . . .'.[18]

This concept of generalized hope may thus provide the key to understanding hope and expectation in a way that is real and meaningful in a palliative context – where talk of future goals for dying persons is potentially problematic. Dufault and Martocchio maintain that generalized hope does involve a sense of future, but one that is essentially open-ended. Because of this openness, it is a sense of expectation that is not threatened when specific goals are not attained. The future is looked to with expectation but in a way that allows for the power of hope to endure even when it becomes clear that any particular goals that may have been set will not be reached.

Hope as the mysterious 'anticipation of the ultimate'

In exploring how hope relates to the concepts of wishing, optimism, the fighting spirit and expectation, the complex nature of hope begins to emerge. At the heart of hope's complexity lies its mystery. The experience of generalized hope is essentially a sense of anticipation and possibility. But if this is not necessarily tied to specific future goals then what exactly is it? Nursing scientists observe hope in dying patients as an 'inner power that facilitates the transcendence of the present situation and movement toward new awareness and enrichment of being'.[19] This is a kind of anticipation of *something other* than the experience of illness in which they find themselves; that is, a state of tension between these experiences and the something other. But just what does this mean? How might we press this towards a more precise definition?

Frankl's account of hope in the concentration camp provides us with some helpful insights. He connects the experience of hope with having a sense of *purpose*: those who are hopeless are those who are 'without a future and without a goal'. At one level, Frankl is saying that hope in the death camp was essentially the experience of 'living for the future', the discovery of a future goal towards which life could be oriented. At the same time, he warns against the dangers of 'robbing the present of its reality' by becoming preoccupied with memories of the past.[20] In other words, even though Frankl identifies the orientation towards a future goal as highly significant in the experience of hope, his emphasis is very much on the importance of the *present*. This points to what seems to be a deeper layer of Frankl's thinking, namely that most essential to the experience of hope is the discovery of an *end* or *purpose* towards which life is oriented. For Frankl this meant living towards a future life of liberation from the Nazis. This is, of course, a goal. But most important to his experience of hope was not the expectation of an event of liberation on a specified date, but the more general sense of living in anticipation of freedom, as a cause worth living for. Here *end* denotes something qualitative, that is, a meaningful purpose that because of its personal significance transcends an otherwise hopeless and purposeless existence.

For Frankl, a person's end or purpose is understood as some kind of meaning or potential meaning that exists within the here and now. Thus he describes a healthy attitude of hopefulness as a state of tension between the circumstances a person has and the possibilities for those circumstances that confront that person within present experience. In the same way that an arch is strengthened by increasing the load laid upon it, thus joining its parts more firmly together, so it is with a person's mental health when they are 'loaded' with a sense of meaning and dynamic tension.

Hope might therefore be defined as the *mysterious anticipation of the ultimate*. In subsequent chapters we will develop this definition theologically. At this stage we can simply understand the human experience of a sense of the ultimate as that which we encounter as our end or purpose. While this may involve the pursuit of specific goals, by no means does our end or purpose in life need to be depicted exclusively in terms of goal attainment. Our sense of the ultimate is far deeper than that. Experiences of failure, disappointment and brokenness may be painfully disturbing, but they need not denote the destruction of what we regard as our end or purpose. We live in hope when this sense of the ultimate is brought to bear on our present experience and creates a dynamic tension. Mysteriously, this fills our present with possibility, with anticipation – even though death may be imminent.

Hope and its relationship with hopelessness

How might we understand the relationship between hope and hopelessness? Some psychologists and nursing scientists regard the two simply as polar opposites. Most, however, see a more ambiguous relationship. Hope and hopelessness are never that far from each other and often seem to overlap in what is essentially an ever-changing process of living with uncertainty.

In a theory known as *learned helplessness*, psychologist Martin Seligman distinguishes between what could be called an *objective* helplessness, whereby an individual cannot *actually* do anything to influence his or her circumstances, and a *subjective* helplessness, where an individual only *perceives* that nothing can be done. The focal point of Seligman's theory is that on the basis of experience an individual *learns* to feel helpless, or not, as the case may be. While the states of being and feeling helpless often correspond, this need not necessarily be so. It should be noted that Seligman talks specifically about helplessness and not *hopelessness*, and that there may be conceptual differences between these terms. Nevertheless, a similar disparity between circumstance and a person's perception of circumstance may be a factor in the ambiguous relationship between hope and hopelessness.

This seems to be the case with David. His diagnosis and treatment present him with what may be the greatest cloud of uncertainty he has ever encountered. At first David develops a coping strategy – that of the fighting spirit. It is a form of hope in that it enables him to envision something of a future, namely his return to work. But he is just a hair's breadth from hopelessness, and it is only a matter of time before he falls over that line. In his hopelessness he becomes utterly preoccupied with death, and as such gives up on life. At both stages, first in his insistence that he will be cured and then in his resignation to imminent death, a distinction may be drawn between perceived and actual hopelessness, where David's feelings do not correspond accurately to the reality of his situation. The point in highlighting such a distinction here is to illustrate the close proximity in which hope and hopelessness dwell. Because they are both born out of the same climate of uncertainty, the relationship between them is more ambiguous than simply one of opposites.

Lynch suggests that there is a creative kind of hopelessness that forms an important part of the hoping process. He argues that hope can only properly come into being in a way that is free of the absolutizing instinct when the reality of limitation is acknowledged. Good hope is not deluded by fantasy, and the one who hopes accepts that certain projects are helpless and not worth hoping for. In this way hopelessness 'becomes a ground where man sets his heel to spring in another direction, with another solution'.[21] However, Lynch is careful to point out that hopelessness does not always function creatively. Problems occur when hopelessness invades our hope in a way that is simply destructive. Then hopelessness obscures the real possibilities that exist; the imagination falls prey to the absolutizing instinct and we become trapped in hopelessness.

Hope and reality surveillance

The distinction we may draw between David's circumstances and his perception of them highlights the concern for a satisfactory reality base in the hoping process. What makes for a *realistic* hope?

David's story illustrates how the quest for a realistic hope is a matter of striving to overcome not only overt optimism but also unjustified pessimism. At least as dangerous as 'false hopes' are 'false fears'. David appears to swing from the first extreme, where he refuses to acknowledge the seriousness of his illness, to the latter, where he will not entertain the possibility that there is still living to be done. In Lynch's framework, realistic hoping might emerge in David if he can recognize that his uncertainty consists of both hopeful possibilities and also hopeless impossibilities and thus resists making an absolute out of either.

One nursing scientist, Beverly Hall, has remarked that health professionals are generally suspicious of any talk of hope in the face of death. She says that whenever she lectures on hope in a palliative context at nursing conferences, the initial objection usually voiced is, 'Aren't you encouraging denial?'[22] Two issues are raised here. First, it seems that a popular assumption is that if a person with a life-threatening illness talks about having hope, they must therefore be denying reality. The question is, *whose reality?* Judging a person to be denying reality is assuming that, unlike that person, one has an objective view of what reality actually is. In many cases it may be that a doctor or nurse does have a more accurate perception of the basis of a patient's particular hope. But to *assume* this suggests a rather judgemental attitude. This raises the question whether it is ever appropriate to label a person's hope as false.

A second assumption Hall points to, and challenges, is that denial can only ever be harmful. Denial can actually function as a very helpful protective mechanism, reducing anxiety while other coping resources are gathered. In her study of the dying trajectory, Kübler-Ross identifies denial as the first and a very necessary stage of coming to terms with the reality of death, functioning as a 'buffer' against shock. She also points out that hope, as in all the stages, can be present in denial.[23] That, of course, is not to say that every act of denial is intrinsically healthy. Most critically, we might ask questions about the scale of a particular denial – that is, its persistency and its intensity, as well as the wider mental health background of the individual concerned.[24]

A particularly sensitive question concerns the extent to which prognosis ought to be disclosed to patients with life-threatening illness. Some surveys report that among doctors in North America the pendulum has swung from an almost universal preference for non-disclosure in the 1960s to a greater preference for disclosure today. Previous belief that it was better to safeguard patients from despair than to inform them of the seriousness of their diagnosis has been replaced by an equally extreme commitment to telling the truth. Some attribute the current preference for truth-telling to a sense of moral obligation among doctors that patients have the right to know the real seriousness of their diagnosis. Others comment on a professional fear of being sued at a later date should it become known that facts were withheld.[25] A major challenge to carers is therefore to balance honesty with the cultivation of hope. This calls for both clarity and sensitivity. In David's case, although no length of time was stated, it was only when his GP told him directly that further treatment would probably not cure him that David broke down in tears. Although initially what appears to be 'false fear' ensues, the episode could be a stepping stone in David's journey of coming to terms with reality.

The pastoral concern for a 'realistic' hope is an essentially practical issue for carers. How we understand the term 'realistic' is, of course, a deeply theological question as well, and it will be taken up later in this book. But now let us probe further into the psychological nature of hope as we ask what psychology and nursing science consider to be its major sources.

What are the sources of hope?

Relationships

Hope is an essentially social experience, as some of the stories in our opening chapter illustrate. While we might wish to ask whether Jane was realistic in her expectation of a miraculous *cure*, she was certainly sustained in some form of hope by the *care* expressed by others who were praying for her. Angela may have been in a very different place spiritually from Jane, but in her request to Sue, the chaplaincy assistant, there appears to be in Angela some intuitive sense that to be prayed for by another person might somehow enable her to feel a little more hopeful. Conversely, it is probably no accident that when David emerges from a state of being withdrawn from interacting with others for a few days, he is in something of a panic, having convinced himself that he is to die far sooner than is really the case.

Within nursing science research, personal relationships are probably identified as the supreme source of hope more frequently than just about anything else. Doctors, nurses, friends and family are all important in supporting and sustaining hope; over and over again patients are reported to say that simply 'being present' is one of the most important contributions that carers can make.[26] Specifically, this has been linked to the importance of 'being needed' and 'being part of something', as well as a basic human need when dying to know that we will not be abandoned.[27] When hope is shared by a community, an individual whose hope is low may be 'balanced' by others whose hope enables them to encourage that person, staying with them in hope. Rarely is everybody's hope exhausted. Hope, then, is *contagious*. While one person may not literally be able to instil hope in another, in 'hoping for' them, a climate is created in which they are more likely to have hope.[28]

Psychologists as well as nursing scientists have long identified a positive link between hope and relationships. In his theory of human development, Erik Erikson stresses social interaction as the context in which hope is born. He identifies the crisis and resolution of 'trust versus mistrust' between the child and its mother as the most foundational social experience. The outcome of that experience will shape the child's ability to hope, an ability that is nurtured as further conflicts between trust and mistrust are encountered along the journey into and throughout adulthood.[29]

Lynch describes how 'Hope is truly on the inside of us, but hope is an interior sense that there is help on the outside of us.' We all have a 'double need of autonomy and belonging'; that is to say, both independence and dependence are equally important components of hope and overall psychological health. It is when either autonomy or dependence is absolutized that an unhealthy defiance or slavish obedience is created, argues Lynch, and so both need to be held in equilibrium.[30]

Research among dying patients indicates that it is the *quality* rather than the *quantity* of caring relationships that matters.[31] In particular, the expression of faithfulness and consistency by giving regular visits, along with an ability to listen attentively, have been highlighted as important attributes of hope-inspiring relationships. The significance of touch has also been stressed, where patients have spoken of their appreciation of carers who greet them with hugs and are willing to hold their hand unhurriedly while they listen.[32] Two independent studies that set out to explore how doctors and nurses contribute to hope in patients with life-threatening illness produced remarkably similar findings. Only when doctors and nurses related to patients with personal 'warmth' rather than cold, clinical professionalism did patients feel hopeful. Five specific signs of such warmth were identified: knowing the patient as a human rather than a 'case'; 'connecting', that is, listening and understanding; taking the trouble to explain treatment rather than merely prescribing it; being welcoming towards the patient; and keeping the patient well informed about his or her condition.[33]

It should be pointed out that there is a danger that carers can become overprotective. Some nursing scientists comment that 'pampering' and an excessive amount of attention to illness can be distressing to patients.[34] There is also a danger that patients may become over-dependent on one particular person who may not be able to provide ongoing support over a prolonged period.[35] While this may be quite unintentional on the part of the carer, Lynch points out that sometimes individuals may purposely set out to make others dependent on them.[36] Such dependency is unhelpful, for it upsets the necessary balance with autonomy that is central to real hope.

Goals and activity

We have defined hope as the *mysterious anticipation of the ultimate*. Hope operates in a way that is particularized, that is, focused on specific objects, but its higher order is that which is generalized, where the sense of possibility transcends the attainment of individual goals. With this working definition it can be seen that although hope should not be understood exclusively in terms of goals, identifying and pursuing goals can function as a very effective way of keeping the dynamic of hope alive. Nursing literature frequently recognizes this.[37] Goals such as living long enough to make a special trip or see the wedding of a son, the graduation of a daughter, the birth of a grandchild, may be the very things that enable people with life-threatening illness to maintain a sense of vitality and engagement with everyday life. Fatalistic resignation may be the poorer alternative, and we have seen how, for a while at least, both Tom and David became withdrawn, entering something of a 'frozen state' as their hopeless preoccupation with death prevented them from seeing any kind of way forward.

The issue of reality surveillance is especially pertinent to setting goals in a palliative context. Once again we may think of David, who began with an insistence that he would return to work and later threw all his energy at getting things in order for what he perceived to be his imminent death. In both cases David had found some sort of direction and as such became engaged with living his life. But in neither case did he recognize the realities of his limitations or the possibilities that could lie before him to enjoy a meaningful life within the boundaries of those limitations. A key task for any carer trying to help David would be to try to enable him to clarify and negotiate the possibilities and the limitations. No easy formula exists for doing this, but flexibility should be the all-important criterion, especially where physical health can fluctuate with life-threatening illness. At times the challenge is to encourage people in David's situation to consider aiming for things they might have too readily written off as impossible. Equally challenging is the need at other points in the journey to support individuals as they revise what is aimed for, laying down those goals that are no longer within reach.

It should be remembered that although hoping in a palliative context involves a process of 'letting go' and working towards an acceptance of death, this does not mean a *passive* acceptance. According to Lynch, hope is formed not out of *primary* wishes that demand immediate satisfaction, but *secondary* wishes that have been examined and have a sense of time – wishes that have the ability to *wait*. In the experience of life-threatening illness, waiting takes on a unique significance, for to hope in the midst of dying involves waiting for death *in hope*. However, this is not a passive waiting; it is *active*. Lynch points out that waiting can be something that happens through apathy, where we simply give up. This is not so with the kind of waiting associated with hope. Rather, to wait in hope 'is a true power . . . it is ready to spring if a possibility appears or an exit opens'.[38] To reinforce our definition once again: hope is the *mysterious anticipation of the ultimate*, a sense of *possibility*. Here lies the significance of goals. The process of identifying, working towards and fulfilling them can be an effective way of nurturing this sense of the possible, maintaining the dynamic of *active waiting* that is such a vital part of hope.

Another reason why the pursuit of goals or aims might be helpful is that it may assist in the reduction of anxiety. Stotland proposes that 'actions of all sorts, whether or not they are directed at attaining hopeless goals causing the anxiety, can reduce anxiety'.[39] In one study, cancer patients report that 'keeping busy' can prevent an excessive dwelling on illness and death.[40] In other words, not only can the pursuit of goals create energy by nurturing a sense of possibility and an active engagement with everyday life; such pursuit can also serve to expend energy, channelling it to creative ends where otherwise it might simply fuel anxiety.

'Keeping busy' may be a popular strategy for coping with anxiety, but tremendous caution is called for. First, there comes a point in the dying trajectory where the individual simply cannot be as active physically and mentally as he or she previously was. Activity can amount to no more than attempted distraction from reality. Here we may simply reiterate that a major challenge to carers is to keep both possibilities and limitations in sight at all times in the attempt to discern the appropriateness of continuing various pursuits. Second, and perhaps more fundamentally, in emphasizing activity there is a danger that a person's *doing* be given more focus than his or her *being*. It is one thing to say that hope is essentially active and not passive, but this must not distort the fact that *active* refers here to the quality of waiting in hope. This means that hope in the face of death must ultimately be understood in terms of something that one experiences as subject: dying is something we *do*, but death is ultimately something that happens *to* us. Hope as we have defined it corresponds to these dynamics. Its active quality is essential to it, and in this respect it is appropriate to explore the *doing* of hope. But ultimately this living, and dying, in hope is about waiting, that is, the state of *being* in hope. We may search for hope. But the most profound hope is something that actually discovers us and lifts us, as a reality greater than and beyond our human strivings.

It is worth mentioning one particular way in which people with life-threatening illness can be encouraged in an ongoing active involvement with life, and that has to do with their participation in making choices about medical treatment. For example, decisions may need to be made about whether a certain course of chemotherapy is appropriate at a particular stage, weighing up the advantages against the disadvantages of the treatment. Nursing scientists often argue that in order for hope to be fostered in patients it is essential that the health care environment be one in which the control of medical treatment is shared between the patient and the health professionals.[41] Earlier in this chapter it was pointed out that the concept of hope, especially in a palliative context, ought not to be defined solely in terms of control and mastery. Nevertheless, in no way does this create any objection to the suggestion that a hope-inspiring environment is one in which the patient is allowed to share in the control over his or her treatment. It simply means that encouraging this sort of involvement is a practical way of cultivating the patient's sense of *possibility* and an active and engaged participation in life that is less fatalistic. Promoting patient involvement in decisions over medical care helps to communicate that illness does not have to mean exclusion from life and its activity.

Imagination

Effective use of the imagination is often identified as a source of hope. For Lynch it lies at its very heart. The capacity to hope, he maintains, depends on an ability to imagine: 'I incline to *equate* the life of hope with the life of the imagination . . . Hope imagines . . . it is always imagining what is not yet seen, or a way out of difficulty, or a wider perspective for life or thought.'[42] The imagination enables one to transcend the immediate situation, envisioning beyond what may appear on the surface to be hopeless circumstances. Lynch's notion of wishing – the vital capacity to pursue what is desirable in life – is foundational here. Only where there is an ability to identify personal wishes can they be taken up by the imagination and formed into hopes.

In the despairing state that Tom describes as 'spiritually frozen', we have an example of someone whose greatest need might be to learn to imagine. Despite a lifetime of church attendance Tom has not discovered a way of personally 'imagining' the promises of Christian hope and what they might mean for him as a human being. As such he finds no assurance or peace in what he has picked up from church culture – to him it is merely religious language. Perhaps his continual attempts to change the subject every time his wife mentions his illness is a way of holding at bay an image of God that is in fact an object of fear – an image that may have haunted him subconsciously for years but has never really been acknowledged and critically examined. Now his fear of dying is brought to the surface and the opportunity is presented to talk with his minister about his feeling of utter despair. In a later chapter we shall pick up Tom's story and see it unfold, but here we may simply note the powerful role that the imagination plays in the act of hoping, along with the despair that can be rendered by a thwarted imagination. Until Tom can imagine something beyond his immediate experience of acute fear, he remains in a state of hopelessness.

In a different way, we can also see a constricted imagination in Jane. An important difference between Jane and Tom is that Jane does hold to a hope of some kind: she imagines that she will be miraculously cured. In the event, Jane dies quite quickly, before her hope is shattered by the realization that such a cure will not be forthcoming. But, like Tom, Jane has not taken hold of the promises of Christian hope in her imagination in a way that engages with the reality of death. She imagines a future, but one that is very narrowly defined in terms of cure.

Lynch emphasizes that the imagination must function in such a way as to appreciate the limitations of what is possible: 'Reality is a better producer of dreams and visions than non-reality.'[43] This means that although it is the imagination that enables hope to envision 'reality' differently than in the state of hopelessness, creating a new sense of possibility, such imagination must nevertheless be aware of life's limitations. Lynch therefore draws a firm distinction between hopeful imagining, and *fantasy* driven by the absolutizing instinct. At face value the distinction may appear to be simply one of degree, fantasy being the unbridled excess of the imagination. But Lynch argues that in fact it is the very opposite: fantasy emerges precisely where there is *no* imagination. Such fantasy represents the rigid, inflexible wishing for absolutes in a way that seals itself off from reality instead of creatively imagining genuine possibilities. Thus the trouble with those whose state of mind is wrought with hopelessness 'is not too much imagination or imaging, but too little'.[44] This is arguably what we see in Tom and Jane.

The link between the imagination and hope is reinforced by Frankl. He says that it was not physical strength that sustained prisoners in the concentration camp, but a 'rich intellectual life' that enabled them to 'retreat from their terrible surroundings'.[45] Frankl describes how he used his imagination to picture himself in the future standing in a warm and comfortable room giving a lecture to an attentive audience about his experiences of the concentration camp:

> By this method I succeeded somehow in rising above the situation, above the sufferings of the moment, and I observed them as if they were already of the past. Both I and my troubles became the object of an interesting psychoscientific study undertaken by myself.[46]

By imagining beyond his present circumstances Frankl

experienced an empowering sense of objectivity about them. But in so doing he did not take leave of present reality, because his imagination made creative use of it, his circumstances providing the material with which he constructed his imaginative vision.

In times of crisis and pain, it can be very difficult to see anything beyond the immediacy of the present with which we are confronted. A challenge for pastoral carers is to encourage those who are dying to cultivate their imagination in ways that enable them to envision something transcendent of such entrapment, bringing to birth that mysterious anticipation of the ultimate that is hope. The examples of Tom and Jane cited here highlight the importance of theological vision – something that will be explored later.

Humour and laughter

A widely recognized source of hope is the emotional uplift experienced in laughter and humour. Hope, of course, is more than emotion alone, but emotion is nevertheless a significant part of hope, and laughter has been described as 'a positive emotion which stimulates a positive attitude'.[47] That is not to say that hope is simply to be equated with 'being positive'. But when we laugh our emotional climate can undergo a transformation that makes us better placed to become more hopeful in our outlook. Thus Norman Cousins regards laughter as 'an igniter of great expectations'. Indeed, he also suggests that it can be beneficial to physical health: 'Laughter is a form of internal jogging. It moves your internal organs around. It enhances respiration.'[48]

Let us resume the story with which we began our opening chapter. Sarah is a young curate who feels overwhelmed with nervousness as she makes her way to visit someone in the hospice. Although she has read a little about the hospice movement, this is in fact the first time she has been to such a place. Upon her arrival she is greeted by a scene that she certainly did not expect: two members of the nursing staff falling over one another, howling with laughter, as the very person she has come to visit gives a somewhat unflattering impersonation of one of the doctors. At first Sarah does not quite know how she should react – she has spent the last hour preparing herself to enter an atmosphere of solemnity. But she soon grasps just how misguided her presuppositions have been.

Sarah's experience highlights what is perhaps a popular misunderstanding of the nature of hospice environments – namely that they are places where we go to die. Sadly, people are sometimes reluctant to accept the support that is offered to them by hospice care because they associate hospices only with death and sorrow. Nothing could be further from the truth! The driving force of the hospice movement is a desire and commitment to enable people with life-threatening illness to live life to the full. Of course, this does not involve sweeping the reality of death under the carpet, and a key task for palliative care is to provide space and freedom for honest engagement with the fear and sorrow that death confronts us with. But it would be profoundly incorrect to presume that for such a task to be undertaken then it is necessary to create an ambience of sombreness and dour sobriety. Hospices are places dedicated to life and hope, to which humour and laughter are central.

So just how might laughter function as a source of hope? The answer could be that it helps us regain and maintain a sense of *perspective*. Some patients with life-threatening illness comment that 'the feeling of delight, joy or playfulness . . . can provide a sense of release from the present moment'.[49] At face value this may seem like escapism. There may be times when that is precisely what is needed. Distraction from the experience of illness can help prevent an excessive dwelling on it, an overt preoccupation that, unbridled, could choke the development of a hopeful outlook. Indeed, even if a patient's sense of humour and laughter were to function as a form of denial, this need not in itself be harmful, for denial can serve as a useful mechanism in the process of coping with illness and coming to terms with death.

On closer inspection it can be seen that laughter creates a

sense of perspective not because it is a way of *forgetting* suffering but because it can actually *empower* the individual in the face of it. Patients in one study made comments such as: 'If I can laugh, I feel like I still have some power,' and, 'I may not have much control over the nearness of death, but I do have the power to joke about it.'[50] Frankl elaborates on this empowering quality of laughter, describing how in the concentration camp a sense of humour functioned as 'another of the soul's weapons in the fight for self-preservation'. The ability to laugh and joke is 'some kind of a trick learned while mastering the art of living'. Frankl explains how he and a friend resolved to invent at least one amusing story daily, about some incident that would happen after their liberation.[51] Humour such as this is empowering because it is essentially laughing in the face of the object of suffering or fear, refusing to be overwhelmed by it. When humour has this effect it enables the individual to feel that they are rising above immediate experience. The 'here and now' is transcended and hope is created.

Spiritual base: psychology and Christian hope

Psychology and nursing science have suggested a strong correlation between the development of hope and the presence of some form of personal spirituality.[52] Indeed, it is not enough simply to describe spirituality as a 'source' of hope, as one influencing factor among others. A practical theology of hope for the dying will understand faith as the very basis of hope. But spirituality need not, of course, refer specifically to Christian faith, or indeed any religious tradition. In our opening chapter we noted that while Angela says that she does not have 'a faith', she nevertheless considers spirituality to be of real importance – enough to ask Sue to pray for her. Thus even when faith is not acknowledged as the basis of hope, it can be seen how personal spirituality is accepted as the climate in which hope forms and develops.

Closely related to spirituality is what we might call a sense of *meaning*. We have defined hope as the mysterious anticipation of the ultimate. It is an experience by which we discover a sense of possibility by looking beyond the immediate present. Purpose and direction are thus encountered *in* the present. In this respect the development of hope is influenced considerably by the discovery of personal meaning in life, as that which fosters a sense of the ultimate. For Frankl, hope and ultimate meaning are intricately interwoven. He describes those in the death camp that had lost hope:

> A man who could not see the end of his 'provisional existence' was not able to aim at an ultimate goal in life. He ceased living for the future . . .

Frankl maintains that hope enables crises to be regarded as challenges where the individual looks beyond the immediate reality and perceives some kind of ultimate meaning towards which life is oriented. Those prisoners who had no hope were those who had no purpose:

> Such people forgot that often it is just such an exceptionally difficult external situation which gives man the opportunity to grow spiritually beyond himself. Instead of taking the camp's difficulties as a test of their inner strength, they did not take their life seriously and despised it as something of no consequence . . . Life for such people became meaningless.[53]

Nursing science has suggested a number of practical ways in which carers might enable patients to discover a sense of personal meaning. Some studies highlight the importance of reminiscence. Kaye Herth, for example, reports that 90 per cent of dying patients whom she interviewed said that recalling uplifting memories was for them an effective hope-fostering strategy.[54] Others emphasize the significance of nurturing a sense of contemplation and appreciation of the moment by highlighting the aesthetic qualities of everyday life. This might involve encouraging patients to enjoy music and other arts, or simply drawing attention to various sense experiences such as the taste of a favourite meal or the warmth of a sunbeam.[55] The renewal of such appreciation can go a long way in enabling a sense of meaning to emerge, which may in turn foster the discovery or rediscovery of a sense of the ultimate that is so central to the experience of hope.

A practical theology of hope for the dying must, however, ask what may be said about the psychology of hope in terms of specifically *Christian* spirituality. Some evidence positively links Christian faith with hope.[56] Faith and its expression through specific· activities such as prayer, fellowship meetings, Bible reading, listening to devotional music and enjoying Christian television and radio broadcasts have all been identified by patients and carers as sources of hope in the face of life-threatening illness.[57]

It should be pointed out that some studies describe how certain forms of belief inherited from the Christian tradition can seriously thwart hope. Connections have been made, for example, between prolonged denial and an insistence that God will cure.[58] Once again, our story of Jane illustrates such a danger. Another example of how religious assumptions can be potentially destructive is the resigned fatalism or profound sense of guilt and fear where God is pictured as vengeful or even tyrannical. One particular study of hope among people with AIDS identifies a disinclination to link belief in God with hope because of a perception among patients that 'religious' people generally stigmatize them, portraying God as one who punishes, especially if they are homosexual.[59] What these things suggest is more a distortion of authentic Christian belief than that belief itself. Not everything that goes under the banner *Christian* is worthy of the name, as reports of this sort testify. The theological nature of Christian hope is the focus of the next chapter. What may be said at the end of this chapter concerning the psychological nature of specifically Christian hope?

The psychologist who possibly offers more insights than any other in response to this question is Lynch, for he explores hope not only as a psychologist but as one who writes from a specifically Christian perspective. Lynch maintains that the life 'in all fullness' promised by Jesus (John 10.10) comes into being as we discover the power of *absolute wishing*. This is the spiritual renunciation of apathy. Hope is born as we dare to imagine how things might be better. But the process can be hindered by distorted forms of Christian belief. Such distortions emerge when the absolutizing instinct encroaches on the images people have of God. This instinct, says Lynch, is the 'father of the hopeless and adds that special feeling of weight that hope-lessness attaches to everything it touches'. So, for example, the image of the vengeful God who wills AIDS as a punishment is the product of the absolutizing instinct that has taken the Christian concept of the God of justice and judgement and grossly misrepresented it. The fundamental belief that God has moral standards is twisted so as to produce an image of God as tyrant. In this way the absolutizing instinct is 'the creator of idols'.[60] It makes absolute that which is not absolute. In other words, it makes what is *not* God, into God.

It might, of course, be objected that *any* belief in God is the product of the absolutizing instinct, since God, by definition, is absolute. It is here that Lynch brings his psychological and theological insights together most fruitfully as he appeals to the nature of the Christian God, evaluating what it means to believe in that God in terms of the psychology of hope. First, in describ-ing hope as 'an interior sense that there is help on the outside of us', Lynch makes the more general anthropological statement that 'interiority and autonomy must come from the outside'. In theological terms, this means that God is the creator whose desire is to bestow autonomy on created beings:

He is more truly God to the degree that he communicates his own autonomy to everything. Even a little child yells with joy when it puts something together that is suddenly able to go under its own steam, without the child's pushing. His normal exultant reaction is: look at it go! Accordingly, even if it is not the fashion so to imagine, we can well imagine God exulting when man comes through with a wish of his own. And we can imagine him thinking: look at it go.[61]

Second, and following on from this, Lynch suggests that

paradoxically real autonomy can only be found when one is fully dependent upon God. It is when God becomes the only absolute that the absolutizing instinct is quelled. 'There is only one God. Nothing else is that big, save in fantasy,'[62] says Lynch; 'the hope of the sick lies in destroying their idols and restoring their souls.'[63] Only when we 'put the absolute in the right place',[64] allowing no person or thing other than God to be God, are the workings of the absolutizing instinct dethroned. Only then can autonomous existence and hope begin.

Letting God be God. That must lie at the very core of the psychology of Christian hope. It is a human encounter, but one that acknowledges the divine as its source. Briefly, it might be noted here that this is precisely what seems to be absent in Tom. God is *not* God to him, but just a word. It is the fear of dying that is the most ultimate reality to Tom. Such fear is consuming him – he cannot see beyond it, and as such he affords it a kind of ultimate status. In Lynch's terminology, it is fear that has been absolutized, and so Tom finds himself spiritually frozen, unable to wish and unable to hope. But as his story unfolds we shall see how Tom's bursting into tears marks a turning point for him. Living hope is not so far away.

We have looked at the psychological nature of hope and considered some of its key sources as described by psychology and nursing science. Now the theological nature of Christian hope requires exploration in the search for a practical theology of hope for the dying.

Notes

1 Viktor Frankl, *Man's Search for Meaning*, ET (trans. Ilse Lasch), London: Hodder & Stoughton, 1962, pp. 72–3. Frankl, like many other writers of his day, had a tendency to use exclusively masculine language to talk of both men and women. Frankl's work is of enormous importance, but it should be pointed out that today we would seek a more inclusive use of language.
2 Ezra Stotland, *The Psychology of Hope*, San Francisco: Jossey Bass, 1969, p. 1.

3 Frankl, *Man's Search for Meaning*, pp. 71, 75.
4 See Richard Lazarus and Susan Folkman, *Stress, Appraisal, and Coping*, New York: Springer Publishing, 1984.
5 Elisabeth Kübler-Ross, *On Death and Dying*, New York: Macmillan, 1969, pp. 138, 139.
6 Judith Fitzgerald Miller, ed., *Coping with Chronic Illness* (2nd edition*)*, Philadelphia: F. A. Davis, 1992.
7 E.g. Norman Cousins, *Head First: The Biology of Hope and the Healing Power of the Human Spirit*, New York: E. P. Dutton, 1989; Jane Gillham, ed., *The Science of Optimism and Hope: Research Essays in Honour of Martin E. P. Seligman*, Philadelphia and London: Templeton Foundation Press, 2000, pp. 143–213.
8 Frankl, *Man's Search for Meaning*, p. 75.
9 Carol Farran *et al.*, *Hope and Hopelessness: Critical Clinical Constructs*, Thousand Oaks: Sage, 1995, p. 11.
10 Sigmund Freud, *The Future of an Illusion*, ET (trans. W. D. Robson-Scott), London: Hogarth Press, 1962, p. 26.
11 William Lynch, *Images of Hope: Imagination as Healer of the Hopeless*, New York: Mentor, 1965.
12 Farran *et al.*, *Hope and Hopelessness*, p. 12.
13 Charles Snyder, *The Psychology of Hope*, New York: The Free Press, 1994, pp. 13–16.
14 Andrew Duncan, 'The Andrew Duncan Interview: Helen's Story', *Radio Times*, 24–30 October 1998, p. 18.
15 Nick Pisa, 'My Secret Cancer Battle: I'll beat it, I'm not going to die, by TV's Onslow', *Sunday Mirror*, 29 November 1998, p. 5.
16 Snyder, *The Psychology of Hope*, p. 2.
17 Karin Dufault and Benita Martocchio, 'Hope: Its Spheres and Dimensions', *Nursing Clinics of North America* 20 (1985), pp. 379–91.
18 Gabriel Marcel, *Homo Viator*, ET (trans. Emma Craufurd), London: Victor Gollancz, 1951, pp. 32, 45.
19 Kaye Herth, 'Fostering Hope in Terminally Ill People', *Journal of Advanced Nursing* 15 (1990), pp. 1250–9, 1256.
20 Frankl, *Man's Search for Meaning*, pp. 70–1.
21 Lynch, *Images of Hope*, p. 60.
22 Beverly Hall, 'The Struggle of the Diagnosed Terminally Ill Person to Maintain Hope', *Nursing Science Quarterly* 3 (1990), pp. 177–84, 179.
23 Kübler-Ross, *On Death and Dying*, pp. 39, 138ff.
24 Mary Ersek, 'Examining the Process and Dilemmas of Reality Negotiation', *Image: Journal of Nursing Scholarship* 24 (1992), pp. 19–25.
25 Eric Kodish and Stephen Post, 'Oncology and Hope', *Journal of Clinical Oncology* 13 (1995), pp. 1817–22, 1818–19; Cheryl

Nekolaichuk and Eduardo Bruera, 'On the Nature of Hope in Palliative Care', *Journal of Palliative Care* 14 (1998), pp. 36–42, 39.

26 E.g. Janice Post-White *et al.*, 'Hope, Spirituality, Sense of Coherence, and Quality of Life in Patients with Cancer', *Oncology Nursing Forum* 23 (1996), pp. 1571–9, 1575; Kate Flemming, 'The Meaning of Hope to Palliative Care Patients', *International Journal of Palliative Nursing* 3 (1997), pp. 14–18, 16; Louann Koopmeiners *et al.*, 'How Healthcare Professionals Contribute to Hope in Patients with Cancer', *Oncology Nursing Forum* 24 (1997), pp. 1507–13, 1509.

27 Herth, 'Fostering Hope in Terminally Ill People', p. 1254; Cathleen Fanslow-Brunjes *et al.*, 'Hope: Offering Comfort and Support to Dying Patients', *Nursing* 27 (1997), pp. 54–7, 54.

28 Janice Morse and Barbara Doberneck, 'Delineating the Concept of Hope', *Image: Journal of Nursing Scholarship* 27 (1995), pp. 227–85, 278; Madeleine Clemence Vaillot, 'Hope: The Restoration of Being', *American Journal of Nursing* 70 (1970), pp. 268–73, 272; Pamela Hinds and Janni Martin, 'Hopefulness and the Self-sustaining Process in Adolescents with Cancer', *Nursing Research* 37 (1988), pp. 336–40, 338.

29 Erik Erikson, *Insight and Responsibility*, New York: W. W. Norton, 1964, pp. 115–17.

30 Lynch, *Images of Hope*, pp. 40, 235ff.

31 Eva Benzein and Britt-Inger Saveman, 'Nurses' Perception of Hope in Patients with Cancer: A Palliative Care Perspective', *Cancer Nursing* 21 (1998), pp. 10–16, 13.

32 Edith Hunt Raleigh, 'Sources of Hope in Chronic Illness', *Oncology Nursing Forum* 19 (1992), pp. 443–8, 447; Judith Fitzgerald Miller, 'Inspiring Hope', *American Journal of Nursing* 85 (1985), pp. 23–5, 24; Herth, 'Fostering Hope in Terminally Ill People', p. 1254; Patricia Poncar, 'Inspiring Hope in the Oncology Patient', *Journal of Psychosocial Nursing* 32 (1994), pp. 33–8, 38. It should be noted that the issue of touch calls for great caution and sensitivity to personal boundaries. This will be developed later in the book.

33 Gina Wong-Wylie and Ronna Jevne, 'Patient Hope: Exploring the Interactions between Physicians and H.I.V. Seropositive Individuals', *Qualitative Health Research* 7 (1997), pp. 32–56; Koopmeiners *et al.*, 'How Healthcare Professionals Contribute to Hope in Patients with Cancer'.

34 Kathleen Smith Baldree *et al.*, 'Stress Identification and Coping Patterns in Patients on Hemodialysis', *Nursing Research* 31 (1982), pp. 107–12, 111.

35 Marilyn Dubree and Ruth Vogelpohl, 'When Hope Dies – So Might

the Patient', *American Journal of Nursing* 80 (1980), pp. 2046–9, 2049.

36 Lynch, *Images of Hope*, p. 45.

37 Hinds and Martin, 'Hopefulness and the Self-sustaining Process in Adolescents with Cancer', p. 337; Raleigh, 'Sources of Hope in Chronic Illness', p. 446; Beverly Hall, 'Ways of Maintaining Hope in HIV Disease', *Research in Nursing and Health* 17 (1994), pp. 283–93, 289–90.

38 Lynch, *Images of Hope*, p. 178.

39 Snyder, *The Psychology of Hope*, p. 78.

40 Hinds and Martin, 'Hopefulness and the Self-sustaining Process in Adolescents with Cancer', p. 337.

41 E.g. Miller, ed., *Coping with Chronic Illness*; John Cutcliffe, 'How Do Nurses Inspire and Instil Hope in Terminally Ill HIV Patients?', *Journal of Advanced Nursing* 22 (1995), pp. 885–95.

42 Lynch, *Images of Hope*, p. 23. My italics.

43 Lynch, *Images of Hope*, p. 200.

44 Lynch, *Images of Hope*, p. 149.

45 Frankl, *Man's Search for Meaning*, p. 35.

46 Frankl, *Man's Search for Meaning*, pp. 73–4.

47 Sonja Sherry Hickey, 'Enabling Hope', *Cancer Nursing* 9 (1986), pp. 133–7, 136.

48 Cousins, *Head First*, p. 313.

49 Herth, 'Fostering Hope in Terminally Ill People', p. 1255.

50 Herth, 'Fostering Hope in Terminally Ill People', p. 1255.

51 Frankl, *Man's Search for Meaning*, pp. 42–3.

52 Farran *et al.*, *Hope and Hopelessness*, pp. 7–9.

53 Frankl, *Man's Search for Meaning*, pp. 70, 71–2.

54 Herth, 'Fostering Hope in Terminally Ill People', p. 1255.

55 Miller, 'Inspiring Hope', p. 25; Hickey, 'Enabling Hope', p. 135; Pamela Brown, 'The Concept of Hope: Implications for Care of the Critically Ill', *Critical Care Nurse* 9 (1989), pp. 97–105, 102.

56 E.g. Verna Carson *et al.*, 'Hope and Its Relationship to Spiritual Well-Being', *Journal of Psychology and Theology* 16 (1988), pp. 159–67; Eva Benzein *et al.*, 'Hope: Future Imagined Reality. The Meaning of Hope as Described by a Group of Healthy Pente-costalists', *Journal of Advanced Nursing* 28 (1998), pp. 1063–70; Richard Fehring *et al.*, 'Spiritual Well-being, Religiosity, Hope, Depression, and Other Mood States in Elderly People Coping with Cancer', *Oncology Nursing Forum* 24 (1997), pp. 663–71.

57 Anne O'Conner *et al.*, 'Understanding the Cancer Patient's Search for Meaning', *Cancer Nursing* 13 (1990), pp. 167–75, 173–4; Herth, 'Fostering Hope in Terminally Ill People', pp. 1254–5;

Raleigh, 'Sources of Hope in Chronic Illness', p. 447; Flemming, 'The Meaning of Hope to Palliative Care Patients', p. 18; Hall, 'Ways of Maintaining Hope in HIV Disease', pp. 288–9.

58 Kübler-Ross, *On Death and Dying*, p. 43.

59 Verna Carson *et al.*, 'Hope and Spiritual Well-Being: Essentials for Living With Aids', *Perspectives in Psychiatric Care* 26 (1990), pp. 28–34, 33.

60 Lynch, *Images of Hope*, p. 106.

61 Lynch, *Images of Hope*, pp. 156–7.

62 Lynch, *Images of Hope*, p. 49.

63 Lynch, *Images of Hope*, pp. 124–5.

64 Lynch, *Images of Hope*, p. 138.

3

The Theology of Hope

From first and last, and not merely in the epilogue, Christianity is eschatology, is hope.

Jürgen Moltmann, *Theology of Hope.*[1]

The pastoral need for theology

What does it mean to hope as a Christian? What is distinctive about Christian hope?

In different ways the stories from our opening chapter ask these very questions. Sarah seeks a renewal of confidence not just in Christian ministry but in *God*. Tom is familiar with the language of Christianity but for him it is painfully empty because until now he has never grappled with the theological heart and substance of Christian hope. Jane, on the other hand, possesses a very clearly defined belief system, but in a way that leaves little room for the realities of pain and death, understanding hope exclusively in terms of miraculous cure. Then we have David, whose striving for something to live and hope for awakens us still further to the need to explore how the Christian gospel carries a 'realistic' integrity. Last, in Angela we are reminded of the challenge to find ways of sharing Christian hope engagingly within our contemporary society, a climate in which we can discern a fusion of spiritual yearning with a marked scepticism towards claims of objective theological truth.

So just what do Christians hope for in the face of death? A simple response to that question is *eternal life*. But what exactly does that mean? Here clarification is needed. Christians commonly talk of 'going to heaven when you die'. This conveys the expectation of an 'afterlife' – the transition, at death, of the soul from time to eternity. But what of the body? According to 1 Corinthians 15, the Christian gospel is completely founded upon the resurrection of the Christ who died and was buried. Thus the Nicene Creed affirms that 'We look for the resurrection of the dead.' But then how might these two tenets of belief be held together? One suggests the entry into eternal life at the moment of death, while the other depicts something of a delay until the Second Coming of Christ at the end of time. Confusion pervades among Christians on these issues, and uncertainty can bring us dangerously close, albeit unwittingly, to a whole host of speculations and superstitions. In *For All the Saints? Remembering the Christian Departed* Tom Wright, the Bishop of Durham, comments:

> My fear is that we have been simply drifting into a muddle and a mess, putting together bits and pieces of traditions, ideas and practices in the hope that they will make sense. They don't. There may be times when a typical Anglican fudge is a pleasant, chewy sort of thing, but this isn't one of them. It's time to think and speak clearly and act decisively.[2]

Although these remarks may be specifically directed to Wright's own Anglican denomination, they arguably represent a major wake-up call to Christians in all the churches. If we are to give an account of the hope that is in us – if we are to actually *live* hope – it is imperative that we sharpen our theological focus and give greater clarity to that hope. Tom Wright himself does this as he takes up the very gauntlet he throws down, and calls upon Christians to rediscover *resurrection* as the primary theme of biblical hope.[3] However we employ images of heaven, they must take their place around a vision of hope that is founded first and foremost upon the resurrection of the body. That, we shall see, is the position that will be taken in this book.

As we develop a practical theology of hope for the dying we shall, however, be drawing on the insights of another major Christian writer for whom resurrection has been of fundamental importance throughout his theological career: Jürgen

Moltmann. Over the years, Moltmann's name has become virtually synonymous with the theology of hope movement that he has pioneered. His work is profoundly relevant to our quest for a model of *living hope* because Moltmann does not simply articulate the *content* of Christian hope, but is chiefly concerned with the very *dynamics* of hoping. Indeed, for Moltmann, these practical dynamics are the essential bearing of all authentically Christian theology.

Rumbold has suggested that a limitation of Moltmann's hope lies in its emphasis on 'community and change; largely this-worldly concerns'. While this may be an important corrective to the other extreme of giving focus exclusively to notions of 'afterlife', Rumbold argues that Moltmann insufficiently engages with the issue of personal hope, which, of course, is of primary importance in the palliative care context.[4] In response i t may be pointed out that Moltmann has in more recent years taken up the specific issue of what he calls 'personal eschatology',[5] which will be explored below. More fundamentally, though, Rumbold's criticism fails to appreciate that Moltmann's theology is really concerned above all else with the dynamics, that is, the actual thrust and movement of hoping. These dynamics are to be found at the core of all resurrection hope, whether we are talking about hoping for the transformation of society, for a better life in this world, or about personal hope in the face of death. Only the symbol of resurrection is wide-reaching enough to embrace all of these dimensions within the same set of hope-dynamics.

A brief history of hope

It is not possible here to present an exhaustive history of the development of Christian eschatology, that is, the doctrine of the last things.[6] It may, however, be helpful to give the briefest outline of its development since the late nineteenth century, in order to sketch roughly the sort of map on which we find Moltmann's thought. We can only really understand

Moltmann's theology when we have an idea of the shape of Christian hope that preceded his thinking.

With the advancing technology of the industrial revolution and rapid expansion of modern Christian civilization, a mood of optimism pervaded late nineteenth-century Europe. The faith of the modern enlightened mind was rooted in progress. Reflecting this, liberal Protestant theology spoke of the kingdom of God in terms of a moral force that was gradually advancing in society. Albrecht Ritschl wrote, 'The Christian idea of the kingdom of God denotes the association of mankind . . . through the reciprocal moral action of its members.'[7] This mode of thought prevailed at length until its foundations were completely shaken by the work of two major biblical scholars. The first was Johannes Weiss; the second was Albert Schweitzer, who gave Weiss's insights more systematic development. In short, these two theologians overturned the popular notion of the kingdom of God by arguing persuasively that for the Jesus of the New Testament, the coming of God's kingdom was a real event that was expected imminently. Schweitzer maintained that Jesus' whole ministry was driven by this expectation, until he eventually realized that it would not come until he went to Jerusalem where he met his death. When this kingdom did not come, the first believers transferred Jesus' hope to the *parousia*, his Second Coming. After a delay of some 2,000 years, though, we no longer hold out with the same dramatic expectation of Jesus' own hope.

In the decades following Weiss and Schweitzer theologians wrestled with the question these two men had raised: what are we to make of the delay of the *parousia* and the promise of the kingdom Jesus left us with? Among many thoughts and ideas put forward in the debate were two that are of particular importance, because in some ways they can still be found in popular belief today, albeit in different forms. The first is *realized eschatology*. This was set out by C. H. Dodd, who argued that Jesus' *parousia* is not in fact delayed at all, since the kingdom Jesus proclaimed came into being in and through his earthly ministry. Thus the kingdom is the existing reality of

God's power in the world, and our challenge today is to rediscover this reality as it confronts us. A second and perhaps
more widely held belief today, however, is Oscar Cullmann's
salvation history. Cullmann emphasized the eschatological
tension between the *already* of Jesus' death and resurrection,
and the *not yet* of his Second Coming. And so the Easter event
is likened to D Day, the decisive battle which has effectively
won the victory. But the Church continues to endure tribula-
tions as war rages until the *parousia*, the V Day on which victory is claimed.

Another area of thought to have made its way into popular
currency has to do with giving emphasis to the *existential
meaning* of Jesus' *parousia*. In different ways, two leading
twentieth-century theologians took the images of a future
promised kingdom of God and sought to appropriate these
images in terms of their significance for present existence.
Rudolf Bultmann did this by 'demythologizing' them. He
acknowledged that hope involves some kind of future expectation, but regarded the biblical references to the 'end of time' not
as historical events to be awaited. Rather, the *parousia* of Christ
meets us in every moment of our lives. Thus Bultmann stressed
the importance of the decision presented to us at all times, that
we might live every hour as though it were the last: 'In every
moment slumbers the possibility of being the eschatological
moment. You must awaken it.'[8] Though working within a
different framework of thought, similarities can be seen with
Paul Tillich's focus on the power of Christian *symbols*. He said
that while eschatology does refer in some way to historical
events at the end of time, primarily it is constituted by 'the symbolic expression of the relation of the temporal to the eternal';
'the symbol of the kingdom of God . . . must be immanent and
transcendent at the same time'.[9] Thus Tillich stressed the importance of 'the eternal now'. Eternity stands over time and thus can
be encountered in every moment and gives meaning to every
moment: 'The hope of the kingdom of God is not the expectation of a perfect stage of history . . . No! The hope of mankind
lies in the here and now whenever the eternal appears in time

and history.'[10] As such, 'Resurrection happens *now*, or it does not happen at all.'[11]

In different ways, Bultmann and Tillich were motivated by a common desire to establish the relevance of the kingdom of God for the present moment. In so doing they both downplayed the theme of a future expectation of the *parousia* as a historical event. This was met with criticism by the lead player on the stage of twentieth-century theology: the mighty Karl Barth. His complaint was that the attempt to encompass every moment with the existential significance of the kingdom of God led to an understanding of eschatology that was too broad to mean anything. He charged that 'little importance can now be attached to a particularly eschatological sphere of hope as Christian expectation of the future . . . we should awaken from this pan-eschatological dream'.[12] Years earlier Barth himself had declared that 'Christianity that is not entirely and altogether eschatology has entirely and altogether nothing to do with Christ.'[13] His concern was to assert that Christian hope is sure and certain and that it provides grounds for complete confidence. Thus Barth stressed the once-for-all nature of what God has done in Christ. As such he conceived of the future kingdom of God as the third form of *parousia*, the first and second being Christ's earthly ministry and Pentecost.[14] Because of the consistency of God, that which is awaited is nothing other than the unveiling of what God has already accomplished: 'It has already taken place; the only thing wanting is that the covering be removed and all may see it . . . The Alpha and the Omega are the same thing.'[15]

In his time, Barth's writing was considered to be so extensive, far-reaching and thoroughgoing that it somewhat dominated the theological world. In 1965 Barth was asked who he considered to be the promising theologians of the next generation. Without hesitation he named one person whose work was just beginning to radically change the way Christian hope was conceived. That person was Jürgen Moltmann.

Theologian of hope: Jürgen Moltmann

The particular work that Barth was referring to was Moltmann's *Theology of Hope*. It became the platform of Moltmann's entire theological career and its title gave birth to a movement of leading Christian writers who, like Moltmann, considered the doctrine of hope to be the defining thrust of theology. Such theologians include Wolfhart Pannenberg, Rubem Alves, Johann Baptist Metz and Carl Braaten. Their contention was that existing theologies had little to say about the future. Thus they called for the eschatological orientation of the whole of theology, that Christians might be renewed with expectation and hope for the future kingdom of God on earth. Of course, the common ground shared by these theologians should not mask the significant differences between their ideas. By no means are they simply derived from Moltmann – each of these voices has contributed to the theology of hope in a way that is distinctive. Furthermore, it might be noted that Pannenberg's thought was emerging before Moltmann was in the public arena. But it is Moltmann's theology that stands out as the most comprehensive treatment of hope itself, and it is thus of unique importance in our search for a practical theology of hope for the dying.

Moltmann's writing falls neatly into two series: his early trilogy of programmatic writings, followed by what Moltmann himself calls six 'contributions' to systematic theology. Our concern in this book is to unpack the main sources Moltmann brings for a practical theology of hope for the dying. A thorough systematic survey of his work is not necessary here.[16] However, the titles of his nine major volumes seem to define the contours of his theology rather well, and so here we shall use these as navigation points as we explore what Moltmann has to say about hope.

Working, hoping, living as a theologian: Experiences in Theology

Let us begin at the end of Moltmann's major works by picking up the title of what might be seen, in Moltmann's own words, as both the 'afterword' and 'foreword' of his theology.[17] *Experiences in Theology* looks back on Moltmann's theological career and describes how 'the road emerged only as I walked it'. As such, Moltmann says the book 'is not intended to be an introduction to my theology, but it is of course my introduction to theology'.[18] Essentially, it is a book about theological method. It is worth mentioning before looking at the major works that precede it because it says something very important about the distinctive nature of Moltmann's theology and its relevance to our quest for a *living hope*.

That special 'something' is that Moltmann writes with his 'lifeblood'. This is a term he once used specifically to describe his approach to one of his earlier books,[19] but there is a real sense in which it captures the flavour of all of Moltmann's work. In this respect it could be misleading to talk of Moltmann's 'thought' or 'writing', as that could imply that his work is the product only of a cerebral, academic exercise. Though it is possible to trace the theological and philosophical sources of his thinking[20] and appropriate to recognize him, as Barth did, as an exemplary scholar, Moltmann is more than an inheritor of his classic German Protestant tradition of dialectic theology. *Experiences in Theology* makes it clear that Moltmann's insights are born out of the joys and pains, celebrations and struggles of life experience. Here is a theologian who not only thinks and writes theology, but who identifies the theological enterprise with the task of *living and hoping*. Of course we might argue that this should be true of all theology, if we believe it to be engaging and relevant to life in our contemporary world. But it is noticeably true of Moltmann's.

Hope itself is Moltmann's primary concern. This, we shall see, is expressed in different ways through the various aspects of his theology, grounded throughout in his personal struggle to find hope in the midst of brokenness. As a teenager he was drafted into the German military and in July 1943 experienced the annihilation of his hometown Hamburg through the RAF's 'Operation Gomorrah', in which 40,000 people burnt to death. One night he narrowly escaped death as his friend standing beside him was blown to pieces: 'I cried out to God for the first time "My God, where are you?" And the question "Why am I alive and not dead like the rest?" has haunted me ever since.'[21] Later Moltmann was taken captive by the British and spent three years behind barbed wire as a prisoner of war. Here, 'weighed down by the sombre burden of a guilt which could never be paid off' and plunged into a depression of 'misery and forsakenness and daily humiliation', Moltmann encountered the 'dark night of the soul'. And yet this was the real genesis of Moltmann's spiritual and theological journey. He writes, 'I cannot even say I found God there. But I do know in my heart that it is there that he found me.'[22]

For Moltmann, then, the work of the theologian has to do with the task of living and hoping. Thus it can be seen how the very engagement of life's sufferings with talk of God is denoted by the question, *God, where are you?*

> That was my question in the face of death. It was not the theodicy question we are all familiar with – the question, how can God allow this to happen? That always seems to me like an onlooker's question. The person who is in the grip of a catastrophe, or is already in the jaws of a mass death, asks differently about God.[23]

This 'asking differently about God' means that anyone who is 'truly' a theologian is someone who knows they are personally involved with the God-question. This is painful; it also embraces life's experiences of joy. Moltmann calls this 'suffering from God and delight in God':

> True theologians must have addressed and worked through their struggles with God, their experiences of God, their fears

of God, and their joy in God. They must have laid themselves open personally to the things they maintain, and must neither suppress their negative experiences of their own selves before God, nor hide their positive delight in God (Ps. 37.4). It is good if we can perceive the theologian in his or her theology – good, if in those who have 'the cure of souls' we can sense the soul that has itself been deeply touched.[24]

Hope is more than just an affective or cognitive human experience. But it does deeply concern human experience, and here we can see how the psychology of hope may be taken up with the theology of hope in a single holistic search for what it means to hope as a Christian. Moltmann's own theology is particularly pertinent to this task because it resonates with his personal encounters with brokenness and pain. In subsequent chapters we will take this further by relating it specifically to the insights of psychology and nursing science. But here we might simply note the 'real life' nature of Moltmann's theology. As such it seems especially promising for a postmodern climate which tends to regard the 'experiential' with more credibility than so-called 'metanarratives'. It is unlikely that somebody like Angela will want to read a book about Christian eschatology as she sits in her hospital bed awaiting surgery. But she just might be intrigued to discover more about the mysterious experience described by Moltmann as having 'found God in my desolation . . . the power of a hope which I can believe, live and die with'. This is what Moltmann calls the *personal* or *subjective* side of Christian faith. It refers to a hope that can only be grasped experientially, not by rational argumentation. It is something best described as a reality that we can only be born anew into: 'We learn to hope if we obey the call.'[25]

For Moltmann hope is not, however, reduced to a matter of human experience alone. While it can only be entered into subjectively, Moltmann stresses that this is only one side of hope. There is also the *objective* side, the truth of God that stands independently of its meaning *for us*. This is the 'reasonableness of faith' – the area of rational argumentation that can only be grasped properly when it is preceded by belief, that is the experience of hoping. Moltmann calls this grasping of reason the movement from *trusting faith*, where we encounter the personal significance of God as an experience of hope, to *discerning faith*, where we step back from our selves and understand God not simply as '*my* Lord' but '*the* Lord'.[26]

Living hope: Theology of Hope

Actually, it is precisely because of this objectivity of God that hope is possible. For Moltmann, authentic Christian hope cannot be founded upon the possibilities inherent in human potential. It is not enough simply to muster our best human resources and hope for the greatest future we can possibly strive towards. Sooner or later our hope will be disappointed. Ultimately, this is because in the face of death we find ourselves depleted of any future possibility, confronted only by brokenness and devastation. Moltmann writes:

> do we not also need a hope which is connected with what we must suffer in sacrifice, in pain, and in dying? We naturally have hope when we are young. But do we not need hope also when we are old and incapable, when we can no longer help ourselves and when finally death robs us of all hope?[27]

If there is any hope at all in the midst of human brokenness and devastation, it must be founded on something that lies beyond and is greater than our human attempts to make a better future. For Moltmann, that 'something' is the transcendence of *God's promised future*. This is the central theme of his *Theology of Hope*.

Originally published in German in 1964, *Theology of Hope* was the first of Moltmann's major works. While his later career follows a much broader theological agenda, the basic thrust of all of Moltmann's thinking can be traced back to the arguments set out in that first volume. It is not a book *about* eschatology, but one that argues for the eschatological orientation of all

Christian theology: 'The eschatological is not one element *of* Christianity, but it is the medium of Christian faith.'[28] Moltmann's protest is that modern theologians such as Barth and Bultmann played down the temporality of eschatology to the point that eschatological discourse had effectively become de-historicized. For Barth, the *parousia* expectation was no more than an unveiling of what Christ has already accomplished, while Bultmann's commitment to demythologization led him to translate all eschatological language into an existentialist framework, emphasizing the present moment. Eschatology was thus emptied of any real sense of future dynamic.

Against this, Moltmann's *Theology of Hope* sets out to rediscover the importance of *God's promise* as a fundamental biblical theme. Biblical history is the history of divine promise, and when any such promise is fulfilled there is always an 'overspill that points to the future'.[29] With this, Moltmann emphasizes the importance of the *novum*, that is, the qualitatively new future that the promised coming kingdom of God denotes.

The sources used by Moltmann in his *Theology of Hope* have been comprehensively documented by M. Douglas Meeks, and there would be little point in duplicating his findings here.[30] However, one particular source deserves to be highlighted, and that is the humanistic Marxism of Ernst Bloch, from which Moltmann derives the notion of *novum*. This is especially important because it serves to illustrate how Moltmann has always sought to give 'an accounting' of the Christian hope by dialoguing with writers of differing worldviews, particularly exponents of Marxist hope. In his *Das Prinzip Hoffnung* (*The Principle of Hope*, 1959), Bloch puts forward an anthropology of hope. He argues that the human condition should be understood in terms of the possibilities that lie ahead. In order to realize these possibilities it is our task to look not to some past golden age but to the future. He writes, 'the true Genesis is not at the beginning, but at the end', speaking of the *novum*, the qualitatively new future that can only be described as the 'not yet', but towards which humanity must strive.[31]

While Moltmann's *Theology of Hope* employs some of the

conceptual framework of Bloch's principle of hope, it is important to stress that for Moltmann, Bloch's *novum* is not radical
enough. Such hope, which only has the innate processes of
history with which to conceive of a future, lacks the radical
newness that only the transcendence of God can bring. Because
for Bloch the future is not conceived as *God's* future, it cannot
confront the reality of death. Moltmann protests: 'There is a
dying where the principle of hope can accomplish nothing.'[32]
Only hope that is robust enough to engage with the reality of
death is worthy of the name. Our innate human potential has
only finite possibilities, but Christian hope in God sees newness
even in the face of mortality.

This brings us to what is really the core thesis of *Theology of
Hope*, namely Moltmann's eschatological interpretation of the
resurrection. The Easter story tells of a *contradiction* between
Jesus' death on the cross and his resurrection. This corresponds
to the contradictions we encounter between present suffering
and the future promised by God; between death and future
life; between brokenness and wholeness. Though cross and
resurrection represent total opposites, in speaking of 'the resurrection of the crucified one' Moltmann asserts that Jesus the
risen Lord is the same man who dies on the Friday. Thus there
is continuity through this radical discontinuity. Indeed, Jesus
maintains his identity through the Easter narrative, but it is only
through this dialectic of cross and resurrection that his identity
may be properly understood. And this is the same Jesus Christ
whose future remains outstanding: 'With the raising of Jesus all
has not yet been done . . . The resurrection has set in motion an
eschatologically determined process of history, whose goal is
the annihilation of death in the victory of the life of the
resurrection.'[33] In hope we thus look to God's promise of the
resurrection, by which all things will be made new, and strive
towards the realization of God's kingdom on earth. Ultimately
only God can make this happen, but in hope we reach out
beyond the present in mission and service in anticipation of
God's promised future.

This fundamental tenet of Moltmann's theology – namely,

that it is in God's promised future that we find hope – has important implications for a practical theology of hope for the dying. We may recall Sarah, the curate who longs for a deeper confidence as she seeks to minister to a dying person. Pastoral carers may indeed find themselves so immersed in a sense of helplessness that it seems overwhelming. Moltmann's theme of contradiction emphasizes the power of the resurrection over and against our human despair. It is a dialectic that contrasts *our* subjective helplessness with *God's* objective promise. But because it is the *crucified* Christ that is raised, the objectivity of that resurrection hope can be encountered in the very subjectivity of our human helplessness, because the crucified one stands in solidarity with us in our helplessness. More will be said about this as we look at Moltmann's second major work, *The Crucified God.* Here we may simply note that Moltmann offers carers like Sarah a way of laying hold of the objectivity of God's resurrection promise even in the midst of feelings of personal inadequacy and despair.

One further important practical implication of Moltmann's *Theology of Hope* worth acknowledging at this point concerns the postmodern context illustrated by Angela. In such a context, which generally regards truth claims as relative, it is not fashionable to attribute objectivity to truth in any way. Christian hope for resurrection is acceptable provided it does not venture beyond its subjectivity as one belief among many. As we have seen, at one level Moltmann affirms the subjective nature of Christian faith – it is something to be grasped experientially: 'Christ as *my* Lord'. But many would resist the objectivity afforded by the phrase 'Christ *the* Lord'. Such theology, it would seem, conveys a metanarrative, a grand story. Does this not immediately erect a barrier between Angela and Christian hope?

It need not. Properly understood, Christian eschatological hope is not a 'metanarrative' or a 'super theory', but an anticipation of the resurrection promise of God. It is the expectation that all will be transformed and made new, though we know not how nor when. It is a hope born out of a narrative, namely the story of the resurrection of the crucified one, but not a *meta*narrative, because we are still presently part of that story, living in anticipation of its end and moving towards the future promised by God. Christian hope is *living* hope. It is something to be encountered, caught up in, invigorated and transformed by. And that may be the very thing that Angela seems to be thirsty for.

Only the suffering God can help us live and die: The Crucified God

Whereas *Theology of Hope* focuses on the resurrection side of Moltmann's dialectic, stressing God's future promise, *The Crucified God* emphasizes the cross, death and present suffering. It seeks to engage Moltmann's eschatology with the reality of pain and death. Moltmann argues that this is important because God's future promise only becomes meaningful through the lens of the cross. Therefore, where *Theology of Hope* highlights 'the resurrection of the crucified Christ', here Moltmann takes up 'the cross of the risen Christ'.[34]

The Crucified God again highlights Moltmann as a theologian striving to give 'an accounting' of the Christian hope by wrestling with real-life issues and engaging with exponents of differing worldviews. In response to the question of the justification of God in the face of the problem of suffering – made devastatingly acute by Auschwitz – *The Crucified God* takes up the challenge of *protest atheism*. Moltmann affirms that 'Protest atheism points beyond both God and suffering, suffering and God, sets them one against the other and becomes atheistic protest against injustice "for God's sake".'[35] In other words, atheism is right in its protest against the traditional 'theistic' notion that God cannot suffer, because

a God who cannot suffer is poorer than any man. For a God who is incapable of suffering is a being who cannot be involved. Suffering and injustice do not affect him . . . But the one who cannot suffer cannot love either. So he is also a loveless being.[36]

Against this, Moltmann asserts the *pathos* of God. God suffers because God loves. Such a God, the crucified God, suffers in solidarity with us in our dying. This is elaborated as Moltmann describes Jesus' death not as the 'death of God' but 'death *in* God'. Traditional atonement theory has one-sidedly stressed the suffering of the Son as he is 'given up' by the Father. Moltmann's response is to give exposition to the different ways in which both the Father and the Son suffer the cross event. The Son is surrendered and forsaken by the Father, but in this act so the Father also surrenders and forsakes himself:

> The Son suffers dying, the Father suffers the death of the Son. The grief of the Father here is just as important as the death of the Son. The Fatherlessness of the Son is matched by the Sonlessness of the Father, and if God has constituted himself as the Father of Jesus Christ, then he also suffers the death of his Fatherhood in the death of the Son.

The most infinite experiences of godforsakenness in death and dying are thus taken up into the very being of God: 'This deep community of will between Jesus and his God and Father is now expressed precisely at the point of their deepest separation.'[37] God's solidarity with us in our godforsakenness, in our suffering and in our dying is thus established. God is with us in the protest against suffering, and in the protest against the justification of suffering. We behold the cross of Christ and see there the God who is at one with us in our own dying. We can lay hold of the resurrection hope because it is the risen one who is crucified and dies with us.

It was in his Nazi prison cell that Dietrich Bonhoeffer decided that 'only the suffering God can help'.[38] *The Crucified God* makes that explicit. We discover resurrection hope not in spite of suffering and dying but in and through that very context, for that is precisely where God is to be found. This reinforces the experiential nature of living hope that is of special relevance to Angela, who is primarily in search of a hope that is not merely explained but actually encountered. Sarah's helplessness may be embraced as the way to resurrection hope, for it is on the path to despair that we discover the God who journeys with us. This is also deeply relevant for Tom, who in his fear of death feels isolated from others and from God. The crucified Christ stands in solidarity with him in his godforsakenness.

The Crucified God is especially pertinent to what we have already identified in previous chapters as the concern for a 'realistic' hope. In different ways this is a live issue for David and for Jane. In David we see the pendulum swing from an initial soldiering on with the insistence that he will soon be well enough to return to work, to a fatalistic resignation that there is nothing left to do but die. Against this, the hope of the risen Christ who is crucified is something that engages both the seriousness of death and the possibilities for life in the face of such reality. For Jane, this offers a more holistic understanding of God's power to heal. Rather than confining hope in God to a miraculous cure, the crucifixion of the risen Christ holds out the possibility of encountering the power of the resurrection in the experience of dying, for that is where God is to be found. These things will be explored in greater depth in the chapters that follow. Here we may simply note that our quest for a living hope demands a theology that discerns God in both life and death. *The Crucified God* offers just that.

Living hope as the Church: The Church in the Power of the Spirit

The last in Moltmann's early trilogy draws together the key ideas developed in *Theology of Hope* and *The Crucified God*. Following the cross and resurrection, the Spirit is at work in the world, transforming it in anticipation of the coming kingdom of God. While it is God who will bring this kingdom into being, the Church does not simply sit back and wait for it to happen. Christians are called to engage in mission in the world, in the power of God's Spirit, striving for as well as pointing to the future that is promised by God.

Moltmann offers us a dynamic way of understanding what it

means to 'be church'. His vision is of a Church 'on the move'. Instead of defining it as an establishment and then describing its missionary function, Moltmann prefers to talk of the Church as something that *happens*, concentrating on the messianic mission in which it is to be found. He writes: 'We cannot say *what* the church is in all circumstances and what it comprises in itself. But we can tell *where* the church happens . . . the church is present wherever "the manifestation of the Spirit" (1 Corinthians 12.7) takes place.'[39] This forward-moving dynamic elaborates the eschatological thrust that runs through Moltmann's early work. Terms such as 'eschatological community' and 'messianic fellowship' are used throughout to express the sense of future-orientation that permeates Moltmann's understanding of the Church. We might say that for Moltmann, the Church is the corporal expression of living hope. It is the 'anticipation' of the kingdom of God in history, the 'working of the Spirit of the new creation' which has not yet come into being in all its fullness.[40]

A theme elaborated in *The Church in the Power of the Spirit* that is of special importance for pastoral care is *worship*. This is a messianic feast that 'renews the remembrance of Christ and awakens hope for his kingdom'; liberation is experienced in the present moment as the worshipping community 'lays anticipatory hold on the joy of redeemed existence'. This is no 'ecstasy that transports us into another world' but it is the 'qualitative alteration of this world'.[41] Here Moltmann develops an area of thought that he initially presented in a brief but fascinating book, *Theology and Joy*. This emphasizes the significance of joy, play, laughter, celebration, beauty and enjoyment against the rigorous moralism of revolutionary movements and western society's work ethic that defines value in terms of function and achievement. Theology has a profound aesthetic quality, highlighting the importance of *doxology*: 'Being aware of God is an art and – if the term may be permitted – a noble game.'[42] Games are often played as a way of distracting attention from hard reality, providing a temporary escapism in a compensatory way. The Christian 'game of freedom' is quite different. Set within the framework of Moltmann's dialectic of cross and resurrection, Christian joy does not flee from sorrow but embraces it:

> Thus both the laughter of Easter and the sorrow of the cross are alive in liberated men. They are not only laughing with those who laugh and weeping with those who weep . . . but they are also laughing with the weeping and weeping with the laughing as the Beatitudes of Jesus recommended.[43]

As Christians celebrate and rejoice in worship the future kingdom of God is thus anticipated in the here and now. This, says Moltmann, is 'playing with the future in order to get to know it'.[44] *The Church in the Power of the Spirit* identifies this 'feast without end' as integral to the life of the Church.[45] While the calling of the Church may be understood in terms of mission, ethics and the pursuit of justice in the world, this can too easily lead to legalism. At the heart of 'being church' is the joy of worship, in which the freedom of God's promised future is envisioned, celebrated and experienced in hope.

Once again, we can see how the experiential dynamism of Moltmann's theology may help to equip us for a meaningful engagement with someone like Angela who is primarily interested in a living hope – that is, something that is real, something that might be encountered, and something that 'works'. *The Church in the Power of the Spirit* challenges us to understand our ministry as something that is alive, vibrant and exciting. As pastoral carers we are not people who are doing a 'religious job'; we are people caught up in the forward-moving thrust of God's Spirit. We do what we do because we dare to lay hold of God's promised future in hope and expectation.

Conceived as an institution, a form of organized religion, the Church seems irrelevant to Angela's angst as she waits to be taken down to the operating theatre. And yet as she overhears Sue praying with another patient, she does not see a representative of an institution. Instead, she senses something of the spirituality of another human being who is seeking to live out her hope in God. Sometimes pastoral carers may feel uncertainty as to whether it is appropriate to offer prayer to people that openly distance themselves from Christian belief. This may have to do with a healthy concern to avoid making a person feel pressured into accepting a prayer that they do not want. Here, of course, it is Angela who actually requests Sue to pray for her. But perhaps this scenario might awaken us to the danger of making assumptions that people who do not outwardly profess Christian faith would never want us to pray with them. The Church as an establishment may be of no interest to most people today. But the opportunity to partake in some way of our Christian living hope, as the mysteriously joyous encounter with God's promised future – that is altogether another matter. To understand church as a dynamic movement – one that is living, vibrant and a joy to be a part of – is something we could do well to rediscover.

The living God of hope: The Trinity and the Kingdom of God

Moltmann's later series of 'contributions' to systematic theology is much broader than his early trilogy. The main continuity is that in his later work Moltmann's thinking about God as Trinity matures and deepens. In *The Trinity and the Kingdom of God* Moltmann again takes up the theme of God's suffering, developing further the implications of the claim that God can and does suffer for and with the creation. Such thinking has been resisted in the past, says Moltmann, through a concern that to suggest that God could suffer would imply a deficiency of God's being. If God must suffer, goes the argument, then God must lack freedom, and cannot really be God. Moltmann meets this line of reasoning by pointing out that God *chooses* to suffer through love. This denotes no deficiency or lack of freedom: it is because of God's infinite love that God freely chooses to suffer. Thus Moltmann emphasizes the pathos of God, writing, 'The experience of suffering reaches as far as love itself.'[46]

In *The Trinity and the Kingdom of God*, the passion of God is elaborated in terms of pathos and suffering as Moltmann develops the central thesis of the book, his 'social doctrine of the Trinity'. God is love. God suffers through freedom in love and 'reveals himself as love in the fellowship of the Father, the Son and the Holy Spirit'. Love can only exist in fellowship and not individually in isolation:

> Because he [God] not only loves but is himself love, he has to be understood as the triune God. Love cannot be consummated by a solitary subject. An individuality cannot communicate itself . . . If God is love he is at once the lover, the beloved and the love itself.[47]

And so the unity of Father, Son and Holy Spirit lies in their *fellowship*. Each receives identity through their relationship in love with the others. Here Moltmann appeals to the Orthodox notion of *perichoresis* to describe the mutual indwelling of Father, Son and Spirit. But he does so in a way that is very much his own, using terms of future-dynamic and forward-movement to give the doctrine an eschatological bearing. According to Moltmann, the triune God is the historical God, the God whose pathos enables us to speak of the God who experiences, suffers and is affected by history. This is because God is *open* Trinity, in whom the 'relations of fellowship' are 'open to men and women, and open to the world'.[48] Geiko Muller-Fahrenholz puts it thus: 'God is not "finished".'[49] As long as the world has not been brought to its eschatological completion, God cannot rest, but continues to suffer with the world, historically, as open Trinity.

Many Christians today, while affirming belief in the doctrine of the Trinity, would probably tend to regard it as a perplexing theological mystery that does not directly engage with the challenges of everyday life. That is a mistake, and *The Trinity and the Kingdom of God* makes the importance of trinitarian theology for living hope explicit. Such theology emphasizes that Christian hope is in a living God. If God is open Trinity, moving us forward to the future in hope and calling us to partake in God's mission in the world, pastoral care is to be understood as the act of *participating in God*.[50] As we care for the dying, we do not simply attempt to tell them about our hope in a God we have 'observed'. Neither is it enough to say that we strive to 'imitate' Christ, as Christian tradition has often stressed. Rather, as we come alongside others who are facing death, we actually partake in God's own history, living the hope of God's future, and inviting those for whom we care to share in the same.

Once again this reinforces the experiential nature of Christian hope, which we have acknowledged is vital in our postmodern context. It is especially relevant to Sarah's concern for a deeper confidence in her pastoral care. Understood as participation in God she may be able to see 'her' ministry as 'God's', openly acknowledging her own human helplessness not as something to feel ashamed of but as the very means by which she grasps hold of the strength and grace of God.

Moltmann's doctrine of God also offers something of enormous importance to Tom. His initial response to his diagnosis is to tell nobody and put on a brave face. Against his intentions, Tom eventually breaks down. The God of *passion*, who is affected by the suffering of history, is the God for whom brave faces are not required. If tears of brokenness can be seen as part of God's own experience, then Tom might just be able to regard them as acceptable. And if Tom can 'own' these tears, allowing them to flow freely as the honest expression of the devastation he feels, perhaps he may begin an open and frank exploration of the promises of hope that have over the years become the unexamined furnishings of the church culture in which he has been immersed. Maybe Tom might come to see his story as part of God's story, and so participate in God in a way that is real and meaningful to him. Such participation involves coming to own the future promises of God's story. That is living hope.

Hope in living creation: God in Creation

Moltmann's doctrine of creation, which focuses on God's *presence* in the world, represents something of a shift of emphasis, particularly when set against his earlier theology which stressed the contradiction between God's promised future and the present experience of suffering and God-abandonment. Some go so far as to identify this change as a reversal in Moltmann's theology.[51] However, a change in emphasis does not necessarily denote a fundamental change in direction. Continuity exists through Moltmann's maintenance of the eschatological theme, though he now develops it in more explicitly trinitarian terms. This debate will be taken up later on; here we will simply unpack what Moltmann has to say about the presence of God in creation.

God in Creation expands Moltmann's notion of God as 'open Trinity'. God is not closed off from the creation, but by the Spirit participates in it, and so the creation itself participates in God: 'If the cosmic Spirit is the Spirit of God, the universe cannot be viewed as a closed system. It has to be understood as a system that is open – open for God and for his future.'[52] This is an expansion of *The Trinity and the Kingdom of God* in that the whole cosmos, not just human history, is depicted as participating in God. For Moltmann relatedness and openness go hand in hand. As 'open Trinity' God 'participates in the destiny of his own creation',[53] and as an 'open system' the universe participates in God. The universe is not static, but must be understood in terms of evolution, process and change. An open system, he says, is an 'anticipatory system',[54] open to God and open to God's future. Creation is not yet finished, but awaits completion in the coming kingdom of God. The Holy Spirit, or as Moltmann likes to put it, the 'Cosmic Spirit', is the power of anticipation animating the open system of creation. The experience of this Spirit in creation thus forms the occasion for hope. Moltmann writes, 'All creations in the Spirit are in intention "open". They are directed towards their common future, because they are all, each in its own way, aligned towards their potentialities.'[55]

What is the future towards which the Spirit directs the creation? Here Moltmann takes up the notion of the *sabbath*. The crown of creation is not humanity, but the sabbath, where God rests, enjoys and savours the goodness of creation. And so the goal of creation, the coming of God's kingdom in all fullness, may be understood as the eschatological sabbath. Moltmann thus calls for a revitalized observance of the sabbath that hope might be nurtured.

> The sabbath opens creation for its true future. On the sabbath the redemption of the world is celebrated in anticipation. The sabbath is itself the presence of eternity in time, and a foretaste of the world to come.[56]

God in Creation offers us a way of understanding the goodness of life itself as the anticipation of God's future. This makes for a more holistic, inclusive concept of hope because it enables us to regard every positive experience of life as part of the prelude to the new creation of God's promised future. Angela's belief in 'something spiritual', though shrouded with uncertainty, can be affirmed as a God-given yearning. This might be taken up by Sue in pastoral conversation as a natural way of sharing something of the living hope that led her to offer as a volunteer on the chaplaincy team.

Affirming and celebrating the presence of God in the fabric of life here and now is of enormous importance for somebody like David. At the point where he resigns himself to death, David's vision of what remains of his life in this world has been eclipsed by his mortality. That mortality is, of course, quite real, but for David it has become the sole definition of reality. As such, he has effectively taken leave of this world even though he still has a life to be lived within it. How pastoral carers might practically respond to David will be taken up in subsequent chapters, but here we might note the fundamental affirmation of all life that is given in *God in Creation*. As long as we are in this world, no matter how close to death we are, life is there to be lived. God is in it, and God bids us to savour the reality of life as the foretaste

of a still greater reality that is to come. Because of this fundamental value that is afforded life itself we are urged to see the
potential that lies within life at every moment. That is not
always an easy thing to do, and at times it may require considerable effort. But if it is true that the living God is to be found
in the living creation, living hope can never be far away.

Living discipleship: The Way of Jesus Christ

Moltmann's volume on christology continues to give focus to
dynamic process and movement:

> I am trying to think of Christ no longer statically, as one
> person in two natures or as a historical personality. I am try-
> ing to grasp him dynamically, in the forward movement of
> God's history with the world.[57]

Eschatological emphasis is expressed through Moltmann's use
of the word *way* in the title of his book. This has a three-
pronged messianic symbolism that captures something of the
'living' dynamic of Christian discipleship. First, the symbol of
the *way* suggests a process of movement towards the future that
is hoped for. All is not yet finished; Christ's future is awaited in
hope. Moltmann takes issue with Barth's inclination to speak
of the *parousia* as the revelation of what Christ already is.
Something new must be expected:

> Christ's parousia therefore does not merely 'unveil' the
> salvific meaning of Christ's death. It also, and much more,
> brings the *fulfilment* of the whole history of Christ, with all
> that it promises.[58]

Second, the *way* conveys the manner in which affirmations are
made about Jesus Christ – namely that they are made in hope,
in anticipation of the *parousia*. This highlights Moltmann's
commitment to Jewish–Christian dialogue that features heavily
in *The Way of Jesus Christ*, and resounds through his career.
The Christian 'yes' to Jesus' messiahship must accept the Jewish

'no' which is based on the present experience of 'unredeemed-ness'. This echoes something of Moltmann's earlier dialectic:

> The 'yes' will in so far adopt the 'no' as to talk about the total and universal redemption of the world only in the dimensions of a future hope, and a present contradiction of this unredeemed world. The Christian 'yes' to Jesus Christ is therefore not in itself finished and complete. It is open for the messianic future of Jesus. It is an eschatologically *anticipatory and provisional* 'yes'.[59]

Moltmann's third use of *way* is to represent the invitation of Christian discipleship: 'A way is something to be followed.'[60] As the community of hope, the Church is called to practise 'the great alternative' and be a 'contrast society'.[61] We discover who Jesus really is only when we enter upon that way of discipleship.

Taken together, these uses of the word *way* help to reinforce the essential openness of living Christian hope as followers of Jesus, which, we have noted, distinguishes it from a 'closed' form of metanarrative. This openness is important because it makes room for the mystery that is a vital part of hope. Such mystery in no way undermines the assurance or conviction that is central to Christian hope; indeed, it actually *expresses* the assurance and the conviction that the future is in God, and as such lies beyond our grasp now. But the assurance and conviction comes as we *live* hope, that is, as we follow Jesus. This means that pastoral carers who seek to give 'an accounting' for their hope (1 Peter 3.15) need not shy away from profound life-questions to which easy answers are just not possible, but can openly acknowledge them as the very context of uncertainty and mystery within which the assurance of Christian hope is encountered and lived. Sarah may thus be released from the burden of feeling that as a minister she must somehow 'know the right things to say'. Her primary calling is to be a disciple of the one in whom she finds hope.

Angela, who longs for spirituality that is real and authentic but is suspicious of religious dogmatism, might well sense a credibility about the claim that Christian hope can be genuine-ly experienced without the need to have truth neatly stitched up. The invitation to travel along the *way* and so experience living hope for herself is more likely to engage with her than simply telling her about the things Christians believe. That is not to suggest that there is no place for apologetics. But it does mean that the experience of prayer, which Angela requests, might sometimes be the most meaningful place to start.

Depicting hope in terms of a journey in which mystery and uncertainty are openly acknowledged may be particularly help-ful for Tom. He might begin to feel that Christian hope could be within reach after all, since finding answers to every last question is not a prerequisite for discovering personal assurance in the face of death. Accepting this might be Tom's first step towards actually starting to wrestle and engage personally with those questions – a process that may be necessary if his 'spiritu-ally frozen' state is to thaw. Then the way of Jesus Christ might start to become Tom's way as he encounters a living hope for himself.

Living presence: The Spirit of Life

We have seen how Moltmann affirms the present experience of God in *God in Creation*. In *The Spirit of Life* Moltmann makes this more explicit than ever. God's Spirit, he says, is 'the divine wellspring of life – the source of life created'.[62] The Spirit in all human beings accounts for a basic orientation to God: 'Because God's Spirit is present in human beings, the human spirit is self-transcendently aligned towards God.'[63] Whenever we experi-ence the love of life, vitality and energy for simply being alive, we experience God's Spirit. This vitality consists not just of joy but also of suffering, and Moltmann echoes his earlier reflections on the pathos of God. Love of life goes hand in hand with the capacity to suffer. A life in which there is no suffering at all is not really a life, but only indifference and apathy. To suffer consciously is the first sign of being truly alive and of living hope.

Moltmann's affirmation of the presence of God in the here and now is nevertheless heavily qualified in eschatological terms. God may be experienced in the present, but this is essentially an experience of anticipation. God is encountered as the presence of the future. As the Spirit of life is experienced now so is the future resurrection life into which the Spirit raises us:

> If according to the Christian hope 'the transfiguration of the body' consists of the raising from death to eternal life, then it is already experienced here and now in the Spirit of life, which interpenetrates body and soul and wakens all our vital powers.[64]

However, the most noticeable development in *The Spirit of Life* is Moltmann's affirmation that God can be experienced in a way that cannot be described in terms of *future*. Specifically, he refers to ecstatic experience, 'the presence of eternity'.[65] He writes, 'In moments such as these the experience of God becomes so intensive that there is no more remembrance and no more expectation. God is pure present.'[66] At first glance Moltmann appears to be altogether taking leave of his fundamental conviction that theology must rediscover its eschatological bearing. It seems a far cry from his critique of modern theologians who have emptied eschatology of its temporality and thus removed its sense of future expectation. Further discussion will be given to this important development later; here it might simply be noted as one of the most contentious points in Moltmann's work, as he ventures further than ever to affirm the presence of God in the here and now.

This affirmation of the living presence of God in the structures of life in this world is of enormous importance to the pastoral care of the dying. Once again, if all spirituality, no matter how vague it may seem, reflects something of a basic God-ward orientation that forms a vital part of our humanity, Angela shares far more common ground with Sue than first meets the eye. Encouraging Angela to see this may well help to break down some of the barrier she might perceive between her and Christian hope.

The breadth of Moltmann's understanding of the presence of God's Spirit – what he calls a 'universal affirmation' of the Spirit in creation – is an important corrective to the narrow vision we come across in Jane's story. It might be argued that Moltmann is too broad in his assertion that 'Every experience of a creation of the Spirit is hence also an experience of the Spirit itself.'[67] Nevertheless, it is a suggestion that refuses to confine the work of God's Spirit to the single hope for a miraculous cure. God is bigger than that. An expansion of vision among those who only recognize the Holy Spirit where miraculous cures occur might enable people in Jane's situation to discern more readily the presence of God even in dying.

Tom, for whom God seems so distant, may find the suggestion that God is to be found within life itself even more alienating. Vitality, love of life and zest for living could not be further away from his experience as he finds himself plunged into fear and despair. But his love of life is probably greater than he would presently recognize, for it is a love that is evinced by the very tears he sheds. Only one who truly loves can truly cry: 'The sighs and cries of prisoners are always the first signs of life they show, and are anything but signs of death.'[68] God, and hope, may be closer than Tom thinks.

Back to the future: The Coming of God

Moltmann's focus becomes once more specifically eschatological in *The Coming of God*. In many ways this book echoes the arguments basic to his earlier work. However, whereas *Theology of Hope* was essentially an argument for the eschatological orientation of all theology, *The Coming of God* grapples with specific dimensions of eschatological expectation, asking what Christian hope means for the individual, for history, for the cosmos, and for God. It is, of course, the first of these – the individual's hope for eternal life, or 'personal eschatology' as Moltmann puts it – that is of particular relevance to a practical theology of hope for the dying. It thus merits closer examination here.

Moltmann understands eternal life in terms of resurrection. Notions of the soul taking leave of the body at death and going to heaven are not derived from the Bible but from Plato's philosophy of the immortality of the soul. Moltmann argues that resurrection is not only a more biblically based hope – it is also more holistic. The whole person, their 'whole life history',[69] is raised. Because it is hope for the raising of an identity that now exists but will be transformed in resurrection, it is not reduced to life *after* death.[70]

But if we do not go to heaven when we die, where do we go? What happens to us between the time of our death and our resurrection at the end of history? Moltmann rejects the doctrine of Purgatory, which teaches that we enter a time of preparation and purification. He also resists Luther's notion of 'the Soul's Sleep', which depicts the time between death and resurrection in terms of rest. Moltmann argues that neither of these doctrines take seriously Paul's words, 'My desire is to depart and be with Christ' (Philippians 1.23).[71] He also maintains that resurrection should not be thought of as something that happens at death, for this contradicts the eschatological hope of the 'Day of the Lord', when all the dead will rise simultaneously, 'in a moment'.

So where are the dead? Moltmann says the dead have 'time' and 'space', 'in the fellowship of Christ'. We cannot know what this is like as we have not yet experienced it, but the dead, like the living, 'are not lost, but they are not finally saved either'.[72] The division between the dead and the living is 'assuredly in the risen Christ . . . In him the dead are enduringly with us who are the living. The common hope for the future of eternal life and the new creation binds us together.'[73] Moltmann's elaboration at this point is somewhat vague. It also appears rather speculative as little scriptural basis is given. At this point it will suffice to acknowledge that what Moltmann offers is something of a response to the need to talk in some way of a real continuity between life in the here and now and a hope that transcends death and encompasses those who have already died. Such a need is especially apparent when Tom's wife Jenny turns to the minister and asks, 'We will see one another again in the next life, won't we?' More detailed discussion will thus be given to the issue in the next chapter.

Another important question that Moltmann takes up is this: 'Is death the consequence of sin or life's natural end?'[74] Acknowledging the connection Paul makes between sin and death, Moltmann also highlights the tradition that regards death as 'natural'. On the one hand, mortality is part of creation in time. 'Nature', of which human bodily life is a part, is 'a time or season of creation which we might compare with winter', and is subject to transience. On the other hand, all of nature awaits the new creation which, says Moltmann, drawing on Hildegard of Bingen, will be like the springtime. So death is not a direct punishment for sin. Nevertheless, we await the 'redemption of the body' (Romans 8.23), when the grace of God 'completes and perfects what that creation was made and destined for'. Only God's grace can bring this about, for the 'frailty of the temporal creation of human beings is like a detonator for the sin of wanting to be equal to God and to over-come this frailty'.[75] In our mortality we crave to overcome it and be like God, and so Moltmann suggests in this sense it is not that 'the wages of sin is death' (Romans 6.23), but 'the wages of death is sin'.[76]

The question of whether death is to be regarded as natural or the result of sin is again one that will be taken up later in this book. Here it is enough to simply recognize its pastoral impli-cations. Should death be seen as the ultimate enemy to be resisted and fought, or might it be positively embraced as part of the created order? This is especially important for Jane, whose focus is entirely on praying that death would not come. While this book is not primarily about the theology of death but about hope, it can be seen that our discussion will have to give at least some consideration to the question of how we regard death itself.

The concluding part of Moltmann's section on 'personal eschatology' in The Coming of God discusses the importance of mourning. Moltmann sets out again his earlier conviction that love and suffering are inseparable. Only the one who loves can suffer. Love for life is thus the context for the work of grief: 'The person who mourns deeply has loved greatly. The person who cannot mourn has never loved.'[77] Moltmann emphasizes the importance of community in the grief process, affirming that 'the community of Christ' is indeed 'the community of the living and the dead, of lovers and mourners'.[78] In this community there is continuity between this present life and life beyond death. Again, however we answer the question, 'Where are the dead?', it is the live concern for just this sense of continuity that causes it to be asked. Jenny is not only seeking some assurance that there will be a future for Tom beyond death, but that there might be a future for them both. As we give further exploration to the doctrine of resurrection we shall see how it engages with precisely these concerns, holding out a living hope to both those who are dying and their loved ones too.

Live issues for a practical theology of hope for the dying

Our journey through Moltmann's major works has hopefully given some idea of the enormous relevance of his theology to our quest for a living hope. More detailed discussion will be given to Moltmann's insights in the following chapters as we seek to develop a practical theology of hope for the dying. But first let us conclude this chapter by highlighting the key issues that are often regarded as the hallmarks of his theology and are of paramount importance for this book. We will also consider some of the debate surrounding these things.

Last things first: the importance of the future

For Moltmann, two fundamental convictions make hope possible: God and the future. First, it is in God alone that we can have hope. Only God is transcendent and thus only hope in God can transcend death. Second, it is the power of the future found in the promise of God, and indeed in the very being of God, that enables the forward-bearing dynamic that is necessary for hope to be generated. Christian hope is eschatological hope, looking to the *parousia*, to the God who is coming to us with the promised kingdom of the future.

Moltmann expresses these convictions by drawing a distinction between two terms that denote the future. The word *futurum* means 'what will be', and refers to the potential that exists within the present but is yet to come into being. Moltmann argues that *adventus*, meaning 'what is coming', is more appropriate for Christian eschatology because the future that is hoped for is the future that God promises to bring to the world. This transcends the mere possibilities that are latent in the world's processes. Only *adventus*, the future that God brings, can be a basis for real hope because it represents the genuinely new, and not something that is simply dormant in the world.[79] It must be pointed out that putting hope in the God 'who is coming' does not denote a passive waiting. Hope is the anticipatory trust in God's future promise that motivates human action. Moltmann thus talks about both 'confidently *waiting*' and 'wholeheartedly *seeking*'.[80] Hope is no mere consolation but the force that compels action and protest. 'God is the future . . . When freedom has come near, the chains begin to hurt,'[81] writes Moltmann. 'In beginning to hope for the triumph of life and to wait for resurrection', the one who hopes 'perceives the deadliness of death and can no longer put up with it'.[82]

The future, then, is vital to Moltmann's theology because his hope is born out of the contrast or contradiction between the future that is anticipated in God and the realities of death and suffering in the present, corresponding to the contradiction between Jesus' resurrection and the cross. This is what gives Moltmann's theology its *dialectic* form. Only where radical *discontinuity* from the present is envisaged for the future can there be hope that things will be better, indeed, transformed.

For all that, unless our vision of hope bears some *continuity* between present experience and the future that is hoped for, the creation as it now is becomes somewhat devalued. If the new creation we anticipate in hope represents the wholesale destruction of every aspect of present reality, then all our strivings and struggles in this life are emptied of any real meaning. Furthermore, we can only begin to envision the future at all by appealing to aspects of our experience with which we are familiar. In the last chapter we saw how vital the imagination is for the psychological process of hoping. The imagination functions when objects of familiarity are depicted in a transformed state. Without continuity between present reality and future vision, that future is unintelligible and hope cannot get off the ground.

An important critical question, then, is whether Moltmann achieves an appropriate balance of emphases between continuity and discontinuity. When we take all of his theology into account, there is strong evidence that he does. On the one hand, his earlier work is arguably more sharply focused on the discontinuity between present and future. That is where the force of his dialectic lies, and is probably what makes his early trilogy so thought-provoking. On the other hand, Moltmann's later work gives more weight to the continuities between the present creation in which God's Spirit is to be found, and the new creation into which it will eventually be transformed. Some critics have suggested that Moltmann contradicts his earlier thinking with this shift in emphasis. That is not really the case, because he retains his basic dialectic, only it becomes broadened. The contradiction between the Friday and Sunday of the Easter event no longer corresponds simply to that which exists between present suffering and future hope. Now the correspondence has been expanded to the more general forces of life against death in creation, as the Spirit of life moves the creation towards the transformation of God's promised future.

Nevertheless, the way Moltmann has related the future with the present has over the years generated considerable debate. The most commonly levied criticism is that Moltmann conceives of hope in God so heavily in terms of the future that he downplays the present experience of God. It has been suggested that Moltmann's eschatology has too much of the 'not yet' and not enough of the 'already'.[83] John Macquarrie draws a parallel with *Alice in Wonderland*, when Alice inquires if she might have some jam: 'She was told that there was jam yesterday and there will be jam tomorrow, but there is no jam today. And unfortunately it is always today.'[84] Moltmann's hope, he argues, will only envision a God of tomorrow, never today.

There can be no doubt that there is a one-sidedness in Moltmann's emphasis of the future that could be construed as denying any present experience of God, especially in his earlier work. Such one-sidedness may be the necessary price to pay for the power of argument found in Moltmann's dialectic. In a letter to Karl Barth, Moltmann once wrote, 'I must champion the truth polemically and onesidedly in the hope that it will itself emerge in the process.'[85] But here it should be reiterated that in order to understand properly the way Moltmann deals with different theological themes and tensions between points of emphasis, we need to appreciate that throughout his career he has tended to take up various complementary perspectives in turn. While one particular book seems to display a one-sided emphasis of one perspective at the expense of others, when set within the overall context of his wider theology it is possible to see how that one book is balanced by the emphasis given to different perspectives in others.

This is certainly the case when it comes to the question of whether Moltmann affirms the experience of God in the present. While *Theology of Hope* radically stresses hope for the future, in *The Crucified God* Moltmann gives focus to God's fellowship and solidarity with us in our present experiences of suffering. In his later work, as Moltmann's doctrine of the Trinity matures, his affirmation of the present experience of the Spirit in creation is developed and integrated within the eschatological structure of his theology. In *God in Creation* the Spirit is identified as the ground of experience in which hope is encountered and the new creation is anticipated. This is developed in *The Spirit of Life* as Moltmann gives the present, mystical experience of God its full weight. Specifically, as we have seen, ecstasy is acknowledged as authentically Christian: 'It is a momentary awareness of eternity.'[86]

At face value this appears to be a reversal of Moltmann's earlier insistence that notions of eternity being present in every moment effectively render the Christian outlook 'timeless' and thus void of any dynamic of future hope. But it is not as simple as that. This is because Moltmann firmly resists the suggestion that anything 'spiritual' should be set against the physical, material world. Spirituality is not an abstraction from bodily life in time and space. Therefore, any mystical experience of God's eternity, though an 'ecstatic moment', should not provide the impetus for a 'flight from the world'. Such moments are 'mystical', but they are nevertheless also understood by Moltmann to be 'eschatological' moments.[87] They are genuine encounters with eternity, in which the experience of time is momentarily suspended, but the eternity experienced is not an eternity *above*; it is an eternity *ahead*. Some have suggested that all Moltmann has ever really done is simply replace a 'vertical' model of transcendence with one that is 'horizontal'.[88] But in response it could be pointed out that there lies the all-important distinction: only when God is regarded as 'ahead' of us rather than 'above' do we discover the forward-moving thrust that is the dynamic essential to living hope.

One further question might be asked here. What sense of future might there be when the kingdom of God is realized in all fullness? Having a future end towards which we are moving generates the forward-thrust dynamics of Moltmann's hope. Without this movement life is meaningless. It is a very similar principle to that which John Macquarrie derives from Martin Heidegger in his suggestion that death gives life meaning. Without an ultimate conclusion, he says, life would be 'just one thing after another, an endless concatenation of contingencies, and that is surely meaningless'. Macquarrie reflects:

It would be like a sentence that wandered on forever and never came to a full stop so that we never learn the sense of it; or like the piece of music that meandered on without the definite form of, say, a sonata movement or a theme with variations; or like a novel or play in which event followed event and scene followed scene without any unifying plot that eventually came to a *denouement*.[89]

Life has meaning as long as we are in the process of moving towards an end, changing and becoming as we hope for that end. But what happens when we reach that ultimate end, when God's kingdom has come? In what sense can eternal life have vitality if a permanent end will replace the processes of becoming that give life its 'living' dynamism? Moltmann offers this response:

> If the process of creation is to be completed through God's indwelling, then the new creation is indwelt by the unbounded fullness of divine life, and glorified creation is wholly free in its participation in the unbounded existence of God. So the indwelling of the unbounded fullness of God's eternal life means the openness *par excellence* of all life systems, and hence also their eternal livingness, not their finite petrification.

Moltmann is talking about an eternity in which the processes necessary for vitality are so transformed that they remain, but without the pain and suffering with which they are correlated in existence as we know it. He refers, for example, to 'change without transience' and 'life without death'. Such eternity is not conceived as static and timeless. Thus Moltmann offers the somewhat paradoxical phrases, 'eternal time' and 'eternal history'. It is out of his conviction that the consummation will be the radically qualitative transformation that Moltmann makes such assertions. He accepts that such a vision is extremely difficult to comprehend when all our concepts are moulded in an existence that knows only of death and 'experiences of transitoriness'.[90] Yet, biblically understood, finitude is not necessarily bound up with mortality, he argues, for angels are finite yet immortal. Resurrection life will be like this, says Moltmann, highlighting Luke 20.36. Just as life in the Spirit is one of being 'changed from one degree of glory to another' (2 Corinthians

3.18), 'so we may assume that there will be a process of transformation of this kind in the "kingdom of glory" as well'.[91]

Raising expectations: the centrality of resurrection in Christian hope

God's promise of resurrection lies at the very heart of Christian
hope. It is foundational for Moltmann's theology, giving it relevance to the quest for a living hope in the face of death, as well
as an authentically Christian identity: 'A Christian faith that is
not resurrection faith can therefore be called neither Christian
nor faith.'[92] Earlier we noted the criticism that Moltmann has
tended to emphasize historical hopes, what Rumbold calls 'this-
worldly concerns'. That may be true, but it is an emphasis that
expounds the significance of resurrection hope as *transcendent*
hope for such concerns. Only a hope that can be maintained in
the face of death is radical enough to form the basis for historical hopes.

In his early work, resurrection is important because, in
its contradiction to Jesus' death, it provides the basis of
Moltmann's dialectic. Hence Richard Bauckham's comment,
'*Theology of Hope* is as much a book about the resurrection of
Jesus as it is a book about eschatology.'[93] Later on, the concept
of resurrection is instrumental for Moltmann as he seeks to
establish the important continuity, which we noted above,
between the old creation and the new. Hoping for the resurrection of this present body gives meaning to the life we now live,
for it looks not to the mere replacement of the present but its
transformation:

> What is hoped for there, after death, as 'the raising of the
> dead', means here the life lived in love . . . Hope for 'the
> resurrection of the body' permits no disdain and debasement
> of bodily life and sensory experiences; it affirms them pro-
> foundly.[94]

Resurrection thus forms the basis of a holistic hope for
Moltmann. It is hope for body and soul, individuals and

society, human history and the whole cosmos.[95] Moltmann affirms the resurrection of the body against the doctrine of the immortal soul because of this holism. Resurrection is no serene *survivalism*. It is not about 'life after death' but 'life out of death'.[96] It takes the harshness of death seriously and acknowledges that only the transcendence of God can be an adequate basis of hope in the face of it. Thus Moltmann says, 'The immortality of the soul is an opinion – the resurrection of the dead is a hope.'[97] Only resurrection hope 'perceives the total mortality of death and the finality of that which is finite; yet it obtains the strength to overcome them'.[98]

These things, we shall see, are foundational for a practical theology of hope for the dying. We have seen in this chapter how Moltmann's theology of hope is future-oriented, driven by the promise of God's coming (*adventus*). The focus of that promise is the resurrection of the body, the symbol *par excellence* (though not *only* a symbol) of the new creation that is not the annihilation of the old, but its transformation and transfiguration.[99] As the discussion gravitates back to the specific pastoral concern for hope in a palliative context, let us now see how Moltmann's theology of hope might be brought into a critical conversation with the perspectives of psychology and nursing science.

Notes

1 Jürgen Moltmann, *Theology of Hope: On the Ground and the Implications of a Christian Eschatology*, ET (trans. J. Leitch), London: SCM Press, 1967, p. 16.

2 N. T. Wright, *For All the Saints? Remembering the Christian Departed*, London: SPCK, 2003, p. xiv.

3 Wright's slim but very readable *For All the Saints?* is published for a wider readership. Its author describes it as a 'kind of footnote' to his more thorough and scholarly volume, *The Resurrection of the Son of God*, London: SPCK, 2003.

4 Rumbold, *Helplessness and Hope*, p. 73.

5 Jürgen Moltmann, *The Coming of God: Christian Eschatology*, ET (trans. Margaret Kohl), London: SCM Press, 1996, pp. 49–128.

6 For a more detailed discussion see John Macquarrie, *Christian Hope*, London & Oxford: Mowbray, 1978; Stephen Travis, *Christian Hope and the Future of Man*, Leicester: IVP, 1980; or Robert Doyle, *Eschatology and the Shape of Christian Belief*, Carlisle: Paternoster Press, 1999.

7 Cited in Travis, *Christian Hope and the Future of Man*, p. 18.

8 Rudolf Bultmann, *History and Eschatology*, Edinburgh: The University Press, 1957, p. 155.

9 Paul Tillich, *Systematic Theology III: Life and the Spirit, History and the Kingdom of God*, Chicago: Nisbet & Co., 1963, pp. 421, 383.

10 Paul Tillich, 'The Right to Hope: A Sermon', in Mark Kline, ed., *Paul Tillich – Theologian of the Boundaries: Selected Writings*, London: Collins, 1987, p. 330.

11 Paul Tillich, *The New Being*, London: SCM Press, 1956, p. 24. Italics original.

12 Karl Barth, *Church Dogmatics IV.3*, ET (trans. G. Bromiley), Edinburgh: T & T Clark, 1962, p. 912.

13 From his 1922 *Romerbrief*. Cited in Carl Braaten, 'The New Theology of the Future' in Carl Braaten and Robert Jenson, *The Futurist Option*, New York: Newman Press, 1970, p. 9.

14 Barth, *Church Dogmatics IV.3*, p. 904.

15 Karl Barth, *Dogmatics in Outline*, ET (trans. G. T. Thomson), London: SCM Press, 1966, p. 133, 135.

16 For a more thorough survey of Moltmann's work see Richard Bauckham, *Moltmann: Messianic Theology in the Making*, Basingstoke: Marshall, Morgan & Scott, 1987; and Richard Bauckham, *The Theology of Jürgen Moltmann*, Edinburgh: T & T Clark, 1995.

17 Jürgen Moltmann, *Experiences in Theology: Ways and Forms of Christian Theology*, ET (trans. M. Kohl), London: SCM Press, 2000, p. xiv.

18 Moltmann, *Experiences in Theology*, p. xv, xxii.

19 Jürgen Moltmann, ed., *How I Have Changed: Reflections on Thirty Years of Theology*, ET (trans. J. Bowden), London: SCM Press, 1997, p. 18.

20 E.g. M. Douglas Meeks, *Origins of the Theology of Hope*, Philadelphia: Fortress Press, 1974; Bauckham, *Moltmann: Messianic Theology in the Making*, and *The Theology of Jürgen Moltmann*.

21 Moltmann, *Experiences in Theology*, p. 4.

22 Jürgen Moltmann, *Experiences of God*, ET (trans. M. Kohl), London: SCM Press, 1980, pp. 6–9.

23 Jürgen Moltmann, *In the End – The Beginning*, ET (trans. M. Kohl), London: SCM Press, 2004, p. 34.

24 Moltmann, *Experiences in Theology*, p. 24.
25 Moltmann, *Experiences of God*, pp. 17–19, also pp. 2–3 and 28ff.
26 Moltmann, *Experiences in Theology*, p. 45ff.
27 Jürgen Moltmann, *Religion, Revolution and the Future*, ET (trans. M. Douglas Meeks), New York: Charles Scribner's Sons, 1969, p. 17.
28 Moltmann, *Theology of Hope*, p. 16.
29 Moltmann, *Theology of Hope*, p. 109.
30 M. Douglas Meeks, *Origins of the Theology of Hope*, Philadelphia: Fortress Press, 1974.
31 Cited in Gerald O'Collins, 'The Principle and Theology of Hope', *Scottish Journal of Theology* 21 (1968), pp. 129–44, 131.
32 Moltmann, *Religion, Revolution and the Future*, p. 17.
33 Moltmann, *Theology of Hope*, p. 163.
34 Jürgen Moltmann, *The Crucified God: The Cross of Christ as the Foundation and Criticism of Christian Theology*, ET (trans. R. A. Wilson and John Bowden), London: SCM Press, 1974, p. 204.
35 Moltmann, *The Crucified God*, p. 226.
36 Moltmann, *The Crucified God*, p. 222.
37 Moltmann, *The Crucified God*, pp. 243–4.
38 Dietrich Bonhoeffer, *Letters and Papers from Prison*, London: SCM Press, 1967, p. 361.
39 Jürgen Moltmann, *The Church in the Power of the Spirit: A Contribution to Messianic Ecclesiology* (2nd edition), ET (trans. Margaret Kohl), London: SCM Press, 1992, p. 65. Italics original.
40 Moltmann, *The Church in the Power of the Spirit*, p. 196.
41 Moltmann, *The Church in the Power of the Spirit*, pp. 261–2.
42 Jürgen Moltmann, *Theology and Joy*, ET (trans. R. Ulrich), London: SCM Press, 1973, p. 49.
43 Moltmann, *Theology and Joy*, p. 53.
44 Moltmann, *Theology and Joy*, p. 36.
45 Moltmann, *The Church in the Power of the Spirit*, pp. 108ff.
46 Jürgen Moltmann, *The Trinity and the Kingdom of God: The Doctrine of God*, ET (trans. Margaret Kohl), London: SCM Press, 1981, p. 51.
47 Moltmann, *The Trinity and the Kingdom of God*, pp. 56–7.
48 Moltmann, *The Trinity and the Kingdom of God*, p. 19.
49 Geiko Muller-Fahrenholz, *The Kingdom and the Power: The Theology of Jürgen Moltmann*, ET (trans. John Bowden), London: SCM Press, 2000, p. 143.
50 See Paul Fiddes, *Participating in God: A Pastoral Doctrine of the Trinity*, London: Darton, Longman & Todd, 2000. Fiddes offers some insightful critical discussion of Moltmann's own trinitarian theology.

51 E.g. William French, 'Moltmann's Eschatology Naturalized', *Journal of Religion* 68 (1988), pp. 78–86, 78–9.

52 Jürgen Moltmann, *God in Creation: An Ecological Doctrine of Creation*, ET (trans. Margaret Kohl), London: SCM Press, 1985, p. 103.

53 Moltmann, *God in Creation*, p. 96.

54 Moltmann, *God in Creation*, p. 205.

55 Moltmann, *God in Creation*, p. 100.

56 Moltmann, *God in Creation*, p. 276.

57 Jürgen Moltmann, *The Way of Jesus Christ: Christology in messianic dimensions*, ET (trans. Margaret Kohl), London: SCM Press, 1990, p. xiii.

58 Moltmann, *The Way of Jesus Christ*, p. 319. Italics original.

59 Moltmann, *The Way of Jesus Christ* , pp. 32–3. Italics original.

60 Moltmann, *The Way of Jesus Christ*, p. xiv.

61 Moltmann, *The Way of Jesus Christ*, p. 122.

62 Jürgen Moltmann, *The Spirit of Life: A universal affirmation*, ET (trans. Margaret Kohl), London: SCM Press, 1992, p. 82.

63 Moltmann, *The Spirit of Life*, p. 7.

64 Moltmann, *The Spirit of Life*, p. 95

65 Moltmann, *The Spirit of Life*, p. x.

66 Moltmann, *The Spirit of Life*, p. 206.

67 Moltmann, *The Spirit of Life*, p. 35.

68 Moltmann, *The Spirit of Life*, p. 105.

69 Moltmann, *The Coming of God*, p. 75.

70 Moltmann, *The Coming of God*, p. 66.

71 Moltmann, *The Coming of God*, p. 105.

72 Moltmann, *The Coming of God*, p. 103.

73 Moltmann, *The Coming of God*, p. 107.

74 Moltmann, *The Coming of God*, pp. 77ff.

75 Moltmann, *The Coming of God*, p. 91.

76 Moltmann, *The Coming of God*, pp. 93–5.

77 Moltmann, *The Coming of God*, p. 119.

78 Moltmann, *The Coming of God*, p. 127.

79 See for example, Moltmann, *The Coming of God*, pp. 25–6.

80 Moltmann, *Theology of Hope*, p. 326. Italics original.

81 Moltmann, *Religion, Revolution and the Future*, p. 61.

82 Moltmann, *Theology of Hope*, p. 214.

83 Richard Clutterbuck, 'Jürgen Moltmann as a Doctrinal Theologian: The Nature of Doctrine and the Possibilities for its Development', *Scottish Journal of Theology* 48 (1995), pp. 489–505, 505.

84 John Macquarrie, 'Eschatology and Time', in Frederick Herzog, ed., *The Future of Hope: Theology as Eschatology*, ET (trans. Frederick

Herzog), New York: Herder & Herder, 1970, p. 122.

85 Jürgen Moltmann, 'Letter to Karl Barth' in Karl Barth, *Letters, 1961–1968*, ET (ed. J. Fangmeier and H. Stoevesandt) (trans. G. Bromiley), Michigan: Eerdmans, 1981, p. 349.

86 Moltmann, *The Spirit of Life*, p. 303.

87 Moltmann, *The Spirit of Life*, p. 18.

88 E.g. Rubem Alves, *A Theology of Human Hope*, Wheathampstead: Anthony Clarke, 1969, p. 61.

89 John Macquarrie, *In Search of Humanity*, London: SCM Press, 1982, p. 238.

90 Moltmann, *God in Creation*, p. 213.

91 Moltmann, *God in Creation*, p. 214.

92 Moltmann, *Theology of Hope*, p. 166.

93 Bauckham, *The Theology of Jürgen Moltmann*, p. 32.

94 Moltmann, *The Coming of God*, p. 66.

95 See for example, Moltmann, *The Coming of God*, pp. 65ff; *The Way of Jesus Christ*, pp. 247–73.

96 Jürgen Moltmann, 'Hope without Faith: An Eschatological Humanism without God', *Concilium* 6 (1966), pp. 14–21, 18.

97 Moltmann, *The Coming of God*, p. 65.

98 Moltmann, 'Hope without Faith', p. 18.

99 Moltmann, *The Coming of God*, p. 70.

4

Living Hope: A Practical Theology

Blessed be the God and Father of our Lord Jesus Christ! By his great mercy he has given us a new birth into a living hope through the resurrection of Jesus Christ from the dead.

1 Peter 1.3

We have looked at how hope is understood in psychology and nursing science and in the theology of Jürgen Moltmann. Our task is to draw from these sources in search of a hope that is theologically grounded as well as informed by those who have worked with and studied human responses to death, dying and situations of potential despair. This chapter will work towards the development of a practical theological definition of such a hope: *absolute hope in God for resurrection*. Based on this model, the subsequent chapter will explore the practicalities of nurturing such hope in pastoral care. Both chapters will be structured around the themes identified in the discussion of psychology and nursing science. This does not mean that priority is given to these disciplines over and above theology, but it is simply a way of presenting theological reflection on hope as a practical theme in response to the issues raised by psychologists and nursing scientists in what are generally practical, clinical settings.

What is hope? Some practical theological descriptions

As we work gradually towards a practical theological definition of hope let us first probe more deeply into its description from a theological as well as psychological perspective.

Hope is a basic and essential human reality

Hope is basic to living itself. Life cannot be sustained without it. The centrality of hope in human existence perceived in psychology and nursing science is also recognized by a number of theologians, Moltmann being one of them. He writes, 'living without hope is like no longer living'.[1] For Moltmann, life itself proceeds from God's Spirit, the 'spirit of life', the source of all vitality. To be alive at all means to have an *openness* to the future that is fundamental to human nature, he argues. This openness is derived from God, the open Trinity of Father, Son and Spirit, to whom humans have a basic orientation. In other words, life only continues as long as there is some sense, however vague, that there is a future to be lived. We might call this our 'natural' human hope, for it is part of our God-given human nature. We may not believe in God, but as long as we believe in a future that is worth living, we maintain this natural, innate hope. It is this basic anthropological phenomenon that denotes a God-ward bearing which pervades what it is to be human, regardless of whether or not we acknowledge it as such. Still another way of putting it is to say that hope and its fundamental openness to the future is inherent in life itself because this very openness is essential to the being of God, who is the source of life.

In the previous chapter we acknowledged the practical significance of a theology that regards all spirituality as reflective of a universal spiritual orientation towards God. In particular, such an affirmation provides a way for common ground to be recognized by Sue and Angela. This could be helpful on both sides of their pastoral relationship. It equips Sue with a way of responding positively to Angela's expression of belief in 'something spiritual', enabling her to see that beneath Angela's scepticism towards organized religion, a genuine yearning for the divine is to be found. From Angela's perspective, a pastoral conversation in which it is suggested that her spiritual leanings, however vaguely defined they may be, are nevertheless indicative of the reality of the God who is far closer than she herself acknowledges, may be the very thing that causes her to re-evaluate her perception of Christianity. She might begin to wonder whether Christian faith is as disengaging as she had thought. Perhaps the most profound way in which Sue might encourage Angela is by praying with her, as requested, in a way that affirms what Angela has tried to express. In her prayer she might find words of thanksgiving for Angela's spirituality and the honesty and openness with which she has shared it. She could then go on to ask God to increase in Angela an awareness of his presence which is in fact already there. This might be appropriately followed by a few moments of stillness, after which Sue could commit Angela to the care of the God in whose presence they are meeting. It would, of course, be crude to suggest some kind of ready-made formula for praying in these sort of circumstances. But an approach of this kind, which affirms the reality of God even in the midst of a person's search-ing for hope and spirituality, may go a long way in enabling such a hope to flourish.

A theology that recognizes hope as a basic component of human nature and as something that reflects an innate God-ward orientation that is woven into the fabric of life itself is a theology that encourages pastoral carers to believe that at least the potential to hope resides in all people. It urges us to main-tain hope *for* hope, whatever the circumstances might be. The innate capacity to hope might be dormant, but as long as there is life, its possibility remains. That is significant for each of the pastoral scenarios we have been following. It is especially rele-vant to Sarah's quest for a deeper confidence in her ministry. She wonders what on earth she might do to be of practical benefit to somebody who is in the final week of his life. The sug-gestion that the God-given capacity to hope already exists in that person might be the very thing that diverts Sarah away from her own feelings of inadequacy, focusing instead on the potential for hope that is never far away. As such she might understand her ministry not as *giving* hope but *nurturing* it. This important distinction highlights two things. First, if Sarah can accept that her responsibility is not to impart something to others, she might feel released from what seems to be a burden of personal helplessness. Second, if she can see her role as one of nurturing and enabling the capacity to hope that is already there, she might begin to grasp something of the tremendous contribution she really can make to the life of a dying person, even in the final stages. Specific practical ways in which she might do this are the focus of the next chapter.

The affirmation of 'natural' hope as a human instinct and a universal spiritual orientation towards God does, however, pose some important critical questions. Does it not suggest a somewhat naïve, overly positive picture of the human condition? If the ability to hope is so basic to human nature, why is despair a reality for so many? Were hope such a natural part of daily experience there would be little point in reading, or indeed writing, this book. Furthermore, is it not the case that the sheer openness to the future of which Moltmann speaks can actually be the source of despair, the dread and terror of our vulnerability as we face the unknown? More fundamentally, Moltmann talks of the world as 'a system open to God'.[2] Is this really so? What about the reality of human sin, where God is shut out? It is clearly not enough simply to recognize that humans *can* hope in God. We need a practical theology that takes account of the reality and pain of the struggle to find such hope.

Moltmann understands sin as 'the self-closing of open systems against their own time and their own potentialities'.[3] In shutting God out humanity closes itself off from the possibilities God gives. As such, the natural human capacity to hope does not mean that men and women always *do* hope freely. The distinction must be drawn between human potential and the distortion of that potential. Hope in embryonic form can be thwarted by a refusal to believe that the future is worth living and working for. Here Moltmann does take seriously the fact that hoping does not come without a struggle:

Enduring hope is not something innate, something we possess from birth. Nor do we acquire it from experience. We have to learn it. We learn to hope if we obey the call . . . Hope is more than feeling. Hope is more than experience. Hope is more than foresight. Hope is a command.[4]

Hope thus requires effort, discipline, resolve and endurance. But how might such virtues get off the ground when we are overwhelmed with despair? How can our potential to hope be realized when we face death, destruction and situations of utter helplessness? The answer is hinted at here in Moltmann's insistence that hope is not acquired from experience. Though hope demands effort, human resources alone are not enough to bring true hope to birth. Rather, hope is something we must be *born anew into*. Hope is a command, and this means that it comes not from within but from without. Hope comes from God, as a gift of grace. Moltmann says: 'We can therefore call salvation in history the divine opening of "closed systems" . . . Thus man's openness to God is brought about by grace.'[5] This is no cheap grace because it commands effort. But this is an effort that is made as a response to what God gives. And just what exactly does God give? Moltmann's theology stresses that in his grace God gives us his *resurrection promise*. Only in response to God's promise can our God-ward bearing potential be transformed into faith and our openness to the future become hope for resurrection as our ultimate future. Moltmann writes, 'Faith is called to life by promise and is therefore essentially hope, confidence, trust in the God who will not lie but will remain faithful to his promise.'[6] In this way Moltmann qualifies the meaning of 'openness to the future'. In and of itself, such openness could indeed be the very source of despair. But an openness to the future that is conceived in terms of God's resurrection promise means a readiness to truly live in hope: 'We find this future in Jesus Christ; he is our future – he is our hope.'[7]

A dangerous implication nevertheless remains. Are we to believe that despair must always be attributed to sin, as the refusal to be open to God's promise and the shutting out of the possibilities God gives? What about the forces of circumstance in our broken world which thwart our capacity to hope? Our struggle to hope may not always be due to a *distorted* potential; sometimes it may simply be *suppressed* by situations of tragedy and pain over which we have no control at all. In those contexts, the suggestion that the struggle to maintain hope has to do with personal sin could create nothing other than a burden of guilt for an individual who is already in the depths of despair. Tom, for example, is terrified of dying, as he cannot currently envision a future. He describes himself as 'spiritually frozen'. God, along with everyone else, seems so distant from him. These feelings would surely only be exacerbated by the suggestion that he is in some way morally responsible for his apparent failure to be more hopeful.

So how might we understand the relationship between the struggle to hope, the grace of God, and the realities of sin and despair, without downplaying or over-emphasizing any of them? Just this question is taken up by Mary Louise Bringle in *Despair: Sickness or Sin?* Bringle asks, 'can I "help it" if I despair?'[8] Sometimes we can, she argues. Despair can amount to a deliberate refusal to trust in divine providence, a shirking of the responsibility to hope. This has to do with our sinful nature, and with effort such despair can be changed into hope. But, Bringle points out, not all despair is freely chosen: 'there also comes a point where I reach the end of my individual resources, where I can no longer imagine a leaven of possibility in a world which feels so oppressively "flat" to me'.[9] This type of despair is more accurately understood in terms of *sickness* because it is 'so paralyzing that no resources we can muster seem capable of mounting any resistance against it'.[10] It calls not for the *effort* of repentance but *healing* by an external source, namely the help of others and ultimately the grace of God. Bringle writes, 'just as we cannot redeem our own fallenness, so we cannot be expected to remedy our own despairing'.[11] But how might we differentiate between these two types of despair? Bringle says the first, which is of a lesser degree, is restricted to some specifiable object and in turn has a specifiable and relatively straightforward solution. An example might be despairing over an untidy home. However, the more pervasive and non-specific despair gets, the more intense it becomes. Most severe is a global despair that has no specifiable object at all. Then despair prevails as the individual can no longer identify any particular 'reason' for it. A correspondence can be seen here with the two orders of particularized and generalized hope identified in Chapter 2, and we will explore this further. At this stage let us simply note that despair, like hope, is multi-layered and ambiguous. Despair can be conceived in terms of sin, as something for which a despairing individual is personally responsible, as well as in terms of sickness, which depends upon some kind of healing from an outside source.

In reality, it is probably rare that despair can be accurately described as either only sin or only sickness. Bringle suggests that pastoral care should respond to this ambiguity of despair with 'a dialectic of effort and grace'.[12] This recognizes that while God's grace is always behind the movement from despair to hope, there will be times when it is more appropriate to emphasize the need for greater effort to be made, and times when it is not. In a pastoral relationship, it would be inappropriate to begin with the assumption that a person in despair only has him- or herself to blame. As such, our starting point should be the quest for the healing of despair as a sickness. Only then can we really expect to meet people in their devastation with warmth and unconditional acceptance at the outset. Anything short of this has the potential to instil in somebody like Tom a destructive guilt. The creation of such a burden by associating his despair with sin will simply suppress yet further Tom's potential to hope.

But not all guilt is destructive – indeed it can be creative, if it enables a person to identify a tangible action that helps facilitate a positive change of some sort. This is the effort of repentance, and may be the very thing that is required if a person's natural capacity to hope is to be realized to its full potential. It may be that an individual is struggling to hope because they have deliberately shunned the possibility that it could be found in God. As such it could be that their own prejudice or cynicism has denied them the spiritual base that not only theologians but also psychologists and nursing scientists identify as important for hope in the face of death, as we saw at the end of Chapter 2. Another possibility is that an individual feels despair as they approach death partly because they have unresolved conflicts in personal relationships and as such are without the presence and support of loved ones, which, again, were identified earlier as a vital part of the experience of hope. A pastoral carer who encounters in a dying person a noticeable bitterness towards an individual or group must be ready to listen to that person's story in a spirit of acceptance, but with an equal readiness to sensitively challenge them with the question of their own responsibility to forgive. In such situations, letting go of past resentments may be required in order to make room for hope. It should be stressed that where such effort is called for, that also is in response to the grace of God – the 'dialectic of effort and grace' does not denote an 'either/or'. It is just that there are times when the grace of God calls for human effort to be made in order to overcome despair, while there are other times when despair would be more appropriately regarded as a sickness in need of healing.

Christian pastoral care should be seen as an expression of God's grace – a grace grounded in God's resurrection promise. It would be a poor expression indeed if individuals in despair were met first and foremost with the challenge to 'try harder'. As such, the healing of despair as a sickness should be given the primacy in the quest to cultivate hope. But this should not circumvent the reality of sin and the basic need for effort to be made towards reconciliation with God and with others. It is important to affirm the natural human capacity to hope in all people, but it is equally important to recognize the suppression and distortion of that potential. Such recognition may be the first step for a capacity to hope to become a living hope.

Hoping and coping

In Chapter 2 we saw how psychology and nursing science closely associate hope with coping, particularly with regard to the way hope can assist in the process of adaptation to illness-related changes. An important issue here is *empowerment*, which is a vital part of hope. Concern was expressed earlier that in a palliative context empowerment should not be conceived exclusively in terms of mastery and control. The *fighting spirit*, a concept closely related to hope that will be given further reflection shortly, may be an important aspect of the experience of hoping, but this must be carefully integrated with the dynamic of *acceptance*.

The question of how people cope with illness, the loss of health and the changes that brings, raises a fundamental question: what do we actually mean by 'health'? This is important, because it is easy to make assumptions about what it means to 'be healthy'. In different ways, David and Jane do just this. They seem to have very rigid understandings of what a healthy state really is, and this could in fact be a contributory factor in the thwarting of their own hope processes. Let us consider why.

Moltmann draws attention to the definition propounded by the World Health Organization: 'Health is a state of complete physical, mental and social well-being, not merely the absence of sickness and handicaps.' Moltmann says that this very popular way of understanding health conceives of it as an ideal. This is problematic, because health implies something that is normative – 'to be a person in the fullest sense of the word is to be healthy'. Definitions of what it is to be human should not be tied down to unobtainable ideals. The real 'strength to be human', says Moltmann, does not lie in living a life of happiness without pain or conflict – such life is altogether unreal. Rather, it is properly understood in terms of the capacity to live with suffering: 'The strength to be human is displayed in the person's capacity for happiness *and* suffering, in his acceptance of life's joy and the grief of death.'[13] This expresses Moltmann's conviction that true humanity reflects the pathos of its creator: 'a man can suffer because he can love . . . he always suffers only to the degree that he loves'.[14] Thus 'without the remembrance of dying, every definition of health is illusory'. Health must not be defined by the 'illusory notions of the modern cult of health', by which it is conceived of as an ideal. Instead, 'we must discover it still more in sickness and in dying'. Once again, we come back to Moltmann's dialectic of cross and resurrection: we do not arrive at the wholeness of the latter without the brokenness and devastation of the former. Resurrection is arguably the supreme symbol of a healthy body, but its true meaning is defined by the suffering of the cross that leads to it. With this in mind Moltmann writes:

> 'Health is the term for the process of adaptation . . . the capacity to adapt to a changing milieu, to become older, to recover one's health, to suffer, to await death in peace.' Health is then 'the ability to cope with pain, sickness and death autonomously'. To put it more simply: 'Health is not the absence of malfunctionings. Health is the strength to live with them.'[15]

It can be seen how David and Jane appear to hold to the sort of ideal that Moltmann describes as deeply unhelpful for processes of adaptation and hoping to develop. They both understand health as the absence of their present conditions, and set themselves on the quest to attain that. As such they are not open to the possibility that life could be lived and even enjoyed without attaining that ideal. For David, illness is something that must be overcome by medical treatment and sheer determination, while for Jane it must be defeated by divine intervention. Neither of them regards health as something that involves a capacity to live *with* illness. By limiting their understanding of health in this way both David and Jane close themselves off from a type of hope that could enable them to adapt to and cope with the reality they face. This is a hope that is essentially empowering, but in a way that does not simply go after mastery, control and an unattainable ideal of health. Dying is part of life itself – indeed as long as we are living we are actually in the process of dying. But with a genuinely living hope that gives us the strength and courage to recognize this truth, dying can be living.

Hope and physical health: resurrection and hoping for the body

There is a sense in which a practical theology of hope that has resurrection as its primary theme may nevertheless engage with David and Jane's desire, despite its narrowness, for healing of the physical body. In Chapter 2 it was acknowledged that some research suggests that hoping may positively affect physical health. In David's case this could be especially important, for when he does grasp the seriousness of his prognosis he does so with a resignation that denies that there could be any life worth living at all. While he may not be 'cured', David's quality of life could nonetheless be greatly enhanced if he could begin to embrace the life that still remains to be lived. This does not have to equate with hoping for a full recovery – it could mean simply resolving to make the most of the time he has left in the given circumstances, perhaps rallying enough energy to undertake particular activities. Jane, who is closer to death than David, may be more limited in the resolutions she is practically able to make. But both David and Jane highlight the significance of the *body* as that which is hoped for. Christians may be tempted to say that our hope ought properly to be located in spiritual, not bodily, expectation. But that does not take seriously enough the fact that our need for hope is located in our human existence which is at once both bodily and spiritual. Resurrection hope looks to the raising of body and spirit, and as such meets David and Jane in their concern for bodily life because it enables us to hope *for the body*. So let us now move from a description of this living hope to a closer look at its definition: absolute hope in God for resurrection.

What is hope? Towards a practical theological definition

Our exploration of psychology and nursing science led us to define hope as the mysterious anticipation of the ultimate. Moltmann's theology understands hope primarily in terms of the resurrection of the body. We shall eventually see these things converge as the different perspectives are brought to bear on one another. First let us consider the practical theological nature of those concepts that Chapter 2 identified as closely related to yet distinct from hope, as this will take us closer to an understanding of hope itself.

Hope and related concepts

1 Wishing and the imagination

Earlier we saw how wishing, though regarded by many as a poor psychological substitute for hoping, is presented by Lynch as an important component of hope. The one who can wish is the one who can make a healthy and balanced assessment of what is personally desirable, free of the distortions of the absolutizing instinct. Such wishes are the raw material out of which realistic hopes are formed. Where active wishing does not take place 'apathy and negativity' exist.[16]

In Moltmann's theology a similarity of understanding can be found. Like Lynch, Moltmann draws a contrast between apathetic existence and a life of vitality in describing the difference that hope makes. God intends for the creation not a life of apathy and indifference but the 'love of life'.[17] Both joy and suffering are part of this God-given vitality as the Spirit of life lives in us, reflecting the pathos of the God in whose image humanity is created.[18] Hope can be seen when such vitality is expressed in the envisioning of a 'wishable future'. Moltmann uses the term *productive fantasy* to describe the creative imagination by which such a future may be envisaged. He does not take fantasy to mean the unrealistic wishes that have been exaggerated by the absolutizing instinct, as in Lynch's framework. Rather, Moltmann's productive fantasy means much the same as Lynch's wishing. It is the productive fantasy that enables us to 'anticipate the still unrealized future in order to anticipate and shape it in thought and pictures'. Moltmann argues that some would deride this as 'mere wishful thinking', but this fails to take seriously the importance of wishing as a dynamic of the imagination in hoping. Modern enlightenment thinking has produced a tendency to approach the future in strictly rationalist terms, but this has resulted in the devaluing of the creative imagination that is required in hoping for the radically new – a newness expressed supremely in Jesus' resurrection. Moltmann thus calls for the rediscovery of the productive fantasy and meaningful wishing. Against Feuerbach, who reduced belief in God to a mere projection of human ideals, Moltmann says that the productive fantasy works positively with projections. They are 'in no way merely compensations for disappointed and suffered reality' but are 'projections into a possible but yet unknown future'. Even illusions are given a positive place in Moltmann's thought here, and he argues against Freud that they need not represent 'gratifications of repressed wishes but – as the word illusion means in its Latin origin – preludes, overtures to the future'.[19]

Putting aside the way that Moltmann and Lynch differ in their handling of terminology (fantasy and illusion are not regarded positively in Lynch's affirmation of wishing), their basic analyses amount to the same thing. Both are saying that an important part of hoping is a vitality by which there is an awareness of personal desires. For Lynch, the emphasis is on wishing as a positive psychological phenomenon that militates against the apathy or the absolutizing instinct that he associates with mental illness. Moltmann's concern is that a wishable future be taken seriously as an eschatological category. It is the eschatological imagination that depicts such wishes, that those who dare to dream of God's promised future can begin to live in hope, in the energy of the Spirit of life,[20] so breaking out of apathetic existence and striving for God's kingdom on earth.

In Chapter 2 it was acknowledged that David, in his insistence that he would soon be returning to work, had fallen victim to the sort of absolutizing instinct that Lynch describes – his desire amounted to the 'wishing of an absolute'. It can be seen how the state of resignation to a supposedly imminent death that subsequently overwhelms David might be described in terms of apathy. He has lost his appetite for living, and by the time he and his wife go to see the vicar – an appointment he makes because he insists the funeral must be sorted out – he is sapped of vitality. How might the vicar respond to David in this situation?

Let us assume that through listening carefully to both David and his wife – a pastoral task that is of paramount importance, as will be discussed later – the vicar has taken on board the basic story as it was set out in the opening chapter of this book. He could try to reassure David that he is not going to die as soon as he thinks by simply refusing to enter into conversation about a funeral. But that is unlikely to engage with David, who has by this stage persuaded himself that the only subject worth talking about is the certainty of his death. At least there is here an open acknowledgement in David that he is ill and is going to die at some stage, which sets the scene for frankness and honesty over realities that could otherwise be denied. A conversation about his funeral could therefore provide the opening that is required for an exploration of the deeper issues. Following the insights of Lynch and Moltmann, one of the most important of these issues is a need to start wishing again, in a way that is less rigid than his previous insistence on returning to work. One way of approaching this might be for the vicar to invite David to tell him about the things that have always been important to him that he would want to be remembered for in his funeral service. The conversation could then be gently moved away from the practicalities of planning a service, focusing instead upon the question of what David values most about his life. In this way David could be encouraged to identify and reflect upon what matters most to him. This just might provide a way of bringing to the surface some of David's wishes that have 'dried up', drawing him out of his state of inertia and enabling him to rediscover a life worth living. As a result he may begin to imagine things that he might possibly be able to do with what remains of his life. And it should be pointed out that even in the very final moments of a life there are wishes to be had, such as the presence of loved ones at the bedside, or the provision of appropriate pain relief. A challenge for carers is to assist in the identification of wishes at every stage of the dying process.

We are working towards a *practical theology* of hope for the dying. It should be stressed that in identifying wishes as the material from which hopes are formed, neither Lynch nor Moltmann means whatever may happen to be the whimsical fancy of the moment. Were this to be the case, hopes so constructed would stand little chance of being realistic, to say nothing of how Christian they might be! Lynch and Moltmann avoid wishing being misconceived in this way by qualifying the concept theologically. For Lynch, only wishes that are not distorted by the absolutizing instinct can be used to form genuine hope. God is the only absolute, and acceptance of this is the key to holding the absolutizing instinct at bay,[21] leaving room only for wishes that are both realistic and at one with the claim of God's lordship. For Moltmann the concept of wish is located firmly in his dialectical thought, talking of a wishable future.[22] By this Moltmann is not referring to whatever future may seem humanly desirable but to the eschatological future: 'We find this future in Jesus Christ; he is our future – he is our hope.'[23] Such a wishable future, dialectically conceived, recognizes the struggles and challenges of the present as it stands in contradiction to it. Thus it is realistic. And because it is located in the crucified and resurrected Christ, and Christ alone, it can only be Christian in nature.

2 Optimism

Another concept related to yet distinct from hope is optimism. We may recall from Chapter 2 that this is generally taken to mean an emphasis on the 'best' that is, the most positive aspects that are inherent in a given situation. From a theological perspective, optimism is found when faith in God is expressed in terms of faith in human progress. That was precisely the essence of nineteenth-century liberal Protestant eschatology, which conceived of God's kingdom as the moral advancement of a Christian society. In the wake of World War One, this was attacked fiercely by Barth, and indeed many other leading theologians, as woefully naïve. They insisted that the eschatological kingdom could only be properly understood as the work of God in Christ, not as some gradual progression towards a morally better society.

Moltmann argues that a Christian theology of hope 'is not grounded in optimism, but in faith'.[24] The dialectic structure of his thought makes Moltmann's vision one of hope rather than optimism. Against any faith in the progress of history, it is in the contradiction between God's promised future and the historical present that Moltmann finds hope. In particular, Moltmann appeals to the use of biblical apocalyptic images that depict a radical contrast between the future that is promised by God and the world as we presently know it. Such images provide a contrast so sharp that no room is left for the blurring of boundaries between human progress and God's *adventus*. Moltmann writes, 'Apocalypticism preserves the Christian doctrine of hope from facile optimism and from false prophets who say "peace, peace, when there is no peace" (Jeremiah 8.11).'[25] Most fundamentally, it is the contrast found in the contradiction between the cross and resurrection of Jesus that spells out the distinction between hope and optimism in no uncertain terms. The raising of the crucified Christ has nothing to do with bringing the best out of a set of circumstances; it has everything to do with beholding the sheer devastation and tragedy of death and accepting that only God can create a future out of that reality. The optimism of progress does not look far enough. Only eschatological hope in God's promise is strong enough to engage with the suffering and evil in history:

> The reason for the apocalyptic hope in the downfall of the world is pure faith in God's faithfulness. It is not optimism. God will remain faithful to his creative resolve even if the world he has created founders on its own wickedness.[26]

Hope and optimism are therefore quite different. This has important implications for pastoral care. It may be that from time to time carers may help to cultivate hope by expressing a sort of optimism that draws attention to the positive aspects of a situation. Angela, for example, is chiefly worried about not regaining consciousness after her operation. In her case, a natural but unfounded fear has actually caused her to lose sight of the health benefits that her surgery will most probably yield. We should not underestimate how far the simple act of highlighting this in conversation might go in reducing her anxiety. Even in contexts of palliative care, when there is little likelihood of physical health improvements, there may be a place for drawing attention to the positive aspects of a situation. For example, a person may have defied a prognosis of six months and still be alive a year later, or they may have experienced a considerable reduction in pain resulting from appropriate medication. These are things that could actually give hope, but can easily be obscured by feelings of depression or resignation created by the experience of living with a life-threatening illness. A carer might enable a dying person to gain a more hopeful perspective by focusing conversation on good things that have possibly been overlooked.

But optimism is not hope, and there could be great dangers in allowing it to function as a guiding principle for the pastoral care of the dying. Marcel says that optimism is an attitude that claims to have better sight: 'If your vision is as good as mine, you are bound to see.'[27] Such presumptuousness could be especially detrimental in a palliative context, where there may be a temptation to respond to depression in dying people with what Kübler-Ross describes as attempts to 'try to cheer them up . . . to look at the sunny side of things'.[28] As Kübler-Ross points out, this sort of optimism can be dangerous as it prevents the contemplation of the reality of death that is necessary for the dying person to come to terms with it. Telling people 'not to be sad' in this way does not allow the free expression of sorrow that is part of the process of accepting the reality of death. Hope, by contrast, is a positive outlook, but one that is more readily open to such reality. Theologically defined, living hope looks beyond death to the coming kingdom of God represented in the resurrected Christ, but does so in such a way that it does not take leave of suffering and death. It is this dialectical nature of hope that makes it far more appropriate than optimism as a basis for the pastoral care of the dying.

3 The fighting spirit

A similar kind of 'positive outlook' that comes close to both optimism and hope and yet is quite distinct, is what we have called the *fighting spirit*. This denotes the refusal to yield. Hope is often depicted as a virtue in these terms. In Chapter 2, and also in our consideration of coping in the present chapter, we noted that while a fighting spirit may be a part of hope, it should not be overplayed so as to obscure the importance of acceptance. This is vividly illustrated by Jane, whose firm resolve to pray for a miraculous cure clearly helped her for a while to carry on hoping for a future, and yet in the end prevented her from really engaging with death itself. Ultimately death is inevitable and must be faced.

There is a kind of fighting spirit that features prominently in the theology of hope. Specifically, a major theme for Moltmann is protest. This represents two very important theological axioms. The first is that God suffers, and does so in protest against suffering. Moltmann argues that atheism is right to protest against the God of classical theism, for that is a God who it is claimed cannot suffer. We cannot justify or explain away suffering, but in the cross we find God's own response to it: God chooses to stand in solidarity with us in our suffering, as the protesting God. Moltmann writes:

> God and suffering are no longer contradictions, as in theism and atheism, but God's being is in suffering and the suffering is in God's being itself, because God is love. It takes the 'metaphysical rebellion' up into itself because it recognizes in the cross of Christ a rebellion in metaphysics, or better, a rebellion in God himself.[29]

Second, hope in the resurrection promise of this protesting God is living hope, placed in the one who defeats death. This converts into action, as Christians are empowered by this living hope to be a protesting people:

> Hope finds in Christ not only a consolation *in* suffering, but also the protest of the divine promise *against* suffering . . . Faith takes up this contradiction and thus becomes itself a contradiction to the world of death. That is why faith, wherever it develops into hope, causes not rest but unrest, not patience but impatience. It does not calm the unquiet heart, but is itself this unquiet heart in man.[30]

It can be appreciated, then, how the themes of resistance and protest, forms of what might be described as a fighting spirit, have a rightful place within a theology of hope, especially if it is to stress the importance of creative action. If it is to feature in a practical theology of hope for the dying it will nevertheless need to be appropriated with great caution. Our story of David illustrates how a person can put up too much or too little of a fight against death. The first extreme of simply resolving to 'carry on as usual' is a denial of the seriousness of life-threatening illness. The second extreme of deciding that there is nothing left to do but die is a denial of the life that remains to be lived. A midpoint between these two extremes is therefore to discover the creativity of the fighting spirit, mediated by the equally important creativity of acceptance.

Kübler-Ross identifies acceptance as the fifth and final stage of the dying trajectory. She emphasizes that while it 'should not be mistaken for a happy stage' it is nevertheless 'not a resigned and hopeless "giving up", a sense of "what's the use" or "I just cannot fight it any longer"'. It has about it a very special kind of creativity, for it is only in acceptance of the reality of death that dying persons experience a sense of 'readiness' to die. In identifying acceptance as the final stage in the process of dying, Kübler-Ross affords it a certain ultimate value.[31]

The dialectical nature of Moltmann's theology of cross and

resurrection enables acceptance to be given a prominent place in understanding hope. Moltmann speaks of the 'resurrection of the crucified Christ' and the 'cross of the risen Christ'.[32] This means that any notion of resurrection power, the power of hope and of protest, is to be found in the cross itself. 'God represents himself and reveals himself in the surrender of Jesus and in his passion and death on the cross. But where God represents and reveals himself, he also identifies and defines himself.'[33] Thus the experience of dying can be affirmed as something in which God is to be found, for though it may be the experience of *godforsakenness*, God has taken this very godforsakenness into himself. Hence, 'God's being is in suffering and the suffering is in God's being itself.'[34] The act of dying can be regarded as something to be positively accepted: God is in solidarity with it. A fighting spirit and a spirit of acceptance therefore need not be regarded as opposites in every respect with the former representing power, strength and creativity and the latter merely denoting impotence, weakness and apathy. Acceptance is to be affirmed as a positive dynamic of hope – it is not simply passive resignation but the creative embrace of death in living hope that is arguably the greatest act of courage. This is a sort of hoping that empowers even when there can be no mastery or control over circumstances.

Though contrasting radically, it is possible to see how the fighting spirit and acceptance are both expressions of courage and creativity in hope. There is something of a correspondence between these dynamics and the ambiguity with which death may be regarded theologically. Should death be resisted or embraced? In Chapter 3 we noted that Moltmann has explored the question of whether death should be regarded negatively as the consequence of sin, or positively as life's natural end.[35] This question is worth taking up here as it has important implications for a practical theology of hope for the dying that takes seriously the dual concern for the fighting spirit and acceptance.

The credibility of the traditional perception of death as the 'wages of sin' (Romans 6.23) possibly lies in the fact that it takes account of the offensive and destructive nature of death.

Perceived as the 'ruinous power contrary to God and hostile to life',[36] death is recognized as the ultimate threat to personal existence and relationships, something that is not part of God's intended purpose for creation. Accordingly, death is regarded as the enemy to be fought. Once again, it should be affirmed that there is a rightful place for the fighting spirit, resolving not to give up too soon. In this sense, seeking, expecting and praying for healing are vital aspects of living in hope. At the same time, the more positive understanding of death as natural recognizes the ultimate inevitability of death as part of the fabric of life. Death is not the ultimate enemy to be resisted, but the ultimate act of freedom to be embraced. This paves the way for a hopeful acceptance of its reality. Once again, Jane's story reminds us of the importance of making room for this.

In pastoral care, the most important practical issue here is that we seek to discern whether it is acceptance or resistance that should be encouraged more strongly at any given stage in the process of dying. Problems are likely to arise if either one of these is stressed at the wrong time. On the one hand, as Kübler-Ross observes, there may be dying persons 'who fight to the end, who struggle and keep a hope that makes it almost impossible to reach this stage of acceptance'. Where this happens, 'the harder they struggle to avoid the inevitable death, the more they try to deny it, the more difficult it will be for them to reach this final stage of acceptance with peace and dignity'.[37] This may have been the case with Jane.

On the other hand, it could be argued that such was the strength of Jane's personal conviction that she would be healed that she did in fact die with a dignity of her own. After all, does one person have the right to decide what 'dignity' must mean for another? It would therefore be equally dangerous to extol the acceptance of death as the 'natural' and therefore 'proper' thing to do, for two reasons. The first is that it risks fostering a premature resignation to fate, like we see in David. The second is that it implies that a reluctance to accept death must be a sign of weakness, or even sin. Moltmann writes:

It is the awareness of death which first creates fear for life, the fear of not getting one's fair share, of not having enough from life, the fear that life will be cut short. This leads to a craving for life, and to greed . . . People like this look at the immortal gods and want to be like them. They break away from their poor, frail, vulnerable and mortal human nature and want to be like God.[38]

Now, we have already acknowledged that pastoral care should not downplay the reality of sin and the possible need for confession and reconciliation. It may be that the making good of broken relationships, letting go of past resentments and making peace with God are prerequisites for the development of hope. But we have also identified the danger of destructive guilt. Pastoral care must beware the danger of making acceptance even more difficult by giving any implication that dying persons should be more accepting of their death than they are. Two things in particular may be reiterated here. The first is Bringle's point that while the struggle to hope *may* be associated with sin, the more severe level of despair is more appropriately understood as sickness that can only be healed by grace. The second is Moltmann's theme of *The Crucified God*. In looking to the cross of the Jesus who has been raised we are reminded that God is with us in our suffering, including the struggle towards accepting death, no matter how godforsaken we may feel. But the struggle itself is not the end of the story – resurrection is. Because this is conceived as the resurrection of the crucified one, the struggle is the very place where we may lay hold of the resurrection promise and so discover a living hope.

4 Expectation alone?

The discussion of psychology and nursing science in Chapter 2 raised the concern that while Stotland defines hope purely in terms of expectation, this does not take into account the complexity of hope. Expectation is a vital part of the psychological dynamics of hoping, but hope means more than expectation alone, as is highlighted in Dufault and Martocchio's proposal of a generalized hope, which is not directed towards specific goals. Identifying and pursuing goals may help to cultivate the process of hoping, but any understanding of the experience of hope itself, if it is to take seriously its mystery and intangibility, must look to greater depths than expectation alone. The most profound and powerful hope is the mysterious anticipation of the ultimate. It has a sense of future but in a way that is essentially flexible and open-ended, not dissolving when particular goals are unattained. So how might expectation be appropriately conceived?

Psychology is not alone in this challenge. A parallel dilemma may be found when the theological nature of hope is explored. Faced with the questions raised by Weiss and Schweitzer concerning the delay of the *parousia*, theologians were subsequently challenged to identify just what Christian hope is directed towards. Very broadly, it is possible to understand subsequent twentieth-century eschatology as a wrestling with this question. In what sense is the Christian hope directed towards a specific eschatological future goal, given the uncertainty about that goal expressed by Weiss and Schweitzer? What is the object, or the nature, of expectation in the Christian eschatological hope? Indeed, is it possible to conceive of eschatology in terms other than expectation? Does Christian hope mean something more complex and profound?

The *realized eschatology* proposed by Dodd sought to make the case that the kingdom of God is not an object of future expectation but a present reality, and so alleviate the difficulty of waiting for something that was not intended to be waited for. Cullmann was more conservative. With his notion of *salvation history* he maintained that the *parousia* remained the rightful object of eschatological expectation, but sought to ease the awkward sense of strain over its delay by downplaying the intensity of an outstanding 'battle' under the emphasis that Christ's decisive victory has already been won. In this respect Cullmann was remarkably close to Barth, who stressed that God's work in Christ is already fully accomplished, and that all expectation must therefore be directed towards the 'unveiling' of this: 'while it is complete in itself', the kingdom of God 'is only moving towards its fulfilment'.[39] Thus Barth subsumed the notion of a specific future expectation under the principle that God's eternal future is equidistant from all times.[40]

The suggestion that eternity is present in every moment is the unifying theme in Barth, Bultmann and in some respects Tillich, which draws the critique of the theologians of hope. Though Bultmann and Tillich approached eschatology from the perspectives of their own different theological systems, both emphasized that eternity lies in the present moment. Their concern was that eschatology should not depict Christianity in such remote otherworldly terms that it obscures the demands of *present* existence. In short, they wanted to establish the relevance of the kingdom of God. For Bultmann this meant demythologizing eschatological references to the future, while Tillich emphasized the symbolic nature of eschatology. What should be pointed out here is that both Bultmann and Tillich sought to highlight the way in which the notion of an end, denoted by eschatological terms such as *parousia, kingdom of God*, or *consummation*, might be understood qualitatively; that is, as the *purpose* of existence. This sort of attempt to give theological expression to a sense of the ultimate in the present, but which transcends the present, might be understood as a theological counterpart to the psychological notion of generalized hope. Both may be seen as attempts to articulate the mysterious experience of hope that is not tied to a specific object of expectation, and yet which does involve a sense of anticipation that transcends the immediate 'here and now'. The parallel is especially striking in the following comment that Bultmann makes on hope as expressed in the Psalms:

> The godly man knows that he always depends on what God will do, so that hope does not always expect something definite, does not fashion for itself a particular picture of the future, but consists in a quite general trust in God's protection and help.[41]

There was nevertheless a significant dissatisfaction with Barth, Bultmann and Tillich. Their dominance in Protestant theology had so stressed the importance of the present that it required the polemic of Moltmann and the theology of hope movement to rediscover the dynamic of future expectation that is such an important part of Christian hope. Here lies the dilemma, and it can be seen how the development of eschatology through the twentieth century may be understood as the attempt to wrestle with it. A comprehensive theology of hope must be one that gives proper emphasis to a sense of eschatological expectation *and* takes account of the mysterious qualitative notion of an existential end that is not defined in exclusively futurist categories but transcends the immediate present, in the present. The problem has been that where theologians have emphasized either one of these vital things, they have done so at the expense of the other. The priority given to the future by Moltmann in his early work, and in the theology of hope movement in general, was a necessary corrective of its neglect, but in making that point the result was a polemic that compromised the significance of the existential 'now'.

Such is the dilemma. At the end of Chapter 3 it was argued that over the course of his career Moltmann has gradually balanced the somewhat one-sided emphasis on the future that characterizes *Theology of Hope*, especially in his later series of contributions where his doctrine of the Spirit matures. By emphasizing the Spirit as the source of life and ground of experience of God Moltmann gives mystical experience in the present its proper weight in a way that does not undermine the significance of eschatological expectation that he expounded so forcefully earlier on. A practical theology of hope for the dying that draws on the insights of Moltmann's eschatology must therefore highlight both of these points of emphasis in his work if it is to take account of the complexity of hope.

Both psychology and theology must wrestle with the question of how expectation should be appropriately conceived in giving an account of hope that involves the pursuit of some object, and yet in its mystery goes beyond such expectation. The dilemma described here is especially challenging for Christian pastoral care in a palliative context. On the one hand, in the face of death Christians look to the objects of eschatological expectation: the hope of eternal life, the *parousia*, and the coming of the kingdom of God in all fullness. At the same time there is a need for deep pastoral sensitivity to the possibility that, confronted with death, the suggestion of future objects of hope may lack meaning. To a dying person such things may have the sound of glib reassurances or pat answers that fail to take seriously their overwhelming feeling that any sense of future is threatened by their impending death. That would certainly be the case with Tom who, for all his familiarity with the themes of Christianity, has never grasped their personal significance and as such regards them as pious clichés. What is needed in these circumstances is a discovery or rediscovery of an awareness of God in the present moment. Then, even in death, a person who is struggling to feel any sense of future may find a mysterious experience of transcendence that reaches beyond the 'here and now', something that might be described as the 'positive glow on life' identified by Dufault and Martocchio. A practical theology of hope for the dying must take account of the dynamic of expectation as a vital part of the experience of hope, but in a way that recognizes such pastoral challenges and so highlights the mysterious power of living hope. This is the power of the anticipation of the ultimate that is experienced in the present and that is not tied to the attainment of any particular goal. This brings us to the very core of Christian hope where just this power may be found: *resurrection*.

The heart of living hope: resurrection

As we move towards a practical theological definition of hope let us now return to what we have identified as its primary symbol in Moltmann's theology, namely resurrection. It is in the resurrection hope that the mysterious anticipation of the ultimate that we have been describing finds its fullest and most complete expression. In the next section we will consider how this is so. First, let us reflect more deeply on its *holistic* nature.

Envisioning the future hope in terms of resurrection means believing that God promises to raise body and spirit. In the New Testament this is expressed by Paul's term, the 'spiritual body' (1 Corinthians 15.44–49). This sounds somewhat paradoxical. The point is, hope that looks to the resurrection does not understand eternal life as an exclusively spiritual concept. Unlike the notion of 'going to heaven when you die', resurrection does not propose a dualism of body and spirit but affirms them together as a unity. This is what the resurrection body means: it denotes the *whole person*, raised and transformed for eternal life.

This means that the body is to be affirmed, even in death, as that which may be *hoped for*. We have already noted how this could offer a way of engaging with David and Jane, providing a point of contact between their hope, which is envisioned in terms of the *curing* of the body, and the resurrection hope, which looks to the *raising* of that same body. While the hopes of cure and resurrection are different in kind, the *locus* of hope – the body – is the same in each case. As such, resurrection enables eternal life to be depicted in a way that is less remote from personal experience than the vision of taking leave of the body in order to 'go to heaven'. With resurrection hope 'bodily' existence is not set against the 'spiritual' – hoping for the resurrection body means hoping for the whole person. Even as death approaches and the ability of the physical body to perform its functions deteriorates, that body nevertheless remains the person who hopes and is hoped for. This establishes the most profound continuity between the present and the future. In Chapter 3 we noted that such continuity is essential if the eschatological future is to be in any way meaningful in the present. Only when there is some correspondence between the two does any kind of contradiction, as in Moltmann's dialectic, carry real meaning. Resurrection hope 'is not a speculation about some far off, posthumous condition',[42] but hope that enables a dying person to discover that necessary continuity between the present and the eschatological future in their own body. Though it may be threatened as illness intensifies and death approaches, the body is not something to be despised, as some kind of prison from which the spirit craves release. Rather, the body *is* the dying person, but it is the same body that will be raised and transformed, and thus may be hoped for.

In our story of Tom it was his wife Jenny who in desperation asked the minister, 'We will see one another again in the next life, won't we?' How might a theology of resurrection hope inform a response to this question? First and foremost, let us establish that the resurrection of the body affirms the raising of *personal identity* for eternity. Sandra Schneiders suggests that the body can be understood as the 'symbol of the self', and offers four insights by way of elaboration. First, the body grounds and manifests *identity through change*. The replacement of cells means that a body is completely reconstituted every seven years, and its visible appearance may alter considerably as it ages. Nevertheless, the person who is that body remains the same. Second, the body is the principle of *personal consistence*. The body makes one distinct from others and 'marks the person off' as an individual 'self'. But the body is not to be understood purely in terms of solitude, for, third, it provides the condition of possibility and the ground of *interaction with others*. It is the spatial location of a person, which allows one to be present to others and identified by them. Fourth, the individual body is the node of a *network of relations among others*. Persons related to one individual are related to each other through that individual. In summary, the body is the principle and location of personal identity, for individuals both 'in themselves' and in society.[43] Together, these four points highlight the strength with which the raising of the body expresses the raising of the whole person we know and love and grieve for. As such, if Tom and Jenny can lay hold of hope for the resurrection of the body, they will discover a hope that affirms that who we are *now* is who we shall be *then*, when God's promise is ultimately fulfilled.

But a practical theology should look beyond Jenny's question and do more than simply identify an answer to it. We must also consider the psychology behind her question. In Chapter 2 we suggested that a form of optimism could be implied in the manner of Jenny's asking – a desperate attempt to grasp at the best thing she can find in the circumstances. In this respect the hope of 'going to heaven' might be seen as a kind of optimism, where death is depicted as a form of progress, the transition from this life to the next.

Regardless of whether or not Jenny is clutching at straws, the resurrection hope certainly does not. In contrast with the serene survivalism suggested by the notion of 'going to heaven', resurrection takes the reality of death far more seriously, and as such represents a more robust hope. The doctrine of the immortal soul maintains that although the body dies the soul, the kernel of the person, lives on. Not so with resurrection, which understands the death of the body as the full and total death of the whole person in their very identity. Nothing survives. The rawness, the sense of sheer destruction that death renders is thus not smoothed over but accepted for what it is. As such resurrection is not 'life after death' but 'life out of death',[44] only allowing hope for eternal life to be voiced when the real annihilating power of the death of the body has been appreciated. That is the power of the Easter narrative, the radical contradiction between the Friday and the Sunday. The totality of death – depicted vividly in Jesus' body on the cross, a body that not only died but also was buried – this totality is shown to be conquered by the raising of that same body, transformed in resurrection glory.

Only when it is accepted that when the body dies the whole person in their identity dies, may it really be appreciated that the resurrection of the body denotes the raising and transformation of that very same person in all their identity. Resurrection does not mean the reuniting of some disembodied spirit with its physical shell, but the raising of the whole person. The resurrection body is different, in that it is transformed into everlasting life that is no longer subject to suffering and death. It means much more than the mere 'revival' or 'resuscitation' of the old body. In this respect there is radical discontinuity between the old and the new, something that, following Moltmann's dialectic, is necessary for hope. But for all this, resurrection does not mean the replacement of the old. There is a fundamental continuity in the personal identity that the body denotes. Hope for the body is thus hope for present identity transformed, but not transformed out of all recognition.

Back to Jenny. How should the minister respond to her question? A simple 'yes' would at least convey something of the vision of continuity between this life and the future life envisioned in the resurrection hope. But such a soundbite answer in its very simplicity would seem trite and pat, hardly taking on board the depth and complexity of angst going on in Jenny, let alone Tom. On the other hand, to avoid giving any answer at all is not likely to engage with the search for reassurance that Jenny's question seems to be pursuing. In the event, the minister decides to take hold of Jenny's and Tom's hands, look at each of them in the eye, and then with a gentle smile give a silent but affirming nod before returning with the open question, 'What are your thoughts?'

Acknowledging once again that it is impossible to spell out any perfect formula for responding to pastoral situations in which carers may find themselves, there are several reasons why this minister's choice of words and actions are very appropriate. First, an answer is given to the question that has been asked – the minister does not try to evade it. Second, the answer is affirmative, communicating something positive to Tom and Jenny about the continuity of this life in the resurrection hope. Third, the manner of the affirmation, though spontaneous, comes across as 'considered' – that is, not mechanical and pre-packaged, but mindful that deep, searching questions deserve more than easy, ready-made answers. By pausing to make proper eye contact and hold hands, the minister expresses a genuine attempt to be personally present with Tom and Jenny in this time of crisis. Fourth, the minister's returning question refocuses the conversation on the couple's beliefs. During such conversation resurrection as the symbol of Christian hope might be explored, but only when the starting point is Tom and

Jenny and the experience in which they find themselves is the conversation likely to engage with them in any meaningful way.

It should be noted that so far no mention of life expectancy has been made to Tom or Jenny. This is something that, with the greatest sensitivity, ought nevertheless to be pursued by the minister in the conversation. It is possible that Tom, rather like David, has decided that he is going to die much sooner than is really likely. Unless the minister clarifies this issue there is a danger that any discussion that focuses on what might be hoped for beyond death will simply reinforce any assumptions that may have been made concerning the imminence of that death.

A 'pastoral conversation' of the kind we see taking place between Tom, Jenny and their minister ought not to be taken in isolation from an ongoing pastoral relationship. It is important to raise this here because of the vast scope of psychological and theological issues that are presented. The sheer breadth and depth of resurrection hope could not possibly be unpacked in one single conversation over a cup of tea. The challenge facing the minister in this story lies not simply in the encounter on this particular occasion, but in the continually evolving conversation with Tom and Jenny as he accompanies them on their journey in the future. Such an ongoing conversation will involve seeking to enable Tom and Jenny to relate the symbol of resurrection to the daily task of living with life-threatening illness – that is, to discover the significance of resurrection as a living hope. So what might this significance be?

First, the symbol of the resurrection body gives value and significance to the struggles we encounter in daily life. The person who hopes for the resurrection of the body may look to a renewed life that is radically different – most notably, one that is free of pain and the threat of death. Yet the pain and tribulation of present experience need not be meaningless. The sufferings and anguishes of our present life history are part of who we are. Personal identity is formed and discovered throughout experiences of both joy and sorrow. Because the resurrection body is the same, indeed, the completion and transformation of the identity that is formed and discovered in present life history, no present struggle is in vain. As conveyed by the scars on the risen Jesus (John 20.27), all present strivings and toils are taken up and transfigured in the resurrection body, and so meaning and significance may be seen in them now because they will not be brushed aside as though they never happened. This does not mean that present suffering is to be understood as instrumental in creating the resurrection body, or that suffering is in some way justified. But it does mean that the body may continue to be hoped for as the principle and location of personal identity, even in the midst of pain and physical deterioration as death approaches.

Second, hoping for the body in this way simultaneously enables the acceptance of death and the affirmation of life to be lived. We have seen how this is a particularly pertinent issue for David and for Jane, although really it is a concern for anybody living with a life-threatening illness. Moltmann asks, 'How can I identify myself with physical life when I have physically to await death and the decay of happiness – and I experience it daily in loss and in disappointments?' Hope for the resurrection of the body affirms both the reality of pain and death *and* the fullness of personal identity that will rise up from them. Thus, 'Love in which a man surrenders himself and identifies himself with this vulnerable earthly life and hope in the resurrection belong together.'[45] The bodily life that leads to death may be embraced because it is this very bodily life that will be raised in resurrection glory. Eternal life is not hoped for 'against' or 'in spite of' the body. Rather, bodily life is the very locus of hope. Resurrection hope is

> the reason for a full acceptance of life here, and means that human beings can give themselves up to the whole of life without any reservation. What is hoped for there, after death, as 'the raising of the dead', means here the life lived in love . . . The resurrection hope makes people ready to live their lives in love wholly, and to say a full and entire Yes to a life that leads to death. It does not withdraw the human soul from bodily, sensory life; it ensouls this life with unending

joy. In expectation of the resurrection of the dead, the person who hopes casts away the soul's protective cloak in which the wounded heart has wrapped itself, so as not to let anything more come near it. We throw ourselves into this life and empty ourselves into the deadly realm of non-identity by virtue of the hope that God will find us in death, and will raise us and gather us . . . In this resurrection dialectic, human beings don't have to try to cling to their identity through constant unity with themselves, but will empty themselves into non-identity, knowing that from this self-emptying they will be brought back to themselves again for eternity.[46]

Moltmann here espouses a *kenotic* theology of resurrection hope. *Kenosis* is a New Testament Greek word meaning 'self-emptying', and denotes a dynamic spirituality modelled on Jesus' own act of emptying himself on the cross (Philippians 2.6–11). It is the free and unreserved surrender of the body whereby death is accepted not as a fatalistic resignation but as an affirmation. Living hope in the resurrection enables the laying down of personal identity in the anticipation that God will raise it, gathered, made whole, and transformed. It is in this kenotic spirituality of resurrection hope that we can see how acceptance and the fighting spirit find their true unity as authentic expressions of courage and creativity. In hoping for the body, looking to its resurrection, we can be empowered to 'let go', and as we 'let go', so we are empowered. Dying thus becomes living.

Let us return again to Jenny's search for an assurance that she will be reunited with Tom in eternal life. It raises another important issue that ought to be highlighted, and that is the *relational* or *societal* dimension of resurrection hope. This needs to be emphasized because while hoping for the resurrection of the body is deeply personal, it should not be misconstrued as individualistic. There are two fundamental reasons for this. First, we may recall Schneiders' point that although the body is the principle and location of personal identity, this does not refer only to the identity of individuals 'in themselves' but also individuals in society. Second, God's resurrection promise refers not to the raising of 'bodies', but to the raising of one body (1 Corinthians 12.27; Romans 12.4–5). The eschatological vision of resurrection ought not to be conceived in terms of a sequence of separate, individual resurrections that occur as each person dies, but as a single communal event as all generations are raised together at the end of history (1 Corinthians 15.23).

Hope for the body is therefore not an individualized hope, but a collective one. This not only reinforces the holistic nature of resurrection hope; it also offers something important to people like Jenny and Tom who long for some assurance that they will be reunited – and that is the vision of 'entering' eternal life together, not alone. The notion of 'going to heaven' carries the popular idea that loved ones are 'up there watching over us'. That is a weak kind of consolation because it conveys a somewhat fragmented and incomplete vision of salvation, depicting the deceased as alive but having to consciously wait for the gradual piecing-together of the network of relationships they left behind. At least, this seems to fall considerably short of the hope of being raised together in a collective resurrection.

For all its shortcomings, it is not difficult to appreciate that the idea of our loved ones 'looking down over us' from heaven is an attractive consolation because it offers an answer to the question 'Where are the dead?' This is a pastoral question, and we need to offer an alternative way of responding to it if we are proposing that resurrection hope is a more adequate conception of eternal life than 'going to heaven'. Perhaps the most logical response is Luther's doctrine of soul sleep, which states that since there is no experience of time for the dead, the interval between death and resurrection can in no way be described as an experience of waiting. This draws on a New Testament metaphor: the dead are 'asleep' (1 Corinthians 7.39; 11.30; 15.6, 18, 20, 51; 1 Thessalonians 4.13–15). Thus while resurrection may not be strictly conceived as something that takes place at the point of death, in being raised at the end of history it will be as though there had been no interval. Luther writes:

Because before God's face time is not counted, a thousand years before Him must be as if it were but a single day. Hence the first man Adam is as close to Him as will be the last to be born before the final Day . . . For God seeth time, not according to its length but athwart it, transversely . . . Before God all hath happened at once.[47]

In this way it is possible to understand resurrection as 'immediate' entry into eternal life. Indeed, it offers us a way of understanding Jesus' words to the dying criminal, 'Today you will be with me in Paradise' (Luke 23.43). It is hard to deny the logical structure of Luther's thinking here. Yet Moltmann feels that in itself the concept of soul sleep does not adequately express Paul's emphasis that dying means in some sense going to be 'with Christ' (Philippians 1.23). Moltmann is perhaps right to stress that the dead, with the living, are all part of what he describes as the 'fellowship of Christ', for this expresses a sense of continuing existence in God between death and resurrection that is difficult to articulate, even with the notion of soul sleep. But Moltmann is somewhat vague here in that he fails to explain just how the dead might 'exist in the same common hope' as the living, without at least implying some notion of a disembodied soul.[48] This implication becomes more explicit when considered in the light of the following passage from *God in Creation*. The context is Moltmann's argument that heaven is part of God's created reality, 'the place of God's presence', but itself unredeemed until the eschatological end:

If, in accord with the general Christian conception, the soul goes to heaven after death, it is not already redeemed there. It waits in its own way for the redemption which will bring the new heaven and the new earth and, in that new earth, the resurrection of the body also.[49]

This is confusing. On the one hand Moltmann staunchly defends the resurrection of the body as the proper way to understand eternal life. Yet at the same time, in seeking to account for the whereabouts of the deceased before the resurrection takes place and also in giving an account of the nature of heaven as God's dwelling place which is nevertheless part of the created order awaiting redemption, he implies a disembodied state that has every appearance of a dualistic immortal soul doctrine.

So just how might we conceive of the location of the dead while we hope for the resurrection? Moltmann's basic contention that the deceased really are dead but are nevertheless, in a very real way, 'with Christ', could be given more adequate expression by drawing on the notion of being held in God's *memory*. Here we might borrow some of the conceptual resources offered by the theological movement known as *process theology*. One of its leading exponents, Charles Hartshorne, suggests that our life history is a 'book of life' and that at death 'the book is finished, but it will not be destroyed. It remains for eternity in the memory of the present God.' Moltmann describes this as a 'fine image', but rightly points out that in itself it is hardly a substantial basis for hope, because in Hartshorne's process theology there is no resurrection life other than this being held in God's memory.[50] What it does offer, though, is a way of conceiving of the state of the deceased between death and resurrection. On the one hand, it fully recognizes that the deceased are dead, with no implication of a disembodied spirit enduring the death of the body. At the same time, there is an assurance that the dead are by no means 'lost', but are safely preserved *in* God, by God's faithfulness and power alone. Such is the strength and depth of God's memory that in faithfulness, God holds the identity of the deceased so fully that, although dead, they are nonetheless really *in* God. This seems to be the sort of vision suggested by Tom Wright as he quotes Cambridge physicist and theologian John Polkinghorne: 'God will download our software on to his hardware, until the day comes when he gives us new hardware on which to run our software once more.' Wright proposes that a strength of this particular image is that it 'leaves vague what the New Testament leaves vague, the question of what precisely someone "is" between bodily death and bodily resurrection', while positively affirming that the dead really are 'with Christ' in a meaningful way.[51]

A practical theology of hope for the dying can in this way give affirmation to Christian hope that is expressed in terms of 'going to heaven when I die'. Strictly speaking, heaven is not conceived here as the destination of the deceased but as the dwelling place of God (Matthew 6.9; Ephesians 1.20; Colossians 3.1). But the affirmation that the dead are *in* God, that is, in God's *memory*, means that there is a sense in which it is possible to say that they are 'in heaven', without undermining the basic conviction that eternal life is to be understood in terms of resurrection. This is important, because it is in response to the pastoral question 'Where are the dead?' that a practical theology most starkly comes face to face with the popular notion of 'going to heaven when you die'. Although it is the contention of this book that resurrection provides the most holistic and robust hope, it is nevertheless important to acknowledge that the hope of 'going to heaven' is well established in Christian theological tradition, and may even represent the most commonly held conception of eternal life among Christians today.[52] A challenge for churches, particularly preachers and teachers, is to enable people to rediscover the primacy of resurrection. However, in the practical context of caring for the dying and their loved ones it is not realistic to expect to engage in critical theological analysis whenever hope is articulated in terms of 'going to heaven when I die'. Following the understanding advanced here, a pastoral carer can support hope that is expressed in terms of references to heaven without any awkward feeling that it might be in some way compromising a conviction that Christian hope is essentially resurrection hope. The language of heaven can be used in prayers and pastoral conversation with a dying person who seems to express their hope in that way. But when such language is employed, care needs to be taken to ensure that the vision of hope is not 'spiritualized' in such a way that it becomes an abstraction and is thus emptied of any meaning.

Anticipating the ultimate: absolute hope in God for resurrection

Resurrection, then, is the key to understanding eternal life. Let us now refocus on the specific dynamic of *expectation*. If it is the case that living hope in the face of death is essentially the anticipation of the ultimate, that is, a mysterious power of expectation that is not tied to the attainment of any particular goal, we must ask how resurrection hope might be the very place where such power is found. If the resurrection of the body is that which is hoped *for*, we need to understand what it is that makes this 'object' of hope more than a 'goal'. In other words, as we look to the resurrection as the most ultimate future expectation, in what sense might this be called generalized hope, something that is far greater than expectation alone?

Absolutely hoping: Marcel's absolute hope

The Roman Catholic existentialist philosopher Gabriel Marcel provides a vital link between the psychological experience of hope as the anticipation of the ultimate and the theological notion of hope, which looks to resurrection. This link is what Marcel calls *absolute hope*. Unlike Dufault and Martocchio, Marcel does not write in a practical clinical context. Neither does he employ theological, eschatological concepts as Moltmann does. But he does offer some tremendously profound insights into what he calls the *metaphysics* of hope, and these are firmly grounded in his belief in God. Rather like Lynch's insistence that only God can hold the absolutizing instinct at bay, Marcel also affirms that God is the only true absolute. Thus Marcel's hope in God is absolute hope. Further consideration of the dynamics of that hope will help us to see how looking to the resurrection of the body is the very thing that enables us to encounter the anticipation of the ultimate.

Earlier we noted Marcel's distinction between 'to hope' and 'to hope that . . . '.[53] This lucidly conveys the difference between generalized and particularized hope. According to Marcel, 'to hope that . . .' means to be caught up in the 'radical insecurity of having'. Such hope reduces itself 'to a matter of dwelling on, or of becoming hypnotized over, something one has represented to oneself'. On the other hand, 'to hope' is not confined to the limits of what the imagination depicts as the object of hope, but is able to transcend the imagination, because this hope is not made conditional. Marcel says that only faith in God makes such hope possible, for only such absolute hope is capable of 'transcending all laying down of conditions'. God is 'the only possible source from which this absolute hope springs' because only God, as 'the infinite Being' by whom all creatures have been brought forth out of nothingness, transcends all objects and thus all conditions of hope. The hope of the believer in God is thus absolute hope, says Marcel: 'The believer is he who will meet with no insurmountable obstacle on his way towards transcendence,'[54] because absolute hope can 'transcend the particular objects to which it at first seems to be attached'.[55] Hope involves living in expectation of such objects, but in itself is a more mysterious, general sense of anticipation that maintains a sense of possibility even if the pursuit of a particular goal is disappointed. *General* here does not mean vague. Marcel says that this hope is 'a mystery' but 'not a problem'; because it cannot be fully articulated in terms of tangible objects it is 'very difficult to describe',[56] but it is nevertheless very real.

Practical theology has given some recognition to this sort of hope. Rumbold describes 'mature hope' that is 'open to possibility' as a deep sense of anticipation that transcends the expectation of specific goals:

> . . . the actual details of a mature hope are not as important as its trust that, whatever may be hoped for, that which actually happens will be for the best. This hope appears more as a personal trust than as commitment to details of a plan for the future.

Rumbold says that this intangible power of hope is 'difficult to express' other than by saying that it is 'trust in God'.[57] Similarly, Lester suggests a *finite* hope that seeks a specific goal, and a *transfinite* hope, which is more open-ended.[58] Lester emphasizes that such open-ended hope is essentially oriented to the transcendence of God. He writes, 'Trusting in the character of God frees us from investing our deepest hope in specific objects, events, or processes.'[59]

As insightful as they are, neither Rumbold nor Lester, as practical theologians, nor Marcel as a theist existentialist philosopher, make any explicit association between this basic notion of absolute, mature, or transfinite hope, and hope in the resurrection. They provide some key conceptual resources to link the psychological experience of generalized hope with a theological understanding of hope in God, but do not venture so far as to spell this out specifically in terms of resurrection hope. So let us now take up just that challenge as we come to what is the core argument of this book, namely: *resurrection hope is the very thing that enables us to anticipate the ultimate.* In other words, looking to the resurrection is the most complete and holistic form of absolute hope. Thus our definition of Christian hope is *absolute hope in God for resurrection*. The resurrection of the body is the *object* of this hope – that which is hoped *for* – but because it is so ultimate, expressing possibility even in the face of death, it transcends all other goals and any conditions they may impose. Marcel's term absolute hope is therefore especially apt because it conveys this very transcendence of resurrection hope.

It is worth mentioning that the significance of such absolute hope is reinforced when considered against Bringle's insights into the nature of despair. It may be recalled that Bringle suggests that the most serious level of despair is precisely that which is not focused on a specific object.[60] Rather, it is more global and all-pervasive. Just as death, in all its sense of finality, can represent such an all-encompassing, generalized despair, so may absolute hope in God for resurrection be the highest order of hope that is sufficiently all-pervasive and transcendent of all objects so as to properly engage with it.

Resurrection as the object *of absolute hope*

It may be helpful here to give greater clarity to the rather para-doxical suggestion that resurrection is that which we hope *for*, and yet is to be regarded as something that actually transcends all *objects*. Strictly speaking, resurrection cannot be called the object of absolute hope because following Marcel's under-standing, absolute hope by definition does not have an object. Absolute hope does not hope *for*, but it does hope *in*, and such hope is *in God*. Marcel's metaphysic of hope is not discussed by Moltmann, but it is possible to incorporate Marcel's absolute hope into Moltmann's eschatology. In so doing we can see how resurrection hope looks to the raising of the dead as its future expectation but in a way that does not reduce that expectation to a mere 'goal', as in particularized hope. Rather, because the resurrection of the body denotes the ultimate transformation of the whole cosmos, it encompasses and indeed surpasses all goals and objects towards which our hopes may be directed.

For all the emphasis Moltmann gives to the eschatological end of history when the dead will be raised and the kingdom of God will come in all fullness, he does not understand this as hope in an object or goal in the strict sense:

> What is called 'the end of history' is, for a Christian under-standing, not an end in the sense of a goal, but release from a life subordinated by the law to goals and achievements into the joy of God.[61]

Moltmann is not denying that there will be an eschatological climax to history; such an event is crucial to his theology. What he is saying is that this eschatological end is so radical that it cannot be likened to any other kind of goal. Hope that looks towards this is therefore a hope that transcends goals, in the ordinary sense of the word; indeed, such hope actually liberates life from the burdensome existence that knows only of pursuing one goal after another. In this respect, then, hope for 'the end of history' is so radical that it transcends any notion of hoping *for* any particular goal, and is most appropriately expressed as hope *in God*. Moltmann, however, is cautious over this. In *Theology of Hope* he writes:

> Our hope in the promises of God, however, is not hope in God himself or in God as such, but it hopes that his future faithfulness will bring it also the fulness of what has been promised . . . It does not merely hope personally 'in him', but has also substantial hopes of his lordship, his peace and his righteousness on earth.[62]

Moltmann's concern is that hope that is not articulated in terms of specific concrete promises of God can too easily become an abstraction. It is not enough simply to say *that* we hope in God; we do also need to spell out *what* it is we are hoping for. Otherwise hoping in *God* could lack content and slip into meaningless sentimentalism – the very thing that leads someone like Tom to regard Christianity as empty and full of pious clichés. Only a hope that engages with *what* is significant for Tom is likely to be 'owned' by Tom personally.

Moltmann, then, affirms the need for some kind of specific imaginable object or objects in Christian hope. But ultimately that hope is not confined to the particularity of such objects. These objects of hope – that is, the things we hope for – are in their totality depicted in the eschatological end, for which the primary symbol is resurrection. Because of its totality and ultimate status, this end can only be found in God, who is by definition the only absolute. Thus the concrete promises *of* God are found *in* God: 'the finite promises point beyond themselves to the eschatological final arrival of God *himself*. For ultimately, the *author* and the *content* of the promise are one.' In this respect, Moltmann affirms the statement, 'We hope in God.'[63]

It is possible to see, then, how ultimately resurrection hope, as absolute hope, does not have an object in the strict sense of the word, but that it simply hopes *in God*. But for the sake of giving this hope concrete expression resurrection is to be identified as its content, as the ultimate promise of God. In this sense it may be referred to as the object that absolute hope hopes for, but it should be stressed that it is qualitatively different from any other type of object, because it is so all-encompassing and radical. Resurrection is all-encompassing because it is both personal and societal, as we have discussed. It is radical because it hopes for life even in death, and as such transcends all goals, the attainment of which would ultimately be threatened by death. It is thus of special relevance in a palliative context, because it is hope that enables dying persons to have a sense of future in the present, even though death approaches. Goals may be set, but even when it becomes improbable that they will be reached, a mysterious but very real *anticipation of the ultimate* prevails, because resurrection denotes possibility even in death, looking to new life that God promises to bring out of death.

It is the nature of absolute hope that only hope that transcends goals can properly enable smaller hopes that are fixed on specific goals to be sustained. Lester says, 'When the horizons of our vision extend indefinitely, there are always possibilities and hope is more secure.'[64] Resurrection hope is in this respect the most indefinite extension of vision. Moltmann writes, 'If the Christian hope means through God the negation of the great negatives of life – guilt and death – how much more must it mean the negation of the many minute negatives of life.'[65] Indeed, it is arguable that only this resurrection hope that engages with death makes any type of hope possible at all. Hoping for resurrection therefore means hoping for hope itself, because only resurrection hope can provide a sufficiently robust basis for all other hopes. Only hope that sets itself upon the ultimate object of resurrection can endure the pain and suffering of disappointment, because only such hope is really absolute. And such absolute status can only be afforded to this object because it looks solely to the God who promises it, and who is the only absolute. In the final part of this chapter we will now give more detailed consideration to what might be meant by a *spirituality* of absolute hope in God for resurrection.

The spirituality of hoping in God

Let us reflect on some of the implications of a spirituality of hoping *in God*. Since that hope is essentially the anticipation of the ultimate, we may regard the spirituality of such hope in terms of a present encounter of the resurrection life in God that is hoped for. As such, if we may consider the possible spirituality of that future resurrection life in God, we may in so doing come closer to an understanding of the spirituality that is encountered in its very anticipation now.

So what might the dynamics of resurrection life in God be like? We may recall that towards the end of Chapter 3 we made the point that although Christian hope looks to the resurrection as the eschatological end, this end is not to be understood as a static and timeless eternity. The processes of *becoming* in time that are necessary for vitality will be so transformed that they will be qualitatively different, no longer accompanied with pain, suffering, transience and death as they are in present life as we know it. Moltmann describes this resurrection life as an 'eternal livingness'. It is life in God's new creation, where God 'dwells in it, and finds in it his rest'. As such, eternal life is understood to be 'a kind of cosmic *perichoresis* of divine and cosmic attributes'.[66] It is thus conceived as a *dynamic* life, an eternal existence that is life in God in the fullest sense.

We can elaborate on the dynamic nature of this resurrection life in God by drawing on some of the insights offered by the Roman Catholic theologian Karl Rahner. He says that eternity as an 'endless running on of time' would be a pointless existence, 'doomed always to roam, without ever finally arriving anywhere'.[67] It must therefore be a qualitatively different existence, 'an existence and life that has God himself in himself as its content'. Rahner stresses that this is 'something we cannot concretely imagine or picture to ourselves here and now', but suggests that eternal life so conceived is dynamic, not static.[68] Traditionally it has been held that, just as faith comes to an end with 'vision', so hope 'is dissolved by "possession", by the "attainment of the goal"'.[69] This, says Rahner, is unsatisfactory, because being raised to eternal life in God does not mean that God is 'attained'. God's absolute transcendence cannot be 'possessed' so that there is nothing left to anticipate, because God is inexhaustible:

> The act of attaining to God as truth in the 'vision' of God in fact allows for the transcendence of this God as the incomprehensible. The event in which this takes place, inasmuch as it is made possible by the divine self-bestowal, is not the act in which the absolute mystery which is God is finally overcome and solved, but rather the act in which this truly unfathomable mystery in all its finality and its overpowering acuteness is no longer able to be suppressed . . . The 'possession' of God – if in spite of what has been said we may still use this term – is that radical transcendence of self and surrender of self which is entailed in the act of reaching out for truth into the unfathomable mystery, and it is also the radical self-surrender and self-transcendence of that love which cannot charm love from the beloved through any act of self-surrender on its part, but lives totally by the love of that which is beloved as based on nothing else than itself.[70]

Hope is not dissolved in resurrection life, but continues to make way for the never-ending transcendence of God:

> In the word 'hope' this one unifying 'outwards from the self' attitude into God as the absolutely uncontrollable finds expression . . . it is a process of constantly eliminating the provisional in order to make room for the radical and pure uncontrollability of God.[71]

Eternal resurrection life in God is therefore anything but a static existence. John Baillie makes this point in a different way in his classic work on the theology of eternal life, *And the Life Everlasting*. He asks whether eternal life is more appropriately conceived as *rest* or *activity*. It is false to think of it 'as a mere period of relaxation, a vast holiday, or the endless Long

Vacation of the lazy student's dreams'. Eternal life is a sort of rest in that it is free of pain and suffering, but not rest in a passive sense. Baillie suggests the term *fruition* to express this: '*Fruition*, then, is *essentially an activity* – a higher activity than the activity of becoming or of unfulfilled quest.'[72] In eternal life there will be 'plenty of room for adventure, and even social service . . . though it will be adventure and service of a different kind. Instead of development *towards* fruition there will be development *in* fruition.'[73] Baillie seems to be using the term *towards* in the same way that our present discussion has suggested the term *hoping for*. The Christian lives towards the resurrection, as that which is hoped for. What Baillie does not entertain is that the notion of *in* might be used to describe the present experience of hope. That is to say, just as in Baillie's words 'development' in eternal life will be development '*in* fruition', in present life it is God who is hoped *in*.

Resurrection life is life *in* God, in the fullest sense: the never-ending encounter of being opened to an ever richer life in God. This makes for a spirituality of hope *in* God in present existence, as the context in which this very transcendence of God is experienced. The one who hopes in God for resurrection may encounter the mysterious presence of God's transcendence, an experience that brings at once both fulfilment and anticipation.

In a specifically palliative context, such spirituality is of tremendous importance. Where dying persons may find the very language of 'future goals' problematic as death approaches, hope may nevertheless be expressed as a mysterious sense of the transcendence of God in the present. As Moltmann says, the moment is experienced as the eternity of God's Spirit: 'as the present of the eternal God it is so profound that both beginning and goal are also contemporary and immediate'.[74] This encounter with God as *absolute*, the one who is hoped *in*, is an experience of fulfilment in the present that reaches beyond the immediate here and now. Such hope in God is a living experience in God's absoluteness, thus creating a sense of possibility even in death. Moltmann describes this sort of mystical experience as *ecstatic*.[75] Literally, *ec-static* conveys a breaking free from the fixed, static sense of 'paralysis' that characterizes hopelessness – what Tom describes as being 'frozen'. This is a spirituality that also holds out an important alternative for David who has given up on life when there is still living to be done. The ecstasy of hope in God offers the prospect of a mysterious sense of liberation from resignation of this kind, bringing a renewed vitality even in death. It is a living hope – something that is organic, dynamic and alive. If this can be grasped by Sarah, who feels ineffective and uncertain about her practical 'value' to someone so close to death, she may well come to discover a renewed confidence in her ministry. As she seeks to nurture in dying persons an awareness of the presence of God, through pastoral conversation, prayer, Bible reading and sharing in worship, she is not merely 'consoling' them. Rather, she is inviting them to take a foretaste of the vitality of the God who is coming to us.

The spirituality of hoping for resurrection

Once again it must be stressed that absolute hope does not have an *object* in the strict sense of the word, because it transcends all objects. What might be meant by a spirituality of hoping *for* resurrection?

Further reflection on the nature and meaning of the resurrection body, as that which we hope for, may help. Let us again take up the Pauline term 'spiritual body' (1 Corinthians 15.44–49). The term expresses simultaneously both the qualitative difference of the new, transformed resurrection life and also the continuity of identity carried into that life from present existence. Schneiders says this notion of a 'spiritual body' becomes conceptually problematic only when *bodiliness* is equated with *physicality*. On closer examination it is possible to conceive of the body without making such an equation. For example, Schneiders points out that the word 'body' may be used 'to refer to very immaterial things such as a "body of evidence" or the "body of an argument". In other words, body has as much to do with unity and consistency as it does with physical solidity.'[76] This means that the 'spiritual body' may be conceived as the 'symbol of the self', that is, personal identity, transformed, with an acceptance of the fact that the exact nature of that transformation cannot be known in present existence. It is hope that the resurrection of the body will happen, but with an openness concerning the precise details of that resurrection. This does not mean that the term 'spiritual body' is an abstraction. But it does mean that while Christian hope must in some ways be formulated in concrete terms if it is not to be lacking in content, hope *in* God must involve a basic trust that ultimately *only* God, as absolute, knows of the exact details of resurrection life. In this respect it is perhaps correct to say that it is more important *that* we hope in God than that we spell out *what* we actually hope for.

Because hope for resurrection is focused on the future 'spiritual body', the present earthly, physical body is the locus of that hope, as we discussed earlier in this chapter. Thus there is a real sense in which hope, as the anticipation of the ultimate, actually enters into a live encounter with it in the here and now, enabling the transcendence of the present. It is possible, therefore, to say that eternal life begins *now* for the one who hopes for the resurrection. Moltmann says that the resurrection is 'an event belonging to the whole of life . . . It will overcome death in the midst of life.'[77] Now, it has already been stressed that resurrection takes the reality of death seriously, and that unlike the doctrine of the immortal soul, it implies no serene survivalism, for it talks of eternal life as God's creation after death, out of death. But it can also be seen that because the body may be understood as the representation of the eschatological *already/not yet* tension, it may be said that eternal life begins in the very experience of hoping for resurrection. This is probably what Tillich is trying to say when he writes:

> Resurrection is not an event that might happen in some remote future, but it is the power of the New Being to create life out of death, here and now . . . Resurrection happens now, or it does not happen at all.[78]

This reinforces the significance of a kenotic spirituality of hope for the dying. Hoping *for* resurrection means that personal identity may 'body forth' in a way that does not mean clinging to the body but is willing to lay it down.[79] Hoping in this way enables a process of *letting go* of life in free acceptance of death, precisely in order that life may be lived. In the very act of laying down the body the new life of resurrection is experienced in hope. Though not specifically referring to resurrection, this is the sort of dynamic that Marcel seems to have in mind in his discussion of absolute hope. He says that hope defined in terms of specified goals is brittle, because insisting rigidly that such goals must be attained is to 'put up limits . . . laying down conditions'. This manifests 'the radical insecurity of *having*'. In contrast, absolute hope in God is

> the inner disposition of one who, setting no condition or limit and abandoning himself in absolute confidence, would thus transcend all possible disappointment and would experience a security of his being.[80]

Absolute hope for resurrection thus means a willingness to relinquish one's grip on life in order to embrace a deeper security in God. This is a spirituality in which *being* is more important than *having*. The being that is hoping *in* God does not cling to the body in 'the radical insecurity of *having*' but freely surrenders the body as resurrection is hoped *for*. Moltmann describes how the body may be regarded in terms of 'having', that is, as an object of possession – something that is expressed in the term '*my* body'. It may also be regarded as that which a person *is*, as in the phrase 'I am some*body*'. Moltmann argues that in modern society where 'The *category of having* has stifled the *category of human being*', the prevalent view of the body is the former of these two. When the body is conceived in this way illness is regarded as something one 'has' ('I *have* a stomach ache'), and thus is distanced from the person. Only when the body is primarily understood in terms of the category of *being* can illness be regarded as part of personal identity

('*I am* sick').[81] This integration is important if illness is to be accepted as part of humanity. As we discussed earlier in this chapter, a holistic concept of health is not one that extols the unobtainable ideal of a life of happiness without pain and peace without conflict. Rather, health is the strength to live with reality, which means a capacity for suffering and joy. The one who hopes for resurrection and so freely lays down the body is one who regards the body as their identity and illness as part of their humanity. This makes for an acceptance of illness and ultimately death as the process of 'abandoning' oneself in 'absolute confidence', in Marcel's words, above.

With these thoughts in mind let us briefly revisit David and Jane one more time. In this chapter we have already considered the need for both a fighting spirit, as the hopeful resolve not to give up too soon, and also an acceptance, as the courage, in hope, to let go and lay things down. David, in his resignation that there is nothing left to do but die, and Jane in her refusal to accept that a miraculous cure may not be forthcoming, illustrate the need for the vital dynamics of the fighting spirit and acceptance. Now we can see how hoping for resurrection provides us with the very resources that are needed for the cultivation of a hope that bears precisely these dynamics. Hoping for resurrection makes the body the locus of hope, and thus provides a way of envisioning a future for the personal identity that is represented by that body and a recognition of the pains and struggles that the same body experiences. This is a daring to hope absolutely, but without taking leave of the daily realities of living and dying in this present body. A number of practical ways of encouraging people like David and Jane to 'body forth' in this way can be suggested.

First, the importance of *touch* should not be underestimated. The simple act of holding the hand of a person while listening, and especially when praying with them, can express more deeply than words that it is that body that is hoped for. One particular way of conveying this when praying is for the pastoral carer to place his or her hands beneath those of the other person, so that the carer 'cups' the hands of the other in their palms. Praying in this way effectively 'upholds' the other person, in their body, before God. Touch, of course, must be used carefully, not least because of the dangers of sexual implications. Different people will have different sensitivities and carers should be mindful of the appropriate boundaries. More will be said about touch in the next chapter, but here it is highlighted because of its significance for the bodily nature of resurrection hope.

Another important ministry in which hope for the body may be nurtured is that of *anointing with oil*. Part of the symbolic power of this pastoral act lies in its very physicality. Unfortunately such ministry can be too rigidly associated either with the last rites or the quest for a miraculous cure, which in the cases of David and Jane would simply serve to reinforce their already constricted outlooks. But offered sensitively, anointing with oil can be a real way of praying for the body to be made whole in a way that looks ultimately to resurrection, accepting that death will come, but also resolving that as long as bodily life continues, there is living to be done.

Yet another practical way of fostering hope for the body is to encourage dying persons to maintain an interest in their physical appearance. This is an area in which close friends and family members who feel unsure as to what they can do to be of help to their loved ones who are dying can make a real difference. Examples of things they could do might include helping to varnish nails or choose a new outfit by browsing through catalogues together. These sorts of everyday things help give greater bodily dignity to the dying person and highlight the importance of the body as that which is hoped for.

Most fundamentally, there is the need for pastoral carers to be ready for openness and honesty in pastoral conversation and prayer. Hoping for the resurrection body is the basis of a holistic care – that is, one that does not seek a way *out* of suffering but a way *through* it. The chances of such hope developing are reduced considerably if pastoral carers take the easier option of avoiding awkward issues. A *real* living hope is one that engages with the real pains and struggles of bodily life and death. And so there may be times when the rather difficult question of what is *realistic* needs to be raised, and challenges may need to be made. How we might go about this in practical terms will be taken up in the next chapter.

In this chapter we have set out a practical theological definition of *living hope*. This is *absolute hope in God for resurrection*. We have probed deeply into its theological and psychological nature. In the next chapter we will turn to some of the practical theological issues encountered in the quest to nurture hope as we care for dying people. How might we enable others to *live* hope?

Notes

1 Moltmann, *Theology of Hope*, p. 32.
2 Moltmann, *God in Creation*, p. 205.
3 Jürgen Moltmann, *The Future of Creation*, ET (trans. Margaret Kohl), London: SCM Press, 1979, p. 122.
4 Moltmann, *Experiences of God*, pp. 19–20.
5 Moltmann, *The Future of Creation*, pp. 122–3.
6 Moltmann, *Theology of Hope*, p. 44.
7 Moltmann, *Experiences of God*, p. 28.
8 Mary Louise Bringle, *Despair: Sickness or Sin? Hopelessness and Healing in the Christian Life*, Nashville: Abingdon Press, 1990, p. 114.
9 Bringle, *Despair*, p. 141.
10 Bringle, *Despair*, p. 126.
11 Bringle, *Despair*, p. 172.
12 Bringle, *Despair*, pp. 145ff.
13 Moltmann, *God in Creation*, pp. 271, 272, 273. Italics original.
14 Moltmann, *The Crucified God*, p. 222.
15 Moltmann, *God in Creation*, pp. 274, 272–3. Here Moltmann borrows quotations from I. Illich and D. Rossler.
16 Lynch, *Images of Hope*, p. 52.
17 Moltmann, *The Spirit of Life*, p. 86.
18 Moltmann, *The Trinity and the Kingdom of God*, pp. 25ff.
19 Jürgen Moltmann, *The Experiment Hope*, ET (trans. M. Douglas Meeks), London: SCM Press, 1975, pp. 23–4.
20 Moltmann, *The Spirit of Life*, p. 3.

21 Lynch, *Images of Hope*, p. 49.
22 Moltmann, *The Experiment Hope*, p. 24.
23 Moltmann, *Experiences of God*, p. 28.
24 Moltmann, *The Experiment Hope*, p. 45.
25 Moltmann, *The Coming of God*, p. 234.
26 Moltmann, *The Coming of God*, p. 229.
27 Marcel, *Homo Viator*, p. 34.
28 Kübler-Ross, *On Death and Dying*, p. 87.
29 Moltmann, *The Crucified God*, p. 227.
30 Moltmann, *Theology of Hope*, p. 21. Italics original.
31 Kübler-Ross, *On Death and Dying*, pp. 112ff.
32 Moltmann, *The Crucified God*, p. 204.
33 Moltmann, *The Crucified God*, p. 192.
34 Moltmann, *The Crucified God*, p. 227.
35 Moltmann, *The Coming of God*, pp. 77–95.
36 Moltmann, *The Coming of God*, p. 81.
37 Kübler-Ross, *On Death and Dying*, p. 114.
38 Moltmann, *The Coming of God*, p. 93.
39 Barth, *Church Dogmatics IV.3*, p. 903.
40 Barth, *Church Dogmatics II.1*, pp. 608ff.
41 Rudolf Bultmann, 'The Early Christian Concept of Hope', in Rudolf Bultmann and Karl Heinrich Rengstorf, *Hope*, ET (trans. Dorothea Barton), London: A & C Black, 1963, p. 11.
42 Moltmann, *The Coming of God*, p. 66.
43 Sandra Schneiders, 'The Resurrection of Jesus and Christian Spirituality', in Maureen Junker-Kenny, ed., *Christian Resources of Hope*, Dublin: The Columba Press, 1995, pp. 97–8.
44 Moltmann, 'Hope without Faith', p. 18.
45 Jürgen Moltmann, *Hope and Planning*, ET (trans. Margaret Clarkson), London: SCM Press, 1971, p. 48.
46 Moltmann, *The Coming of God*, pp. 66–7.
47 Cited in Moltmann, *The Coming of God*, p. 101.
48 Moltmann, *The Coming of God*, p. 106.
49 Moltmann, *God in Creation*, p. 183.
50 Moltmann, *The Coming of God*, pp. 73–4.
51 Wright, *For All the Saints?*, pp. 72–3.
52 It should be stressed that an analysis of the anthropological and biblical arguments involved in the debate concerning whether eternal life should be conceived in terms of resurrection or the immortal soul is beyond the present scope. A classic critique of the doctrine of the immortal soul is John Baillie, *And the Life Everlasting*, London: Oxford University Press, 1934. For a defence of the doctrine see Paul Badham, 'Does Religion Need Immortality?' in Arthur Berger *et al.*,

eds, *Perspectives on Death and Dying*, Philadelphia: The Charles Press, 1989, pp. 209–20.

53 Marcel, *Homo Viator*, pp. 32, 45.

54 Marcel, *Homo Viator*, pp. 45–7.

55 Marcel, *Homo Viator*, p. 32.

56 Marcel, *Homo Viator*, p. 35.

57 Rumbold, *Helplessness and Hope*, p. 66.

58 Lester, *Hope in Pastoral Care and Counseling*, pp. 63ff.

59 Lester, *Hope in Pastoral Care and Counseling*, pp. 66.

60 Bringle, *Despair*, pp. 115ff.

61 Jürgen Moltmann, 'The Liberating Feast' in Johann Baptist Metz and Jürgen Moltmann, *Faith and the Future: Essays on Theology, Solidarity and Modernity*, Maryknoll, New York: Concilium/Orbis, 1995, p. 106.

62 Moltmann, *Theology of Hope*, p. 119.

63 Moltmann, *The Experiment Hope*, p. 50. Italics original.

64 Lester, *Hope in Pastoral Care and Counseling*, p. 65.

65 Moltmann, *Religion, Revolution and the Future*, p. 120.

66 Moltmann, *The Coming of God*, p. 295.

67 Karl Rahner, *Theological Investigations XIX: Faith and Ministry*, ET (trans. Edward Quinn). London: Darton, Longman & Todd, 1983, p. 171.

68 Rahner, *Theological Investigations XIX*, p. 176.

69 Karl Rahner, *Theological Investigations X: Writings of 1965–1967* 2, ET (trans. David Bourke), London: Darton, Longman & Todd, 1973, pp. 247–8.

70 Rahner, *Theological Investigations X*, p. 249.

71 Rahner, *Theological Investigations X*, p. 250.

72 Baillie, *And The Life Everlasting*, p. 232. Italics original.

73 Baillie, *And the Life Everlasting*, p. 234. Italics original.

74 Moltmann, *The Spirit of Life*, p. 39.

75 Moltmann, *The Spirit of Life*, p. 18.

76 Schneiders, 'The Resurrection of Jesus and Christian Spirituality', pp. 100–2.

77 Moltmann, *The Coming of God*, p. 66.

78 Tillich, *The New Being*, p. 24. Italics original.

79 Schneiders, 'The Resurrection of Jesus and Christian Spirituality', p. 102.

80 Marcel, *Homo Viator*, p. 46.

81 Moltmann, *The Experiment Hope*, pp. 160–2. Italics original. See also *Religion, Revolution and the Future*, pp. 56f.; *Hope and Planning*, pp. 47f.; *The Future of Creation*, pp. 141ff.

5

Nurturing Hope

May the God of hope fill you with all joy and peace in believing,
so that you may abound in hope by the power of the Holy Spirit.

Romans 15.13

We understand absolute hope in God for resurrection to be a
gift of God's grace. It is grounded in God's resurrection promise. As such, we cannot *give* it to others as something that can
be mechanically induced by following some kind of formula.
Christian hope is organic: it is something to be *lived*, as the
resurrection promise is anticipated. But as we live in this anticipation so we may *nurture* this hope in others. We look for ways
of enabling them to cultivate that same kind of anticipation that
we have described. In this chapter we will consider some of the
practical issues that may be encountered as we seek to do this.
Once again, we will follow the themes identified in our discussion of psychology and nursing science. We will explore some
of the major sources of hope as well as the quest for a hope that
is *realistic*. First, we probe further into the relationship between
hope and hopelessness.

Living hope in the midst of death and hopelessness

We may recall that psychology and nursing science generally
regard hope and hopelessness not as polar opposites but as two
ambiguously related realities that may be encountered in the
same yet ever-changing process of living with uncertainty.
Moltmann suggests that hopelessness effectively amounts to the
failure to recognize this uncertainty. Drawing on the thought of

Joseph Pieper, he identifies two forms of hopelessness: 'presumption' (*praesumptio*) and 'despair' (*desperatio*):

> Presumption is a premature, selfwilled anticipation of the fulfilment of what we hope for from God. Despair is the premature, arbitrary anticipation of the non-fulfilment of what we hope for from God. Both forms of hopelessness, by anticipating the fulfilment or by giving up hope, cancel the wayfaring character of hope.

It is possible to see both of these forms of hopelessness in David. In his initial refusal to accept the seriousness of his cancer there is a certain presumption that he just could not die. Conversely, his later preoccupation with dying suggests the very despair that Moltmann describes here as a 'giving up'. Moltmann regards both types of hopelessness as 'forms of the sin against hope'.[1] We may recall that in Chapter 4 we considered how Moltmann understands sin as the closing of 'open systems', and how hopelessness may thus be conceived as the shutting out of the possibilities of the promised future of God. The pastoral implications of associating despair with sin were discussed there and need not be repeated here. What is worthy of mention again, however, is that the sheer openness to the future, which Moltmann sees as so integral to hope, could also be seen as the very source of despair. The uncertainty of the open future is the breeding ground for hopelessness as well as hope, and it is perhaps because of this shared territory that we see a rather ambiguous relationship between the two.

Marcel says that hope can *only* be experienced in the same context in which the possibility of despair equally exists: 'Hope is situated within the framework of the trial.'[2] He makes it a point of emphasis that 'the less life is experienced as a captivity the less the soul will be able to see the shining of that veiled, mysterious light'.[3] It is precisely in those situations that could be deemed hopeless that hope is really encountered.

The ambiguity of the relationship between hope and hopelessness is conveyed in Moltmann's dialectic of cross and resurrection. When Moltmann says that 'Christ's death on the cross is "the significance" of his resurrection for us,'[4] there is a deep acknowledgement of the fact that the meaning and profundity of resurrection hope is to be found only in and through the experience of the hopelessness of the cross. In this respect hopelessness is therefore part of hope itself, for only out of the former does the latter arise.

These things have important implications for the pastoral care of the dying. Despair can be kept in perspective. If hopelessness is not diametrically opposed to hope then hope may never be all that far away, even though hopelessness seems to have the upper hand. Lester says, 'I use the word despair to describe disturbances of the "hoping process" in which our capacity to hope is lost, blocked, distorted, or in some manner impaired.'[5] Lester's account of despair depicts it as simply the polar opposite of hope,[6] and so there is an inner consistency in his comment. The problem is, this does not allow for the possibilities for hope that exist precisely in the midst of despair. If in despair 'our capacity to hope is lost', then despair is far more than a 'disturbance' of the hoping process. However, when it is recognized that hopelessness is one and the same context for the discovery of hope, then it need not be seen as the termination of all possibilities, but the very beginning. This is not naïve: it is based on the conviction that resurrection hope is only arrived at via the cross.

The basic 'unifying theme' in Rumbold's book on helplessness and hope in palliative care is the experience that he summarizes as feeling there is 'nothing more to do'. Relatives, friends, professional carers and dying persons themselves frequently experience this.[7] But, argues Rumbold, it is precisely in the midst of this encounter that hope is to be found:

> To really hope we must open ourselves to the pain of false hopes being broken down, the challenge and threat of new possibilities being opened up. We must search within ourselves for the meaning of our own lives, and struggle to reaffirm this meaning in the face of death.[8]

Hope in the face of death may only be found when other hopes are exposed as inadequate and are thus stripped away. Then only hopelessness remains. But when this is entered into new possibilities are exposed:

> Thus the prelude to resurrection is our powerlessness, a recognition that we are helpless in the face of death and finitude, and that only God can bring meaning out of this situation.[9]

This reinforces what was said in Chapter 4: absolute hope in God for resurrection involves a *kenotic* spirituality. Hope is encountered in the process of freely surrendering oneself, laying things down and letting go. Part of this process is the entering into hopelessness, the very context for hope. In terms of pastoral care, Moltmann describes this as 'diakonia under the cross'. Caring for the dying is a 'ministry to those in so-called hopeless situations'. It is not something that provides carers with feelings of success, in the sense that solutions may be found. Rather it is a ministry in which effective care is where the carer has a readiness to 'die daily'.[10] This is the kenotic principle that lies at the heart of living and dying in hope. Rumbold reflects:

> The helper then has the choice of abandoning the relationship and withdrawing, or staying and sharing the other person's helplessness.[11]

> To try to organize a helping relationship so that the risk of suffering is eliminated, or to withdraw as soon as helplessness threatens, is to frustrate any possibility of real ministry.[12]

Pastoral care in a palliative context must be able and willing to share in hopelessness. But when it is understood that even in this hopelessness hope is to be found, such a pastoral relationship may be entered into with hope. Sitting with Tom as he shares his feelings of devastation and bursts into tears may not have the outward appearance of a hopeful situation, and being the minister in that scenario may not be easy. But it is in the shedding of Tom's tears that he begins to be open for the first time about his feelings. Later in this chapter we will consider what he shares; here we may simply acknowledge that it is only when he reaches hopelessness that a glimmer of hope begins to shine in Tom. We can also see how David's hopelessness may be regarded as the seedbed of hope. When David goes with his wife to visit the vicar to discuss funeral arrangements, the vicar could just see the victim of a tragic illness who has nothing left to do but get ready to die. But a more hopeful discernment would perceive in this situation an opportunity to enable David to talk about his disappointments and fears, as the first step towards identifying possibilities that still lie ahead for David – possibilities that might engage him once again with the life that is there to be lived.

Hopelessness then may be regarded as the context for the birth of hope. It is this basic axiom that perhaps most needs to be grasped by Sarah. She wants to feel that visiting her church member who is dying will have some kind of positive influence, but she feels utterly helpless. Perhaps in discovering the kenotic principle described here she may be enabled to integrate her feelings of hopelessness into her ministry of nurturing hope, understanding them in terms of her own 'diakonia under the cross' with the dying person she is visiting. It is a cross that leads to resurrection promise. There, in the midst of dying, living hope is to be found.

Let's get real: hope and reality surveillance

A living hope that is found in the midst of hopelessness, which sees resurrection promise in the cross, is a hope that is not escapist. It is a hope that dares to stare death in the face and, without downplaying its pain and anguish, affirms the life that is to be lived. Let us probe more deeply into our practical theological concern for a realistic hope. Specifically, this concern is highlighted by our stories of David and Jane. They illustrate how individuals can stake everything on the hope that life-threatening illness can be overcome, with medicine or by a miraculous cure. Such hope can be very brittle, having the outer appearance of strength, but easily shattered when placed under the strain of reality. In David's case, the denial of death is traded for the denial of life as the dashing of his hope of physical recovery leads him to give up on living. In Chapter 2 we considered how unrealistic hoping could function as an adaptive coping mechanism, part of the process of coming to terms with reality. However, in Chapter 4 it was suggested that the very narrowness of David and Jane's thinking could actually make for a maladaptive way of coping. A key question for pastoral care must therefore be whether it is ever appropriate to challenge the hopes that are held by those who are dying, and if so, how.

What is 'reality'? Utopia and Christian hope

David illustrates how a hopelessness that is resigned to fate can be as unrealistic as a hope that denies the seriousness of life-threatening illness. If both hope and hopelessness can be unrealistic, the question raised is, therefore, *what is reality?*

This question features prominently in theological discussions of hope. Resurrection hope is committed to being 'realistic' in that it does not seek to be mere 'pie in the sky when you die'. Death is taken seriously by Moltmann's dialectic of cross and resurrection, which expounds a hope that cannot be grasped by circumventing pain and suffering but which is found in and through these realities. At the same time, the very radical nature of resurrection hope, as *absolute hope*, challenges what is perceived to be the limits of 'reality'. Because it is God who is hoped in as ultimate reality, the boundaries of what is possible are blown open in hope. Moltmann writes:

> Hope alone is to be called 'realistic', because it alone takes seriously the possibilities with which all reality is fraught . . . In its eyes the world is full of all kinds of possibilities, namely all the possibilities of the hope of God.[13]

There is then a kind of dual concern over the issue of 'realism'. Hope should not take leave of reality yet at the same time challenges what are actually perceived to be the limits of reality. This dual concern is manifest in the ambiguity with which theologians treat the concept of *utopia*. For example, Rubem Alves affirms utopia as a vital part of the hopeful imagination that dares to envision alternatives to the status quo. 'Prophecy and utopia', says Alves, 'see the future as a task. They want to "make room for the possible, as opposed to a passive acquiescence in the present actual state of affairs . . . "'[14] Alves' argument is that 'realism' tends to function as an ideological tool used to suppress such hopeful imagination and keep things as they are. The one who dares to hope is deemed 'unrealistic' – 'He must abdicate his will and bow down to the "reality" of life. He must be converted to "realism".'[15] Thus:

> To dispose of utopias as irrational products of consciousness is to refuse to hear the voice of life itself . . . To say that a vision is utopian reveals almost nothing about the vision itself, but definitely unveils the logic of the system that passes this judgment.[16]

Theologians talk of 'the utopian function' of Christian eschatology, by which hope imagines and so challenges the status quo.[17] The term is not used without qualification. For example, liberation theologian Jose Miguez Bonino is cautious to distinguish the kingdom of God from utopia, pointing out that the former is distinctively *God's* initiative, as well as being a hope for history and one that defines action in the present, which utopia lacks.[18]

Moltmann captures the theological ambivalence over utopia:

> Hope and the kind of thinking that goes with it consequently cannot submit to the reproach of being utopian, for they do not strive after things that have 'no place', but after things that have 'no place *as yet*' but can acquire one. On the other hand, the celebrated realism of the stark facts, of established

objects and laws, the attitude that despairs of possibilities and clings to reality as it is, is inevitably much more open to the charge of being utopian, for in its eyes there is 'no place' for possibilities . . .[19]

On the one hand Moltmann affirms the creative use of the 'productive fantasy'[20] and in this respect Christian hope may be seen as utopian.[21] At the same time, hope that is defined by the dialectic of cross and resurrection 'leads faith away from the illusions of history and utopias of the future back to the cross of Christ'. Hence Moltmann talks of 'the iconoclastic power of Christian hope' by which 'the prohibition of images is fulfilled in the destruction of images of religious fetishism on the one hand and of religious dreams of the future on the other'.[22] Eschatological hope is essentially *critical*. As absolute hope in God it holds finite hopes in check, preventing them from becoming absolutes. Lynch says that hoping in God is a matter of putting the absolute 'in the right place'.[23] In this respect it exercises a challenging role against finite hopes that claim to deliver more than they really can. Yet it also dares to hope beyond what might be assumed to be the 'sensible limits' of possibility, and is as such the challenge to hope for more.

Pastoral care writers Rumbold, Lester and Capps also express the dual concern over the issue of realism in hope described here. First, there is a recognition of the need for a reality base and that there can be such things as 'false hopes'. Rumbold describes how a 'lasting or mature hope is formed through a process of testing and clarifying reality; that is, through struggle'.[24] Such hope only emerges as the layers or 'orders' of denial are gradually broken down.[25] Lester uses the term 'Golden Calf Syndrome' to describe the way finite hopes are made absolute: 'A future story that has no transcendent reference is substituted for the sacred story.'[26] Against this, Lester says that Christian hope is set in the memory of the sacred story of the Judeo-Christian tradition, which dares to believe that 'God is ultimate reality, not ultimate fantasy'.[27] Capps proposes that the reality base of a person's hope is strengthened as he or she learns to 'let go' of 'failed hopes and of the self who envisioned them'.[28] This is a special type of *modesty*, says Capps, by which the hoping person acknowledges 'the finiteness of one's own existence'.[29] This 'letting go' once again underlines the kenotic nature of hope in God for resurrection.

Second, these pastoral care writers also stress that hope serves to expand the parameters of what is perceived to be 'reality'. Capps says that 'When we hope, we envision eventualities that are not yet realities but yet appear to us as potential realities.'[30] There is a sense in which such 'potential' is part of reality itself, but which may only be seen through the eyes of hope. Hopelessness, which does not see this potential, is rooted in unreality. Lester writes:

> People become vulnerable to despair to the degree they separate themselves from reality by attaching their hoping process to fantasy and illusion (such as in mental illness) rather than to reality.[31]

Daring to hope, then, involves imagining the future transformation of reality, but in a way that remains 'in touch' with that reality as it is presently experienced. To live in hope is to defy reality without taking leave of it. When the status quo is too readily accepted, the present can effectively be absolutized. When the status quo is denied completely, the future can be absolutized. Hoping in God as the only absolute makes for a vision that does not allow absolute status to be given to present conditions or to individual objects of aspiration.

As for David and Jane, we need to ask whether we see in them something of the absolutizing instinct at work. Arguably, we do. David begins by rigidly fixing his vision on a rapid recovery that will allow him to return to work. As soon as he grasps the false nature of this absolute he latches on to another, namely the conclusion that only death awaits him now. Jane's absolute – her insistence that she will be miraculously cured – remains the same right up until her death, the very death that she refuses to accept as a possible reality. But for all this, is it ever appropriate for carers to challenge people like David and Jane with the suggestion that their perceptions of reality might be false?

Whose 'reality' is it anyway? Perspectives in pastoral care

In our discussion of nursing science in Chapter 2 it was suggested that a judgemental attitude could be implied in the assumption that carers possess a more accurate perception than patients as to what is an 'appropriate hope'. Within a palliative context we might also ask whether any one person has the right to define what constitutes a 'dignified' death. In Chapter 4 it was argued that while there is a place for the dynamic of the *fighting spirit* in hope, this must be qualified in order to emphasize the importance of *acceptance* of the reality of death. But Paul Fiddes, quoting a doctor, claims that for some, 'the dignified way to die will be in fighting to the last'.[32] Perhaps that is the case for Jane. The point is, a practical theology of hope for the dying that seeks to discern what is an 'appropriate', that is, 'realistic' hope, needs to be aware of the relative nature of human judgement. An issue of power is implicit here, as Lester points out: 'Pastoral caregivers must avoid stepping into the omniscient position of thinking that *we* know definitively what reality is in a given situation for a particular person.'[33]

Here the matter of *perspectives* in the experience of hope is highly pertinent. In the search for a realistic hope we must ask, *whose reality?* The perspectives of nurses, family members and other carers are *specific*, and so it may be argued that they differ considerably from that of the dying person. However, though the perspective of each person is specific in that it is the experience of their own particular being, it need not mean that it must be so completely different from others. Fiddes makes a very significant point here. His argument is that it is inaccurate to draw a sharp distinction between the experiences of dying and death. Specifically, he is criticizing Moltmann's suggestion that in the cross the Father experiences death while the Son experiences dying:

If we follow Moltmann's view that the Father only suffers bereavement and not dying, then we make too wide a division between one person who suffers the dying and another who suffers the death.[34]

Now it is arguable that Fiddes does not fully appreciate the trinitarian union of the suffering of death and dying that is established by Moltmann's doctrine of *perichoresis*. This doctrine has gradually matured in Moltmann's thought over a period of time that stretches way beyond the writing of *The Crucified God*, in which the point Fiddes contests was set out. After all, when Moltmann writes, 'The Fatherlessness of the Son is matched by the Sonlessness of the Father,' there is a fundamental assertion of the unity of the Father and Son in suffering.[35] Furthermore, in his own trinitarian thought Fiddes seems to overplay the notion of Father, Son and Spirit as 'persons *as* relationships' rather than 'persons *in* relationship'.[36] Thus his own logic leads him to a reluctance to assert that the Father and Son *as specific persons* may have specific experiences of suffering in the cross. For all this, Fiddes nevertheless points out that it is possible to establish a false dichotomy between the experiences of dying and death. He suggests that while 'we do not experience ourselves *as being dead*; we cannot literally suffer our own bereavement', as we come alongside others who are dying we do in fact 'experience our own death in anticipation':

> We discover about death from experiencing the running out of time; we experience death as the final deadline, the last boundary in the face of which we feel time passing. We feel the death of others as an offence against love because they no longer have time for us, and we can no longer spend time on them; but in our own being too we experience the same sense of loss of time in the face of death.[37]

For the purposes of our present discussion, the point is that while dying persons and their carers are different individuals in a pastoral relationship, their specific experiences and perspectives are not so totally different as they may initially appear. These specific experiences and perspectives are united in the fundamental human encounter with mortality. Ultimately, we are *all* dying persons. The role of 'carer' in a palliative context should not imply that he or she is in some way 'outside' of the dying process itself. Furthermore, resurrection hope unites both individual and society, which means that it is a hope that encompasses both 'patient' and 'carer'. The point is that a practical theology of hope for the dying should envision a fundamental unity of dying persons and pastoral carers in the quest to find hope in the face of death. This provides a basis for pastoral care to exercise a critical and challenging role concerning 'reality' and how it might be perceived in hope, in a way that affirms the fundamental equality of perspectives in pastoral relationships and thus does not imply the assumption of superiority of perception on the part of carers.

Let us come back specifically to David and Jane. Their perceptions of reality may be quite different from the perceptions of other people who are caring for them. Nevertheless, if it is the case that the absolutizing instinct is operational in David and Jane as we have suggested, choosing not to challenge their perceptions as 'unrealistic' could be to their detriment. 'False hope' is a value-laden term. But this does not mean that it should be avoided through fear of implying a judgemental arrogance. A preoccupation with the relative status of perceptions of reality in pastoral care should not be allowed to dissolve the critical task of facing up to the dual concern over realism in hope that we have described. It is precisely this concern over 'reality' that constitutes a fundamental 'value' in a practical theology of hope for the dying – the identification of a hope as 'false' does not amount to condescension because such an assessment expresses just this value. Pastoral care, in its commitment to reality, has a responsibility to challenge a dying person's perception of reality where his or her hopes are either 'false', that is, unrealistic, or where that person underestimates, overlooks, or denies the potential possibilities for hope that really do exist. As Roland Riem says, 'Confrontation will happen wherever integrity engages with illusion.'[38] Let us then take up the question of *how* such confrontation might take place.

Seeking and speaking truth in love: confrontation in pastoral care

Clearly, a carer's 'confrontation' of a dying person's perception of reality must be done with the greatest sensitivity. This is not least because 'denial', as we have noted from Kübler-Ross, can function as an important coping mechanism, a 'buffer after unexpected shocking news'. As such, a dying person may simply come to terms with reality in his or her own time without any need of intervention. Indeed, Kübler-Ross says this is usually the case.[39] Nevertheless, it should be considered how pastoral care might go about 'confrontation' when intervention is required. Here Riem points to some insightful comments of Alastair Campbell.[40] Campbell says that 'the person of integrity is first and foremost a critic of self, of tendencies to self-deception and escape from reality, of desire for false inner security in place of the confrontation with truth which integrity demands'.[41] This reinforces the above-mentioned importance of recognizing that both the carer and the dying person are united in the mortality and the susceptibility to fail to grasp reality that is part of our common humanity. The pastoral carer who recognizes that they too are dying and acknowledges the limits of their own human perspective is better placed to confront dying persons with the challenge that their hope or lack of hope may be unrealistic.

The second point Riem draws from Campbell concerns the actual practicalities of confrontation. How in practical terms might sensitivity be combined with frankness and honesty? Campbell highlights the importance of *listening*. Specifically, he suggests that there is a certain power in the act of listening whereby the listener simply remains silent when reality is denied. For example, let us imagine that Jane is visited by the chaplain of the hospice to which she has been admitted. They begin a conversation and it is not long before Jane tells the chaplain of her certainty that she will soon be home because God is going to heal her as he did before. At this point, the chaplain could look, purposefully, deep into Jane's eyes and say nothing verbally, yet through the very act of silence express more than words can adequately articulate. Campbell stresses the significance of this sort of creative use of silence:

> When someone is desperately asking us to help them deny the reality of their pain, it requires great strength to stay silent. Yet silence is often our greatest service. By remaining *with* people, but at the same time refusing to take the escape from pain they seek, we can restore their courage to voice their deepest fears and express the anguish they find so threatening.[42]

This is a way of confronting denial with gentleness and in a way that expresses pastoral support even in this refusal to conspire with the denial. Rumbold stresses that 'the helper's role initially is that of listener'. He also points out that in the early stages of dying such listening should not involve 'arguing about the realism of those wishes and hopes' that the dying person has.[43]

A question that may be asked, however, is how pastoral care might venture beyond the act of silence. Campbell is right to say that the power of silence must not be underestimated, but it is important to consider what action might follow if the listener does not manage to challenge the dying person's perception of reality in this way. Encouraging reality surveillance does not equate with the blunt confrontation of dying persons with the medical facts of their illness. However, there will be times when information has to be disclosed for the first time, or needs to be restated, or when what has hitherto been implicit may need to be made explicit. What resources might there be besides the use of silence?

An enormously important tool here is *memory*. This is a deeply theological theme. Christian hope is grounded in 'reality' because it remembers the reality of what God has done in history, supremely in the death and resurrection of Christ, and is thus empowered to look to the future and challenge the way 'reality' is now perceived. In Moltmann's words, 'hope exists in the mode of memory, and memory in the mode of hope'.[44] Memory can also function as a practical resource in pastoral care. As listener, the carer may encourage the dying person to explore what Rumbold describes as his or her 'personal salvation history'. This is an exploration of past experiences that

> have proved to us certain things about the trustworthiness of life – events have worked for good even though life has been at points difficult and confusing. This basic trustworthiness of life, and the meaning found through reflection on the past, is the basis for our present hope and trust . . . 'I was in trouble and delivered from it here, and here, and again here in my life. Now I once again face the unknown, but I believe somehow it will be all right.'[45]

Earlier we noted that the value of reminiscing on past experience as a hope-fostering strategy has been recognized in nursing science.[46] Lester also talks about helping persons to 'locate reality' in hope by encouraging them to pursue 'a realistic grasp of her or his history and its influence on the present . . . Staying in touch with reality means accepting one's freedom to make projections into the future and create one's own future stories.'[47] Resurrection may be hoped for as the faithfulness of God in the past is remembered. Rumbold says:

> This sort of life review can become personal salvation history, the story of God's acts within his [the dying person's] life that makes it possible to look ahead to his death and still wish and imagine possibilities in the face of this apparently impenetrable barrier.[48]

So how might we enable David and Jane to explore their life stories? In Chapter 4 it was suggested that the vicar who is approached to plan David's funeral could take this up as an opportunity to encourage David to talk about the things that he would like to be remembered for. In so doing David might just

begin to identify and reflect upon those things that are meaningful to him. Now we can take this further and add that such a
conversation could be a way of enabling David to trace his life
story and recognize past experiences of living with difficulty
and uncertainty – experiences through which he can affirm that
'basic trustworthiness of life' to which Rumbold refers. This
could be a way of helping David to envision the continuation of
that same story as the life that is still there to be lived.

For Jane, the telling of her story already plays a major part
in the formation of her future outlook. She looks back to an
earlier experience of healing and readily affirms God's hand in
it – the very hand she now believes will heal her again. This
genuine conviction is both a strength and a weakness for Jane –
it is the foundation of her hope yet also its very stumbling block.
She draws from her past and so finds a form of courage for the
future, but the way she does this is constricted. This is because
Jane's memory is focused primarily on just one experience, and
her hope is fixed exclusively on its repetition. There is no reason
to bring the reality of her previous experience into question –
indeed it would seem to be an appropriate pastoral response to
join with Jane in affirming it as part of her personal 'salvation
history'. But a challenge for a pastoral carer would be to
encourage Jane to tell *more* of her story, so that her experience
of healing might be more consciously located within the overall
context of her whole life. Until she does this, Jane seems to see
God only in the miraculous, and not in her experiences of suffering. Furthermore, she might also be encouraged to recall
more of the biblical story, in order to explore the place of Jesus'
healing ministry within the wider 'salvation history' in which
Christian faith is set. Jane has an openness to talk about her
faith, and so finding a window of opportunity to do this would
not be difficult. In such a conversation, attention might be
drawn to the signs and wonders in Jesus' earthly life, a life that
led to his death on the cross. The greatest miracle of all, Jesus'
resurrection, could then be highlighted as the primary theme for
Christian hope. Until Jane makes a closer connection between
her experience of healing and the resurrection promise to which

it points, she seems to be prevented from forming a hope that truly accepts the reality of death that we all must face.

There can be no pretending that a conversation with Jane such as this would be easy or straightforward. But encouraging Jane to talk about these things might just enable her to begin to integrate her experience of healing more thoroughly with the wider scope of her life story and also to set that story within the Christian salvation story. Only when that happens is her hope really likely to be expanded in a way that sees God in dying as well as in living, and in a way that sees not *cure* but *resurrection* as the greatest form of healing, and as the most fundamental object of Christian hope.

Encouraging and enabling dying persons to tell their life story thus has tremendous potential as a strategy for exploring what they perceive to be 'realistic'. But two critical questions may be asked. First, what about those life stories that tell primarily of pain and failure, in which there is very little apparent evidence for what Rumbold calls the 'basic trustworthiness of life'? Second, what about those who do not profess Christian faith and who would therefore choose to exclude references to the memory of God's faithfulness in recounting their own story?

In response to the first question it should be pointed out that a person who perceives their life as nothing but a trail of tragedy and sorrow in which there is no meaning to be found is precisely the person whose perception may change through the experience of exploring that life story with another who has the ability to come alongside them and listen. Reflection on that story may have only ever taken place in isolation; in the presence of a listener things may be exposed that had never been perceived before. Hope in pastoral care and counselling thus emerges as a person is helped to discover their personal story and so envision the future of that story. That is Lester's thesis. He writes, 'Our storied history, created by memories, provides us with the sense of groundedness necessary for having an integrated self.'[49] Personal stories that seem to tell of only pain and suffering may find hope when set within the 'Christian sacred story':

Through the symbol of the cross, Christianity affirms that suffering is a reality within the human condition . . . Our sacred story includes the belief that God is present with us, suffering with us, saddened on our behalf, and working in mysterious ways to be known unto us.[50]

Moltmann's dialectic of cross and resurrection strengthens this point. This dialectic remembers the 'sacred story' in hope by stressing the presence of God in suffering and that resurrection hope only emerges out of the hopelessness of the cross. Pastoral carers can give focus to this story through Bible reading, sharing communion, and giving special emphasis to the images of cross and resurrection when praying with the dying.

Our second question takes us back to Angela, who we have said reflects something of our contemporary postmodern context. Angela is sceptical of organized religion and so distances herself from Christian faith, but she readily invites Sue, the chaplaincy assistant, to pray with her, expressing a deep concern for 'something spiritual'. Here is a deeply reflective person who quite openly shares something of her past with Sue, but who does not automatically describe her story in terms of the memory of God's faithfulness. Angela may never choose to interpret her life in that way. But here we may recall Moltmann's affirmation of the universality of God's Spirit. According to this, there can be no compartmentalizing of 'the sacred' or 'the secular' because 'every experience of a creation of the Spirit is hence also an experience of the Spirit itself'.[51] It is possible that in the process of reflecting on her life story and on the question of personal meaning, the question of God might emerge and Angela may become consciously exposed to the basic God-ward orientation of her humanity. Of course this does not mean that she will thus by necessity come to hope in God for resurrection. But it does mean that a basis for 'giving an account' of this hope (1 Peter 3.15) may be established. Carl Braaten says that this basis may 'enlarge the sphere of understanding' so that the Christian message of hope might become meaningful: 'A person moved by the question of hope for the future may discover that biblical faith in God speaks that same language.'[52] Perhaps, then, Angela may in time come to see how the Christian salvation story is actually one that engages deeply with the searching and yearning of her own personal life story.

As far as the issue of confrontation in reality surveillance is concerned, the challenge facing Sue is to help alleviate some of Angela's acute fear that she will not regain consciousness after surgery. It would be a crude oversimplification to suggest that a pastoral conversation and short prayer with Angela would provide some kind of 'quick-fix' here. But is there anything that Sue may be able to do, even in the limited confines of this single encounter, that might go some way towards challenging and consequently reducing some of the irrational fear in Angela? Once again, there can be no neat formula, but a good place to start might be for Sue to listen to Angela with a particular readiness to pick up on any comments she might make that sound vague but which convey important interpretations of life that she may never have really thought through. Often people will reflect upon life and describe their hopes and fears by using phrases that can easily pass by unnoticed because they have become rather clichéd. Examples include, 'These things are sent to try us', 'There's always someone worse off than you' and 'There's probably some reason for all this'. The profoundly serious implications of such remarks are generally masked by their vagueness. But when used in pastoral conversation they can present an opportunity for carers to confront perceptions of reality that may never have been either acknowledged or examined.

Let us imagine that Angela says to Sue, 'Whether or not I make it through the operation, I suppose some good will come out of all this in the end.' Sue could respond with a gently affirming nod and a smile, and the question, 'What sort of good thing do you hope might come out of it?' A response such as this refocuses the conversation on the question of what we might hope for. But more fundamentally it provides a way of making what is implicit, explicit. Angela may find herself becoming more self-aware and more conscious of the irrational nature of her fears as she verbalizes her thoughts and feelings. Rather than Sue simply telling Angela that her fears are unfounded and that surgery is far more likely to help her than harm her, opportunity is created for the irrational nature of those fears to be exposed as Angela elaborates on them herself. She may be more likely to 'grasp' reality when it confronts her in her own words than through the words of another person.

A good working principle for challenging a person's perception of reality is thus to find a way of enabling them to arrive at the point of confrontation of their own accord. We have considered how this might be accomplished with the use of silence, or by encouraging them to reflect on their personal 'salvation history', or possibly by asking them to clarify and so make explicit thoughts and feelings that have not previously been brought to the surface and properly evaluated. Whichever of these means of confrontation are employed, it is important to remember that some people may *never* come to terms with reality. This seems to be the case with Jane. In such situations a pastoral carer might be tempted to think they have failed. It should be remembered, however, that pastoral care cannot *force* people to perceive reality in any given way, just as it cannot force anyone to hope. Our aim is to *nurture* hope, and that can only happen where hope is chosen freely.

Working with the sources of hope

In Chapter 2 we identified some of the things that psychology and nursing science consider to be the main sources of hope. We want to know what strategies pastoral carers might develop for fostering hope in dying people. We need to be cautious, however, lest we think that all that is needed is to translate such sources of hope into working formulae. Nurturing hope is not that straightforward! Nursing scientist Martha Stoner writes:

> When I read the early, anecdotal accounts of hope written by nurses, I have a mental image of drops of hope being 'instilled' in a patient's vein. Oh, that it were that simple.

Nursing interventions related to hope are at least as complex as the concept itself.[53]

There are no easy ways of nurturing hope in others. But when we consider what are commonly regarded as the sources of hope from a psychological perspective, and evaluate these things theologically, it is possible to identify real ways in which pastoral carers can make a practical difference.

Relationships

We may recall from Chapter 2 that psychology and nursing science stress the importance of relationships in the process of hoping, identifying hope as an essentially social experience. Marcel's metaphysics of hope also recognizes that 'hope is always associated with a communion, no matter how interior it may be. This is actually so true that one wonders if despair and solitude are not at bottom necessarily identical.'[54] David and Tom may be cited as testimony to this observation, for they each appear to be most despairing at the point where they have avoided talking with anyone about their thoughts and feelings. We need community, relationships and social interaction if hope is to take root in us.

A similar conviction finds expression in Moltmann's theology with the emphasis he gives to *fellowship* as the context in which hope is encountered: 'The experience, life and fellowship of God's Spirit come into being when Christ is made present and when the new creation of all things is anticipated.'[55] Fellowship is not simply a gift of the Spirit, says Moltmann; it is 'the eternal, essential nature of the Spirit himself'.[56] Following Moltmann's social doctrine of the Trinity, which emphasizes that the 'trinitarian fellowship' is 'open to men and women, and open to the world',[57] this means that God is experienced *in* fellowship. The Spirit as the 'divine wellspring of life'[58] is not simply the source of each individual life but the origin of all community:

Life comes into being out of community, and wherever communities spring up which make life possible and further it, the divine Spirit is efficacious. Wherever community of life comes into being, there is also community with God's life-giving Spirit. *The creation of community* is evidently the goal of God's life-giving Spirit in the world of nature and human beings.[59]

The individual believer finds hope as he or she encounters God's Spirit and becomes a new creation. But just as primary is the experience of *community*:

> . . . in these experiences of the Holy Spirit, hope is assured, because future is anticipated – the future of the new creation: the rebirth of the cosmos to glory, the blessed community of creation which joins all separated creatures, and the direct fellowship with God of the creation united in Christ and renewed in the Spirit.[60]

This does not mean that community and hope are only experienced within the Church, but Moltmann does stress that the Christian community is the 'messianic community' – the 'fellowship of hope'.[61] This is not only the place where eschatological hope is experienced; it is also the fellowship that 'acts messianically', as the community 'on the way', living in hopeful anticipation of God's resurrection promise and thus functioning as the presence of a 'contrast society' in the world.[62] The Church 'is like an arrow sent out into the world to point to the future'.[63] Other theologians also draw attention to the calling of the Church to function as the eschatological community or fellowship of hope. Braaten says the Church is 'on the way'[64] in eschatological anticipation, the 'eschatological community of hope that exists for the world'.[65] Alves argues that the present community of hope is 'the future actually taking place in the present. The community is a "sample" of the "not yet," the *aperitif* of a banquet still to come.'[66]

How then, in practical terms, might local churches venture to be communities of hope? Here we may draw on two particular images used by Jesus to describe the calling of the Church: salt and light (Matthew 5.13–14).

1 Eschatological salt of the earth: the Church as the scattered community of hope

The image of salt sets before us the challenge of being a scattered missionary presence in the world. Christians are called to *live hope* in our daily contexts of work and leisure. This is a *personal* challenge insofar as it is the charge of every individual Christian. But it is also a *corporate* calling because every individual is called to be a representative of the scattered community of hope. Lester says:

> At its best, the church is extending community, particularly to those who have minimum hope. The church provides a surrogate family that accepts the hopeless into an intimate fellowship and cares for them in ways that awaken hope.[67]

As a scattered presence in the world, the Church as the community of hope seeks to nurture its hope in others by the open sharing of its own fellowship, building community and making friendship with and among those who do not have these things. Moltmann offers the term *open friendship* to describe this ethos. He writes, 'Open and total friendship that goes out to meet the other is the spirit of the kingdom in which God comes to man and man to man.'[68] It is his conviction that 'every act of caring has its origins in Christian friendship'.[69]

This has important implications for the way pastoral carers might perceive their role. It challenges us to rediscover the simple yet profound importance of establishing a basic companionship in pastoral relationships. As Riem says, 'Pastors come from the community of faith to offer community to the world.'[70] But the scattered community of hope that is represented is distinctive, because it embodies the resurrection hope in which it 'abounds' (Romans 15.13). Thus Lester writes:

Even in the face of the grim reaper the pastoral person represents the God of promises. We engage people as stewards of a tradition that proclaims possibility even in the face of the very real experience of death.[71]

Giving 'an accounting for the hope' that is in us (1 Peter 3.15) thus amounts to far more than simply *telling* others. Set within the context of friendship as the basis of pastoral care it would be more accurately described as an act of *sharing*. This means that Christian apologetics ought not to be divorced from personal companionship with those in whom we seek to nurture hope. As Moltmann says, 'The arguments have to be spread out on the table; but the story has to be told at the table too.'[72] Once again we are reminded of the experiential nature of *living* hope – the very thing that we have noted as especially important for the postmodern context represented by Angela. Christian truth claims may seem like just another implausible metanarrative to her (although it is unlikely that she would describe them in such terms). But encountering Sue as a living person with a living hope – a member of the scattered community of hope – clearly carries a certain credibility, as is evinced by Angela's request to Sue for a prayer.

If local churches are to understand themselves in terms of scattered communities of hope it is vital that an emphasis on the 'priesthood of all believers' (1 Peter 2.9), that is, an every-member ministry, be rediscovered. Sadly it is often the case that the visitation of the dying is locally regarded as the exclusive task of the minister or specifically assigned pastoral carers of some sort. Friendship cannot be defined in such narrow terms – it is the calling of all Christians, as members of the scattered community of hope. We should not underestimate the extent to which hope can really be nurtured in people who are dying when they are just reminded that others have not forgotten them. Simple gestures such as cards or flowers and personal visits are some of the practical ways in which this can be done. Of course, there is a need for sensitivity to the possibility that a dying person may not wish to be constantly surrounded by visitors, especially when they are feeling tired. But this sensitivity might too easily be translated into an excuse with which to mask a reluctance to visit through fear of personal helplessness in 'not knowing what to say'. After all, we do not need to be trained pastors or counsellors in order to express friendship. Furthermore, let us not assume that the only thing a dying person wants from a visitor is the opportunity to explore their innermost thoughts and feelings about dying. An important part of the church's pastoral care for the dying is to enable such deeply personal conversation, but as vital is simply to provide basic companionship where isolation and loneliness may be the alternative. In this respect, a church member who is willing to express friendship by popping round to chat about football or gardening can be just as much a source of hope to someone who is dying as an ordained pastor who comes to offer prayer ministry.

We can nevertheless be a little more specific about the qualities that make an expression of friendship more hope-inspiring. Our discussion of nursing science in Chapter 2 noted that it is the *quality* rather than the *quantity* of caring relationships that matters. Specifically highlighted was the importance of regular visiting, listening and a sense of personal warmth. Similar findings emerge in a study by Paul Ballard *et al.*, where a group of practical theologians and palliative nursing scientists investigated the qualities looked for in a chaplain by cancer patients in a hospice day centre. In addition to a specific identity and expertise that a chaplain is expected to bring to the 'spiritual dimension', such a person is primarily appreciated when they bring a 'genuine humanity' to the pastoral relationship – that is, a sincerity, approachability and a sense of humour. Also mentioned are the qualities of 'availability' and 'openness'. Such a chaplain is 'willing to take people on their own terms' and has an ability to listen.[73] These qualities can all be construed as basic attributes of friendship.

Without denying the value of specialist skills such as counselling or theological expertise, a practical theology of hope for the dying that understands the pastoral relationship primarily in terms of friendship is one that affirms the significance of simply 'being there'.[74] This reinforces the importance of *listening* that we have already identified. Indeed, listening is a skill, and one that should not be underestimated. Rumbold points out that a concentration on 'tasks which exclude listening' can function as a means of avoiding a genuinely close relationship with dying persons. In a pastoral relationship even 'tasks such as prayer and reading scripture may be used to keep our distance from another person'.[75] In listening the pastoral carer communicates that he or she is really there with the dying person. A similar thing may be said of physical *touch*. Rumbold comments that a dying person may be frequently touched for the purpose of medical examination and treatment, but this does not communicate the care and concern that may be expressed by the simple act of sitting with that person and holding their hand.[76] Riem describes the language of touch as 'the way in which being present-in-love is expressed bodily'. The importance of touch was raised towards the end of Chapter 4, and it should be reiterated here that pastoral carers should be mindful of the danger of sexual implications and respectful towards personal boundaries. A person may not want to be touched. But used sensitively it is a way of communicating the message: 'You are not alone: whatever happens, I am with you.'[77] With listening, touch is a way of expressing friendship and conveying that one is present with the other.

At the risk of oversimplifying the complex and varied needs of those who are dying, it may yet be that a basic willingness to just 'be there' is the most profoundly helpful way in which pastoral carers can nurture hope. We may struggle with the simplicity of that claim – especially if we are in search of theologically grounded, psychologically insightful guidance over what to say or do in the face of apparent hopelessness. But it does mean that Sarah, who mentally rehearses the 'script' for her visit as she crosses the hospice car park, can be assured that before anything else it is her very presence, in friendship, that can make a genuinely positive difference to the level of hope in the church member she has come to visit. Her willingness to sit quietly with that person will probably be of far greater value than any amount of words she has prepared. And yet for all its simplicity, the willingness to 'be there' is not to be regarded lightly. The pastoral carer who approaches the dying person as a friend is one who is willing to become vulnerable, accepting 'the risk of helplessness'.[78] This is no easy task and it is possible to find ways of avoiding such vulnerability. Rumbold describes how chaplains may retreat behind liturgy rather than risk a 'personal encounter with a dying patient'.[79] The willingness to 'be there' in friendship for the dying person is simple yet also demanding. But as long as we are a truly scattered community of hope we can expect to feel vulnerable.

As a model for pastoral relationships in caring for the dying, friendship establishes a sense of *mutuality* between persons. Moltmann says that in friendship, we look neither up nor down at the other.[80] It is 'a bond between people for their own sake'.[81] This means that 'the poor, the sick, and the rejected', or indeed anyone to whom pastoral care is expressed, 'are *subjects* in the kingdom of God, not the objects of our sympathy'.[82] Thus it might be more apt to speak not of caring *for* but caring *with* others in friendship. The community of hope is scattered so that it might be truly alongside those who do not otherwise have community and who are struggling to find hope. This is especially appropriate in a practical theology of hope for the dying that stresses the shared mortality that is basic to the human condition. Both persons in the pastoral relationship, as has been argued, share a common humanity in which the reality of death and dying is fundamental. The pastoral relationship in which this is openly recognized and affirmed is one in which perceptions of what may or may not be 'realistic' hopes can be challenged in a way that need not imply an attitude of condescension.

The mutuality established by friendship is also a way of helping the pastoral relationship to achieve the right balance of *autonomy* and *dependency* that is essential to a healthy sense of community. The 'double need of autonomy and belonging' described by Lynch must be noted here.[83] On the one hand, the

experience of friendship in community is one of being supported by others. This is essentially a willingness to receive, and
in dying this involves a laying down and letting go of one's
own independent strength, allowing others to give. In this
sense dependency is fundamental to friendship in community.
Acknowledgement of the mortality that is basic to our common
humanity opens the way to the free acceptance of help from
others. Michael Wilson writes, 'Good community depends on
mutual service,'[84] and, 'The key word of the Christian gospel is
not service but friendship.'[85] Unless receiving is emphasized as
much as giving, people are divided into 'haves and have-nots',
in which those cared *for* are treated as objects and held at
arm's length. In friendship the very notions of giving and receiving are displaced by *sharing*: 'There is a mutual sharing of
God's gift of presence when both those who give and those
who receive represent Christ to one another.'[86] Thus 'certain
things like hope and a sense of human worth cannot be conveyed by a giving/receiving relationship but are communicated
by a sharing relationship such as friendship, colleagueship or
companionship'.[87]

On the other hand, the willingness to accept help and support
from others in friendship does not equate with a thwarting of
personal *autonomy*. In Chapter 2 it was noted that psychology
and nursing science highlight the danger of encouraging a sense
of over-dependency. Rumbold warns of the temptation for
carers to adopt a 'mothering attitude'. This might provide a
helpful short-term reassurance to a dying person that the carer
has a real concern for him or her. Nevertheless, Rumbold points
out that carers who become 'locked into a mothering stance'
tend to 'interpret everything the patient says at a child's level'
and because they are then 'not open to relate as adults with
another adult, the patient's communication is devalued or dis-
counted entirely'.[88] When the pastoral relationship is understood in terms of friendship, a sense of mutuality helps prevent
this. If friendship is, as Moltmann says, 'existence *with* others',[89]
the relationship is one of dependency that does not consume
autonomy but exists in a healthy equilibrium with it. Similarly

Capps, drawing on Erikson's developmental theory, highlights the importance of autonomy in hope as an essential part of the process of establishing relationships of trust. According to Erikson, 'For the growth of autonomy a firmly developed trust is necessary.'[90] Capps makes the point that true relatedness is in fact the capacity to be alone, and this is a sign of a hopeful attitude, for it means that 'the absent other has been internalized and one "feels related" to the other even when she is absent'.[91] Autonomy that is born out of relatedness is thus understood as the ability of the individual to see possibilities and make free decisions based on them. Such autonomy should be distinguished from a masochistic urge to resist all outside help, 'where the capacity to be alone degenerates into a defiant declaration of one's capacity to go it alone'.[92] The distinction lies precisely in the fact that autonomy is grounded in relatedness – it might even be described as a sense of belonging to community that has been internalized. For the purposes of our present discussion we can add that this is a scattered community – something beyond and bigger than ourselves that we belong to, yet a network of relationships that may not always be located in the same place at the same time. But now let us consider what it might mean for that community to be *gathered*.

2 Eschatological light of the world: the Church as the gathered community of hope

The second image of church that we find in Matthew 5 is that of being together in what is a more obviously corporate way. The Church is called to be the lamp on the lamp stand; the city on the hill. In a sense, of course, light is also 'scattered' – radiant and diffuse. But here Jesus talks about prominent, focused points where light shines. Such images depict the Church as a gathered community of hope, and they complement the importance of being scattered. Where there is no gathering together there is the danger of fragmentation – fellowship then becomes diluted and its identity is unclear. But where a church is only ever gathered and never grasps its calling to be a scattered presence, it is in danger of becoming a ghetto. What then might we say about the importance of this 'togetherness' of the gathered community of hope?

Earlier we considered the significance of encouraging individuals to explore their *story* as a way of surveying reality. Hope is nurtured as a meaningful past is remembered and projected into the future. Story is also a vital part of the gathered community of hope. Lester, for whom narrative is central to the hoping process, emphasizes the importance of community in this respect. He says that hope is discovered as the community not only narrates its story in the past tense but also envisions it in the future.[93] This comes close to Moltmann's concept of the 'messianic community' as a 'story-telling fellowship'.[94] Rumbold says, 'Our story with God is the story of our participation in his community, and our experience in community is the basis of our hope.' He suggests that the community is the location for 'dying well', because the story of the dying individual forms part of the communal story in which hope and meaning are discovered.[95] Pastoral care for the dying should therefore be less concerned with rectifying specific problems, as in approaches to health care that seek only 'cures', and more given to the task of creating and sustaining community.[96]

Robert Jenson highlights the practical significance of community in hope in discussing aspects of Christian worship. He describes worship as *drama* in which the worshipping congregation, as 'the community of a particular narrative communication' tells the eschatological story. Jenson asks, 'Why do we celebrate the eucharist instead of just having a reading of Mark 14?'[97] His answer is that worship as drama is the community narrating the eschatological story *dialogically*. Worship should involve every member of the gathered community, telling the story with its liturgy and through the sharing of bread and wine. The physical layout of places of worship should be such that members of the congregation face one another. The space provided for worship should be 'wholly a stage. And there must be no auditorium, for here there are no spectators; the telling and acting-out is done not for the worshipers but between the worshipers.'[98] Jenson also stresses that prayer is the 'appeal to the person of the future' and is most fundamentally a communal practice: 'the believer's "private" prayer is but an extension between times of his common prayer'.[99]

Moltmann takes up the importance of community in worship as he discusses eucharistic practice: 'The Lord's Supper is in its very essence a fellowship meal.'[100] It should be central to the regular worship of the Church because in 'eating and drinking in remembrance of Christ's promises, this meal is eating and drinking unto hope'. Hope is cultivated communally, drawing on the memory of the community: 'Eschatological hope is celebrated in the power of this memory.'[101] It is 'a foretaste of the feeding of all humankind in the kingdom of God', and is therefore the 'feast of freedom', the occasion for joy.[102] With this, Moltmann also stresses the importance of the *openness* of the Christian community, expressed by the Lord's Supper as the 'open feast',[103] the eschatological fellowship meal that is open to the whole Church, to the whole world, and to the future. Once again we may note that only a community that strives to be a scattered missionary presence in the world as well as a gathered fellowship is likely to have this sort of openness.

The pastoral literature on hope reinforces this stress on community as a gathered presence, and its significance in the process of hoping. Lester says, 'Hope is communal and relational, not isolationist and separatist.'[104] Rumbold writes, 'Hope can be shared, not given. It is a quality which emerges within human community.'[105] Pastoral care should therefore 'call people into community as participating members'.[106] Capps maintains a focus on hope for the individual, but nevertheless points out that it is the task of the Church as community to represent and keep alive a 'hopeful orientation to life'.[107] Simon Robinson says that hope is to be found 'in the experience of the pastoral community', specifically through the dynamic of agape. This is the ground of hope because the experience of agape sets life free from 'conditionality', thus presenting the individual with a sense of possibility in freedom for future living.[108] Here Lester, Rumbold, Capps and Robinson each highlight something very important about the nature of the Church's evangelistic calling: the Church's mission is not simply about making individual Christian disciples, but about making Christian disciples *in community*. We are to give an accounting not of '*my* hope' but '*our* hope' – remembering that Peter's first letter and its missionary imperative was addressed in the plural 'to the exiles of the Dispersion' of Asia Minor (1 Peter 1.1). Christian hope – *absolute hope in God for resurrection* – is not just a mere commodity, a personal resource for the benefit of the individual. Rather, it is a collective reality that we encounter most fully only when we understand it as something that we become a part of. As Alves puts it, '"Repent": throw away your old stethoscope and find a way of hearing the heartbeat of the future already pulsating in a community. And "be baptized": join it.'[109]

If building community in this way is to be taken seriously as part of the mission of the Church, evangelism cannot be reduced to a mere matter of pursuing church growth. Planting churches and growing existing churches should be regarded as a key task in the work of nurturing absolute hope in God for resurrection, because it involves building up gathered communities of hope. As individuals find a personal place within such communities, as they discover fellowship and a sense of belonging, so a living hope is nurtured. It is often said that people experience belonging before they experience believing. We might add to this that belonging is as such also the path to hoping.

It may be true that in Britain today many people, in the words of sociologist Grace Davie, 'believe without belonging'. Davie's point is that while formal church membership and attendance at church services decline, the majority of British people persist in believing. However, Davie herself heavily qualifies her claim by pointing out that such believing tends not to represent the postmodern sort of conscious 'pick and choose' spirituality that we have in this book epitomized in Angela. Rather, says Davie, 'believing without belonging' denotes 'the fall-back position acquired by British people when they simply do nothing; an *ordinary* God indeed'. It is belief in an 'ordinary God' because all it really amounts to is a vague and nominal assent to Christianity as a historical religion.[110] The point we may make in our present discussion is that belonging is in fact an integral, indeed, defining feature of the sort of believing that really nurtures a living hope in individuals. As such, evangelism is more than *telling* people about Christian hope – once again, it is about *sharing* it, encouraging others to partake in the gathered community of hope. This means something far deeper than simply inviting people to come to church, as a mere act of attendance. It means enabling people to experience a sense of personal belonging, so that they too might encounter this *living* hope.

It might be the case that David, who approaches the local vicar because he wants to make arrangements for his funeral, has the sort of 'belief' that Davie describes. He was brought for baptism as an infant in the local Anglican church, and was also married there. But apart from the occasional Christmas carol service, David never goes to church. Nevertheless, he regards both the church and the vicar as 'his' – not because he has a close relationship with them but more because it is his 'fall-back position', to borrow Davie's term, when he wants to 'get everything in order' for the death to which he has resigned himself. Now David's instigation of the meeting to discuss his funeral actually presents the vicar with a genuine opportunity to encourage David towards a greater and more personal partaking in the community of hope. It could be suggested, gently but positively, that David and his family might be more effectively supported at this difficult time by coming along to church, where they can meet friends who mutually support one another. In no way should any implication be given that church attendance is any kind of 'condition' for the holding of a funeral. But it could be expressed that the church is more than a building in which funerals are held: it is a community whose desire is to help people to live life to the full at every stage, including anyone who might be facing life-threatening illness. The point would not simply be to try to persuade David to 'go to church' – that could understandably be construed as a crude attempt to manipulate a religious practice at a time when David is most vulnerable. Rather, the aim would be to enable David to experience a sense of personal belonging, to feel part of the community of hope and so encounter something of that hope for himself.

Let us now recall Tom and his wife Jenny. What might some of the more detailed practical implications of what we have said be for them? Tom has been immersed in his local church all his life, and yet he has never really 'owned' Christian hope personally. At face value this may seem puzzling, if we understand belonging to be a vital part of the experience of hoping. But on closer examination we might ask whether Tom has ever really grasped a sense of personal belonging to his church in any depth. He has over the years found a certain solace in the security of continuity and familiarity with the culture and tradition of the church, hence his constant resistance to any kind of change. But for all his faithfulness Tom has never made close relationships with others. He has always been a very private man, reluctant to disclose his deeper thoughts and feelings to anyone other than Jenny, hence his insistence that no one else be told about his heart disease. However, Tom's diagnosis creates for him the most acute crisis situation of his life: never before has he felt so starkly confronted with his mortality. Because of the shell he has erected around himself, Tom now feels isolated and alone with his profound fear of death. Yet he cannot break out of this 'frozen' state – he despairs simultaneously over his isolation *and* the thought of talking to anyone else about it.

In the event the 'ice' is broken as Tom's emotions overtake his resolve and he bursts into tears as he sits with his minister. For the first time in years Tom allows another person to enter the sanctuary of his deepest and most personal thoughts and feelings, relaxing the guard that usually maintains the 'safe distance' between himself and other people. This requires tremendous courage from Tom, because he now makes himself vulnerable. But in this very act of vulnerability a relationship of trust is brought to birth. Tom encounters what is for him a very new experience of *community*. What is most personal to him is now *shared*. For Tom, this is the beginning of feeling that he truly *belongs*, because now he is not so totally alone. Of course, he has only ventured to allow one other person, the minister, into his personal sanctuary, but this is a tremendous break-through, since it means that Tom's network of relationships of trust does now extend beyond Jenny and himself. In this simple yet profound act of sharing Tom now has a form of personal ownership over the church as a community that he did not previously have. This could well prove to be the first stage of a new sense of belonging and the journey into hope. In time it may be that Tom will feel able to share some of his concerns with one or two others and so receive support more widely. But for now we can note once again the importance of listening in this situation. It was through the minister's willingness to sit in silence and really listen to Tom that a climate of confidence and trust was created, in which Tom was able to be open and honest.

As for Jenny, we may recall her specific quest for a hope by which she may envision a future reunion with Tom – 'We will see one another again in the next life, won't we?' Such a concern reinforces the significance of gathered community in Christian hope: we discover hope *as* community, that is, in the experience of fellowship, as we hope *for* the resurrection of community and of society. Absolute hope in God for resurrection looks not to the raising of individual *bodies*, but the collective resurrec-tion *body*. In practical terms, this calls for churches to empha-size our collective hope by seeking to nurture a genuine sense of personal togetherness as the gathered community. Moltmann talks of 'the body language of social experience of God',[111] by which he refers to bodily, sensory experience as the vehicle for encountering hope in fellowship with others. Specifically, the laying-on of hands in prayer, shaking hands and embracing in the liturgical exchange of 'the peace', and sharing in the Lord's Supper are given as examples of such experience.[112] These are all ways in which local church services and meetings can seek to emphasize bodily existence and so highlight *hope for the body* as an essential experience of the gathered community of hope.

As we *live* hope together, so we may envision our resurrection life together.

Goals and activity

In Chapter 2 we noted that according to psychology and nursing science the pursuit of goals is a key to the cultivation of hope. Having aims, even as death approaches, encourages an active engagement in life. Hope – that is, *living* hope – involves the acceptance of death but not passively. We explored this in greater detail in Chapter 4 with the suggestion of a kenotic spirituality in which both acceptance and a fighting spirit are not conceived as bipolar but as mutual expressions of the courage and creativity of hope. The appropriateness of this spirituality in the face of death is reinforced by the way in which it corresponds to the dynamics of dying itself, for death is both something we do and something that happens to us. Dying and living in hope is a process in which we are at once both active and also required to wait in expectation. Moltmann's notion of *adventus* expresses this. In hope we await the coming God, but this is an active anticipation. Activity and waiting go hand in hand – as Johann Baptist Metz puts it: 'Jesus' call: "Follow me!" and the call of Christians: "Come, Lord Jesus!" are inseparable.'[113] Roman Catholic theologian Edward Schillebeeckx expresses it this way:

> The Christian knows that he receives the future to make it – he does not simply receive it as a 'present' that is given to him, but receives it to 'make it' himself, to bring it about. On the one hand, eschatological hope is not a passive state of waiting for the future, but, on the other hand, neither is it self-redemption, as though the promised future could be realized by human achievement.[114]

Eschatological hope presents us with a responsibility to work towards goals, but this active engagement in life is set within the prevenient expectation that it is God in whom we hope: a 'dialectic of effort and grace', to borrow Bringle's phrase.[115] A vital feature of this dynamic of what might be called *active waiting* in hope is *patience*. Moltmann says that 'hope only remains alive through patience . . . This patience alone is able to survive the tension of the hope of history.' This is because it 'accepts the "cross of the present" in the "power of the resurrection"'.[116] Marcel also talks of such patience. Aware of the resisting, protesting nature of hope, which he refers to as its 'non-acceptance', Marcel asks, 'How, if I do not accept can I avoid tightening myself up, and, instead, relax in my very non-acceptance?' He suggests, 'If we introduce the element of patience into non-acceptance we at once come very much nearer to hope.' Activity and waiting are thus combined in Marcel's phrase 'to take one's time'. Just as an examiner might say to a candidate, this means, 'do not force the personal rhythm, the proper cadence of your reflection, or even of your memory, for if you do you will spoil your chances'. This is 'the secret affinity between hope and relaxation'.[117]

Pastoral carers can thus find both theological and psychological grounds for seeking to help those who are dying to identify and pursue goals in a spirit of *active waiting*. As we mentioned in Chapter 2, examples of such aims might include the making of a special trip or attending a family wedding or other significant occasion. Hope can be nurtured by encouraging the dying person to talk about plans or forthcoming events, and also by remembering such things when praying with them. On the one hand, it is a way of cultivating an active engagement in life and a sense of vibrancy that is vital to the process of hoping. In nurturing the creative resolve involved in making everyday plans the basic interest in life that sustains absolute hope in the face of death is kept active. Seeking goals energizes the sense of expectancy that finds its ultimate expression in absolute hope. At the same time, this absolute hope in God for resurrection is essentially the awaiting of a gift of grace. This means that the disappointment of failing to attain goals, such as making that special trip, need not lead to the collapse of hope because such absolute hope is not defined by those goals. Lester says:

We do not move into despair when we lose a finite hope because we have not lost our basic, foundational, transfinite hope. We do not have to be afraid to fail, for ultimate hope is open-ended.[118]

Danger emerges when individual goals are allowed to define absolute hope. When this happens, they are afforded the absolute value that is not theirs. So Lynch argues that we should 'put the absolute in the right place', allowing the most ultimate hope to be in God alone.[119] The absolutizing instinct is the compulsion to idolize individual goals, but when God is identified as the only absolute, other hopes are held in their right perspective. Indeed, while the pursuit of goals can help to foster the process of hope, more fundamentally it is the ultimate, absolute hope in God that makes smaller hopes possible and enables new goals to be identified when the pursuit of previous ones has been disappointed. As Lester says, 'we can hope in these finite goals *because* of our transfinite hope, not *instead* of our transfinite hope'.[120] Absolute hope, then, does not depend on the attainment of individual goals, for it is greater and more mysterious than the expectation of them, as has been discussed. But where goals are successfully reached absolute hope, as a more general sense of expectation, a 'positive glow on life',[121] is cultivated. Lester writes, 'The ultimate hope can be found in finite hope because finite hope contains the signs of God.'[122] Carers should not be reluctant to encourage dying persons to pursue goals, provided it is emphasized that flexibility concerning the nature of such goals is required.

How, in practical terms, might future goals be brought into pastoral conversation? Sensitivity is required if carers are to avoid giving the impression that they are just bypassing an individual's struggle to envision a future of any kind. Sometimes it may be possible to introduce and maintain a sense of expectation in the conversation simply by asking questions or making passing references that depict the individual in the future in some way. For example, Angela's fear is that she will not regain consciousness after her operation. Having listened to Angela, allowing for these fears to be the focus of the conversation for a while, Sue might go on to ask her about family and friends and when they might be visiting. She could ask how long it is likely to be before Angela is able to return home. The conversation could lead into the subject of Angela's career or a particular hobby that is dear to her, and so Sue could ask when she might be resuming such things. In this way attention is drawn to Angela's future as Sue suggests an assumption that there really *is* a future ahead for Angela. Let us reiterate that conversation of this sort should not be introduced before there has been opportunity to explore the struggle to find hope. The reality of Angela's fears should not be downplayed in any way, or she could suspect that she has not been properly listened to or understood or taken seriously. But by giving focus to the future continuation of some of the things that represent everyday life for Angela, Sue may well be able to nurture in her a greater sense of expectation, and with it a deeper level of hope.

Let us recall David once again. We have already suggested that one way of encouraging David to envision some kind of future might be for the vicar to ask him what he would want to be remembered for in his funeral service. In identifying those things that are particularly meaningful for David in this way there is a possibility that the conversation could gradually take up the question of how some of them may still have an ongoing future in David's life. For example, while David may not be in a position to resume the antiques business that he has always hoped for, he might be able to attend one or two auctions, an activity that has been a longstanding enjoyment of his. But how might such a pastoral conversation venture beyond this? What further might be done by the vicar in order to encourage David to engage more actively with such possible goals?

One concrete way in which the vicar may help to nurture a measure of greater expectation in David would be to arrange to meet with him again, perhaps in a couple of weeks. Although this may seem like a very simple thing, the very act of writing an appointment in the diary makes the statement that there is an expectation of some sort. It is a way of saying to David: 'This meeting today is not the end of the story; we will see each other again soon.' It also raises the question, 'What will you be doing in the meantime?' The assumption is thus conveyed that there is a future for David to live for, even though there may need to be some flexibility over what might be undertaken in that time. It also creates a kind of informal 'framework' in which David might be encouraged to think about aims, work towards them and then reflect upon them when he next meets with the vicar – establishing a form of 'accountability' for David beyond his family.

This sort of 'action and reflection' process is in fact deeply rooted in the spirituality of Christian hope. The active pursuit of goals is the experience of reaching forward in hope. The attainment of them is the occasion for joy, a savouring of what has been reached, and a renewed sense of anticipation. These dynamics are expressed theologically in what Moltmann describes as

> two archetypal images of liberation: the exodus and the sabbath. The exodus from slavery into the land of liberty is the symbol of external freedom; it is efficacious, operative. The sabbath is the symbol of inner liberty; it is rest and quietude.[123]

Life in hope is therefore ordered 'not in a linear sense but rhythmically', says Moltmann, for in eschatological expectation time is experienced in the rhythm of 'inward and outward movements, in tension and relaxation'.[124] The weekly sabbath is the rest and celebration in joy and anticipation of the eschatological sabbath, which is the goal of creation – 'God's eschatological Shekinah'.[125] Moltmann is not advocating a slavish adherence to sabbath observance for the sake of religious legalism, but is highlighting a dynamic principle of *living* hope. The sabbath represents the periodical relaxation in the midst of hope's restlessness and contemplation of what God has done and is going to do – the 'presence of eternity in time, and a foretaste of the world to come'.[126] This is not a static rest, but part of the vibrant anticipatory experience of time as life is lived dynamically in hope:

> In the rhythm of the sabbath, which healingly interrupts the flux of time, God's rest is experienced, the rest which, as well as being the goal of creation, will also be the end of history . . . In the expectation, time vibrates and dances.[127]

Reaching goals are points of satisfaction that punctuate hopeful living. Taking stock of them, savouring what has been accomplished, can thus serve to renew the greater absolute hope in God that sustains life even as death approaches. A practical theology of hope for the dying that takes this principle on board recognizes the importance of not only pursuing goals but also highlighting those that have been reached. Pastoral carers who help dying persons to recognize goals as they are attained may help in identifying them as occasions for thanksgiving, encounters with the faithfulness of God and foretastes of the eschatological hope in God for resurrection. So the next time he meets with David, a key task for the vicar would be to try to give a focus to something that David has done or resolved to do since their last meeting together. This could be something as relatively major as having booked a family weekend break or as small as simply looking on the internet for forthcoming antiques auctions. However seemingly exciting or mundane such things might be, it is important that David is encouraged to take a more active engagement with the life that is there to be lived.

Once again, following the model of friendship as a model for pastoral relationships, a friend is one who truly shares our joy when we attain our personal goals. Pastoral carers can encourage dying persons by expressing joy as goals are reached. Also important is identifying goals that have been reached in the past. This reinforces the value of exploring the dying person's story. Reminiscing on past accomplishments can nurture a sense of satisfaction and encourage reflection on those life experiences that may be recognized as foretastes of what is still to come. Here the use of the imagination may be especially important.

Imagination

We have considered how hope might be nurtured in Angela and David by envisioning goals. Essentially this involves *imagining the future*. With both Angela and David the immediate concern is to enable them to form visions of hope that depict the continuation of this present life, *in* this present life. Absolute hope in God for resurrection can sustain such hopes because it looks beyond them to that which it anticipates as the ultimate future – namely, the raising to eternal life. This is a radical, transcendent hope, and so it calls for the radical use of the imagination in order for it to be meaningfully envisioned. As we explore this in more depth we shall see how the imagination is a vital theological component of hope, in a way that complements the importance given in psychology and nursing science to the use of the imagination for nurturing the hoping process.

'Christian hope . . . is not imaginary, but it is irreducibly imaginative.' So write Richard Bauckham and Trevor Hart in *Hope against Hope: Christian Eschatology in Contemporary Context*.[128] Their conviction is that it is Christian hope that expresses the very transcendence that is needed to blow open the human imagination that is otherwise 'constrained by the conditions of the immanent'.[129] Where the imagination is limited by the possibilities of the immanent, 'there is little genuine hope to be had'.[130] Bauckham and Hart attribute a contemporary lack of hope in society to 'the postmodern failure of imagination'.[131] They refer here not to the lack of imagination in contemporary society but its misuse:

> . . . not wanting to be bothered with a despairing snared world, we postmodern individuals retreat instead into our private televisual and computerized virtual realities which, unlike the 'real world', we can programme, control and edit to our own advantage and personal delight.

In such a society, 'imagining has no aspiration to transcendence, no forward moving and potentially liberating direction'. Instead, imagination retreats into 'individualistic fantasy' rather than daring to hope for a better future.[132] Postmodern society gives priority to the present:

> . . . with its throwaway culture, its emphasis on the immedi-
> ate and the instantaneous, its feverish drive to squeeze as
> much as possible into time as a limited commodity, its frag-
> mentation of time into allocated quantities, and its obsessive
> organization of time, we live increasingly in the present and
> its prolongation.[133]

This concurs with what Moltmann has described as the 'anam-netic culture' of contemporary society in which technology is exploited in order to 'vanquish the power of passing time' and 'make all times simultaneous to ourselves'.[134] Technology itself is not the problem, but the social inertia it breeds. This is a serious threat to humanity. It is the product of a postmodern solipsism that has come to believe that there is very little one can do to change things, so the imagination might as well be spent constructing a private world of simulation and virtual reality in pursuit of personal fantasies that are not interrupted by the pains and sufferings of the wider world. Thus

> it is possible to ignore with impunity the piercing eyes of the
> starving child or the bewildered refugee whose face is beamed
> across the globe into our private space by satellite TV, or to
> turn a blind eye to the mugging or the racist attack taking
> place on our own doorstep. Such things, we might come to
> suppose, are not our proper concern and should not be
> allowed to spoil our day. So we draw the curtains or reach for
> the remote channel changer.[135]

Bauckham and Hart's analysis of postmodernity is one that proclaims that opium itself has become religion. Against this escapist use of imagination that anaesthetizes real hope, they call for the Christian eschatological vision to awaken the imagination from its postmodern slumber. Hopeful imagination 'fuels the engines of our movement into the future',[136] for hope is 'the capacity to imagine otherwise, to transcend the boundaries of the present in a quest for something more, something better, than the present affords'.[137]

The transforming power of absolute hope in God for resurrection thus lies in its capacity to imagine transcendentally – that is, in its daring to hope even in the face of death. Arguably, that is the very force that is expressed through the dialectic nature of Moltmann's theology, which stresses the radical contradiction of Jesus' resurrection against his death on the cross. We may dare to hope even when death confronts us because our imagination is set free to anticipate a future that radically contradicts what otherwise seems to be the finality of our death. Moltmann writes:

> Theology always includes the imagination, fantasy for God and his kingdom. If we were to ban the images of the imagination from theology, we should be robbing it of its best possession. Eschatologically oriented theology is dependent on a messianic imagination of the future, and sets this imagination free.[138]

Imagining in hope is for Moltmann the very task of theology. In *The Coming of God* he defines theology as '*imagination for the kingdom of God* in the world, and for the world in God's kingdom'.[139] Moltmann acknowledges that this is no easy challenge when he remarks: 'It is difficult to say anything at all about the future . . . How much more difficult it must be to say anything about the ultimate future of the whole world!'[140] Of course, Moltmann, the theologian of hope, is not suggesting that nothing be said about the future, only that it is difficult to find 'ways of describing what is as yet hardly imaginable in this impaired life'.[141] True to the dialectic nature of his theology, his point is that such is the radical contradiction between the present and the future, even the eschatological imagination is strained to find adequate images of hope. As he wrote earlier:

'The resurrection pictures, which have been attempted, are pitifully inadequate because the colors for painting the future must be taken from the already spoiled palette of life in the here and now.'[142]

The use and limits of the imagination in hope bring us back to something that we have already identified as a significant issue relating to the symbol of resurrection, and that is the double need for both *continuity* and *discontinuity*. On the one hand, Braaten says, 'Eschatological imagination is filled with visions of new things,'[143] and Alves comments that it is only in naming the things that are absent that this imagination 'breaks the spell of the things that are present'.[144] The eschatological imagination must envision a hope that is so radically new (*novum*) that it is discontinuous with the present. At the same time, as Bauckham and Hart point out, this newness can only be imagined and expressed 'using language, appealing to pictures and states of affairs, drawn from this old order, the world as we know and are used to talking about it'.[145] This has to be so, for it is the only material we have for constructing an imaginative vision. But caution must be exercised in the use of the eschatological imagination, given that such material is fundamentally limited, owing to the fact that it is, as Moltmann says, 'drawn from this impaired life here'.[146]

Daring to hope in the face of death thus calls for a creative and free use of the imagination, but not an *unfettered* use, to the extent that it loses sight of its own limitations. Bauckham and Hart argue that the truly hopeful imagination is, on the one hand, free from a literalism that possesses eschatological images of 'directly predictive force'. At the same time, it should not be reduced by a programme of relentless demythologization that effectively regards eschatological images as merely 'a way of clothing general features of the human condition in imaginative form in order vividly to express the truth about them'.[147] Bauckham and Hart suggest a 'rhetoric of the unsayable', a term borrowed from the literary critic J. Bellemin-Noel, as a way of understanding the use of imagination in hope:

In the same moment this rhetoric both says and does not say, describes yet does not attempt to describe. It tells us that what is hoped for is not containable within the categories of the familiar, but to the unfamiliar itself it can only point obliquely by way of exaggerations, denials and disruptions of the known.[148]

A sense of ambiguity must be preserved if the eschatological imagination is to be kept alive but in a way that does not solidify into a rigid literalism that betrays the dynamic openness to the future that hope is about.

An example of this sort of rhetoric can be found in the old Negro spiritual songs, where hope for liberation from slavery is fused together with hope in the face of death in the same eschatological vision. Heaven is used as an imaginative expression of this vision, a way of imagining the future hope, drawing on the familiar in order to envision that which is not present.[149] It is a kind of 'rhetoric of the unsayable' because it ventures to articulate in vivid picture language an eschatological hope that is full of mystery but no less real for that. As Theo Witvliet writes, the African slaves integrated the biblical stories into their own experience and 'transformed them into something that was tangible and concrete'.[150] By constantly connecting the language of heaven with the Exodus story, the historical hope for liberation and hope for eternal life was depicted in the same vision – the image of freedom from slavery. Witvliet quotes this traditional song. It fuses two visions into one: crossing the Red Sea out of slavery into freedom with crossing the River Jordan and the 'mighty Myo', the West African river of death:

My army cross over
O Pharaoh's army drowned!
. . . We'll cross de river Jordan,
My army cross over;
We'll cross de danger water,
My army cross over;
We'll cross de mighty Myo,
My army cross over.[151]

Here some of the important dynamics of the use of the imagination in the process of hoping can be seen in action. Hope reaches out imaginatively for that which is discontinuous with the present reality of suffering and death. Continuity exists within the discontinuity as images of the familiar are formed into a hopeful vision. Hart likens this movement to the process of modulation in music when a piece shifts to a different key. When the change is unanticipated the two passages seem completely unrelated and the sensibility of the listener is jarred. The transition must be smoothed. The composer does this by taking a chord belonging properly to the old key and using it in a way that is also proper to the new one, 'thereby transforming its significance, and effecting a harmonious bridge between the passages'. Hart talks of 'God's skilful modulation from the key of death into the key of life'. By imagining, 'the power of God's future can be genuinely present and effective in the midst of a world which, as yet, cannot bear it'.[152]

Now let us draw the discussion back to the specifically pastoral question of how the imagination may function in the cultivation of hope among the dying. Resurrection hope is hope *for* the body, the 'symbol of the self'.[153] Hoping for this involves envisioning not the destruction of present identity but its transformation. The body is the locus of hope as both continuity and discontinuity are envisioned in and for it. This absolute hope in God for resurrection transcends everything finite, and thus cannot be comprehended in the ordinary sense, only envisioned, hence Bauckham and Hart's comment: 'Resurrection is in origin not a concept, but an image.'[154] Thus we can affirm the resurrection body as the primary imaginative symbol of hope – that is, the key image that enables us to dare to hope in the face of death.

We may recall that a major reason why the resurrection body is so important is that it gives absolute hope in God some kind of *content*. Without this, hope in God is in danger of becoming an abstraction and can slip into meaningless sentimentalism. The resurrection body thus provides a basic frame for the work of the imagination in hope that will avoid this danger. If such hope is to be meaningful, it must be in some way imaginable.

Only then can it be envisioned, expressed, communicated, shared – accepting that any single image employed is provisional and contingent, for only God, not the images themselves, has absolute status.

So how, in practice, might a pastoral carer enable someone to envision a future hope for the resurrection body? Ann Townsend, a hospital chaplain, describes her pastoral experience with Jean, a cancer patient. She talks of how the struggle to find a topic for conversation led eventually to the discovery of one thing they had in common: Southend. It was a place that was personally significant to each of them for different reasons. Townsend describes how this provided the raw material with which the imagination could function as a source of hope:

> As Jean grew progressively weaker, and her pain harder to bear, we would go together in imagination to Southend. We'd walk along the pier, buy cockles and winkles and candyfloss, and join the crowds watching Punch and Judy or listening to the band. 'Going to Southend' became an activity important to both of us. Mysteriously it somehow seemed to begin to hold out hope to her that the end of her despair, pain and hopelessness just might be something that could only be described as 'good' . . .
>
> On the morning I was due to leave for holiday, I went to say goodbye to Jean . . . She clung on to me tightly: 'We keep on talking about Southend', she said. 'Am I ever going to get there in the end . . . or will I get lost on the way?' I took a deep breath, swallowing back the tears that threatened to overwhelm me. 'You'll be there very soon, Jean . . . that *other* Southend is quite close now . . . not too far to go.' Her face relaxed, she closed her eyes and I knew that she had understood what I had not spelled out for her. I kissed her goodbye. On return from holiday I heard that she had died just two hours after I had left her.[155]

Here is an example of how the exploration of a person's story, reminiscing on meaningful and satisfying experiences of the past, might be cast in the future tense. This is an imaginative reflection, and takes place here in the context of a pastoral relationship that may be described as friendship, as common ground between parties is used as the basis for the reflection. It also gives us an idea of the sort of way in which we might, in a postmodern society so suspicious of 'metanarratives', seek to bridge the gap between our Christian story of hope and the personal narratives of individuals. Images of the life that we know now may be cast in the future as a way of depicting the resurrection life for which we hope. Capps describes this sort of future visioning as a form of 'projection'. He heavily qualifies his use of this term, stressing that he does not mean the unconscious act of ascribing one's own ideas to others as psychoanalysis usually understands it. Rather, he is referring to the sort of projection that is made in photography. In the strict sense, photographs are illusory in that they represent something that is not really present. But it is precisely in this illusory nature of the photograph that its value lies. Capps thus describes images of hope as 'creative illusions'.[156] They are projections because

> they envision a future that is technically false and unreal, as it does not exist, and yet it is profoundly true and real, as it expresses yearnings and longings that not only exist but are often more real than the objective world. When we hope, we envision eventualities that are not yet realities but yet appear to us as potential realities.[157]

Against Freud's critique that religion places limits on allowable projections, restricting the image of 'providence' to an exalted and rigid father figure, Capps points out that Christian hope is anything but fixed and static in its projections. Rather, and here Capps draws on Moltmann, God is viewed 'in dynamic and future terms, such as "I will be what I will be" (Exod. 3.6) or "the coming of God"'.[158] Such images are 'catalysts for change', ways of envisioning the realisable. Furthermore, there is a sense in which images of hope are *self-projections*: 'we project *ourselves* into the future and envision our existence being different from what it is at present'.[159] Imagining the future is not abstract or impersonal; it is the act in which we are motivated into striving towards its realization now. Capps himself does not specifically highlight the image of the resurrection body. But it is precisely that, the supreme image of hope and the *ultimate* image of self-projection that enables us to imagine a meaningful future even in the face of death.

Let us return to Tom once more. We have previously noted that in his 'spiritually frozen' state of despair, his greatest need may be to learn to imagine. In a sense, 'God' seems an empty word to Tom – a mere piece of meaningless religious jargon that fails to engage with his dread of dying. However, deep within Tom's subconscious, 'God' is in fact a real object of fear. Until now this has never really been brought to the surface and examined. But as Tom begins to talk openly for the first time about his acute fear of death, he tells the minister that he has been terrified of dying for as long as he can remember. Intrigued by this comment, the minister wonders whether Tom may have experienced any particularly traumatic bereavement in his early life, and so he asks a few questions about Tom's childhood. In fact, Tom did not have any such experiences, but as he describes his memories of growing up the minister notices how fiercely strict Tom's father seems to have been. Tom was forced to attend church and Sunday school from an early age, any misbehaviour would be punished harshly, and a moral code that 'only good people go to heaven' was instilled in him.

The conversation between Tom and his minister continues over several subsequent pastoral visits. It gradually becomes apparent to the minister that Tom's lifelong record of church attendance seems to stem largely from a deep insecurity that he has unconsciously harboured since childhood: unless he goes to church every week, he will be punished by God when he dies. As Tom recalls the fear of his stern father that took root in him as a child, an association with the fear of damnation emerges, and Tom describes how his father would tell him in no uncertain terms that hell awaits anyone who does not live 'a worthy life'.

Now Tom's health crisis has confronted him with his mortality, and as he contemplates dying, his father's threat of hell is the only thing he sees. Death itself is almost personified in the image Tom has of his father. This object of fear is so acute for Tom that it has become ultimate reality to him – he has *absolutized* it, so that *it* is 'God'.

So it is that the challenge facing the minister is to help Tom to find what are for him new and different ways of imagining God and the future beyond death. This is no straightforward task, and it is something that can only really be worked at over time. But it is the *resurrection body* that provides the framework for such imagining and the making of what Capps calls 'self-projections' into the future. It may be precisely here that the minister finds common ground for nurturing hope in both Tom and his wife Jenny, by focusing on the affirmation that in the resurrection life they will indeed be reunited, stressing the communal nature of resurrection. That, as we have seen, was the concern voiced by Jenny at the outset. But for Tom this has an added significance. Unlike his father, Jenny represents unconditional love and acceptance to Tom. Indeed, she is the only person to whom Tom has ever really felt close. With Jenny, Tom feels he has nothing to prove because he knows that he is loved by her unreservedly. Just as Townsend drew on memories of Southend to enable Jean to envision resurrection life (above), so Tom might be encouraged to imagine an eternal future with God in terms of the unconditional love and acceptance that he has experienced in this present life with Jenny.

Let us not pretend that helping Tom to imagine a future in God in a positively hopeful way would be easy. His fear of dying and his negative images of God run deep. But Tom turns a significant corner in making himself vulnerable with the minister. The ice of his 'frozen state' has been broken with the shedding of his tears and his dread of death and of God that has haunted him for years has now been brought to the surface. With the minister's ongoing provision of a pastoral relationship of friendship, creating a context in which Tom can continue to feel that he can share openly and be listened to, the images of fear may begin to be unmasked and displaced by images of hope.

The experience of humour: laughter as an emotional uplift

The centrality of the imagination in hope does not mean that hoping is a purely cerebral enterprise. As hope imagines the future resurrection of the body there is a real sense in which this future becomes an experience of the heart. Witvliet describes how the emotional experience of hoping in the midst of slavery was expressed in the black spiritual songs:

> That there is life from death, conquest in defeat, joy through all pain is sung and confessed in the songs of the slaves, but not explained. That does not mean that this mystery can simply be accepted as an abstract truth of faith dictated from above. It does mean that their concrete mode of thinking was opposed to the form of knowledge which cannot be experienced and lived through. Their knowledge of faith was a knowledge from the heart.[160]

Hope is an emotional experience. Nursing scientists Dufault and Martocchio thus speak of the *affective dimension* of hope.[161] This is also reflected in Moltmann's theology which, we may recall from Chapter 3, is essentially *experiential* in nature. On the one hand Moltmann writes, 'Hope is more than a feeling. Hope is more than experience . . . Hope is a command.'[162] That is to say, hope in God's promised future should not be reduced to a matter of human emotion. On the other hand Moltmann takes the passions very seriously, and central to his theology is a doctrine of divine *passibility*: God is not unfeeling, but suffers and rejoices with the creation. The pathos of God is affirmed, and true humanity is understood as that which can freely express the rich diversity of human feelings. Moltmann thus writes, 'Is mourning the reverse side of love, and is its pain the mirror-writing of love's delight? The greater the love, the deeper the grief.'[163]

Our concern in this book is for a *living* hope – something that can be experienced. That is what our postmodern world thirsts for, as we have illustrated with Angela. Pastoral carers should therefore be encouraged to regard the free expression of emotion by dying persons as a natural and healthy part of hope. Tears of sorrow and hopelessness can form part of the hoping process. Resurrection hope is found via the cross, and in the context of this dialectic, feelings of sadness and despair can be embraced as part of the emotional fabric of hope. Our story of Tom gives us a glimpse of this. But what may be said about the place of humour and laughter?

In Chapter 2 we considered how psychology and nursing science describe the experience of humour and laughter as a source of hope. This is also an important theological theme. It is difficult not to see a certain sparkle in 1 Corinthians 15.55: 'Where, O death, is your victory? Where, O death, is your sting?' Moltmann writes:

> From the earliest times, Easter hymns have celebrated the victory of life in an exorcism of mockery, ridiculing death, pouring scorn on hell, and facing the lords of this world without fear . . . Easter sermons in the Middle Ages and even later are said to have begun with a joke. Laughter takes away the seriousness of a threat, disarms it.[164]

Joy is a longstanding theme in Moltmann's writing. In exploring this Moltmann emphasizes the significance of play, festivity and celebration. He asks the question: 'How can we laugh and rejoice when there are still so many tears to be wiped away and when new tears are being added every day?'[165] His response is that in celebrating and rejoicing in God's promised future Christians experience something of that future in its anticipation: 'We enjoy freedom when we anticipate by playing what can and shall be different and when in the process we break the bonds of the immutable *status quo*.'[166] Here Moltmann follows a theme presented by Harvey Cox, who argues that '*festivity* – the capacity for genuine revelry and joyous celebration, and *fantasy* – the faculty for envisioning radically alternative life situations' are 'absolutely vital to human life'.[167] Thus 'Man is *homo festivus* and *homo fantasia*.'[168] In play and celebration we hope imaginatively. This present life is affirmed but also, because festivity, in its excess, displays contrast with 'everyday life', possibilities for the future are envisioned.

Play and laughter are thus closely related to the imagination. Alves says that play 'creates an order out of imagination and therefore out of freedom . . . here imagination assumes flesh – takes the impossible and treats it as if it were possible'.[169] It 'brings the vision of the future'[170] – this is the 'playful intention of the imagination'.[171] Christian worship, especially eucharistic worship, is precisely where God's future promise is celebrated in playful and joyful imagination. Here the drama of Easter is rediscovered, but as Braaten points out, not simply as a memorial:

> Instead, our remembrance of Jesus arouses expectant joy because he was raised to be the Lord of the future. In Holy Communion we declare that we are leaving the old world behind in joyful anticipation of the new.[172]

Moltmann talks of the joy that is experienced as God's victory over death is celebrated in the Lord's Supper, a feast that 'lays anticipatory hold on the joy of redeemed existence'.[173] Perhaps a significant challenge for churches today is to rediscover a renewed sense of joy in worship. Arguably one of the greatest strengths of what is often labelled the 'charismatic movement' is precisely this sort of vibrancy. Such joy, when it is genuine, does not mean the superficial froth of a contrived emotionalism, but the natural rejoicing that flows spontaneously from the profound sense of liberation that is authentic to the experience of living hope.

A practical theology of hope for the dying must therefore stress the importance of worship in pastoral care. As dying persons share in the worship and celebration of the Christian community so they may be taken up in the experience of joy as resurrection is anticipated in the face of death. Such joy in worship enables death to be laughed at in hope. It may not be possible for a dying person to attend church services and meetings in the final stages as his or her physical health deteriorates. Whether in hospital, hospice or at home, it may be appropriate for a small group of friends, rather than just the individual minister, to visit and share in a communal act of worship.

Concern might be expressed that the value of Christian worship is not something to be measured in terms of the practical pastoral functions it may provide – however noble such functions may be. That is to say, worship, understood as the playful imaginative anticipation of the future, may be seen as a source of hope, but its value and purpose lies first and foremost in *glorifying God*. But a false dichotomy could too easily be assumed. This is because *giving* glory to God and *receiving* joy in worship are inseparable. In the words of the Westminster Catechism, the supreme end of humankind is to 'glorify God and enjoy him for ever'. When God is glorified God is enjoyed, and when God is enjoyed God is glorified. To encounter true joy is to glorify God by sharing in God's creative purpose. Moltmann says this is 'like a great song or a splendid poem or a wonderful dance of his fantasy, for the communication of his divine plenitude. The laughter of the universe is God's delight. It is the universal Easter laughter.'[174] A 'true theologian' is thus one who both suffers and *delights* in God, and Moltmann describes the theology of such enjoyment and delight as 'dance and play before God in what we might call theo-fantasy', traditionally known as *doxology*.[175] The point is that the 'pastoral value' of worship, as a practical source of hope that nurtures joy even in the face of death, cannot be separated from the fundamental purpose of worship which is to glorify God, for such glorification is to be understood in terms of *enjoying* God.

The experience of joy is important for hope in the face of death because there is a real sense in which it is an experience of the resurrection that is hoped for. Moltmann writes: 'When the Spirit of the resurrection is experienced, a person breathes freely, and gets up, and lives with head held high, and walks upright, possessed by the indescribable joy that finds expression in the Easter hymns.'[176] This is a 'new livingness and exuberant joy', and may be understood as a foretaste of the 'feast of eternal joy' in which 'all created beings and the whole community of God's creation are destined to sing their hymns and songs of praise'.[177] Eternal resurrection life, according to this vision, will be one in which God is glorified and enjoyed eternally. Resurrection life in God is not a 'fixed' eternity but a dynamic, everlasting encounter of being drawn ever deeper into God. Joy then may be understood as an indescribable experience in which the most intense feeling of satisfaction coexists with an equally intense longing for more but in a way that does not undermine the sense of satisfaction. This indeed comes very close to the account that C. S. Lewis gives of his experience of joy, that 'unsatisfied desire which is itself more desirable than any other satisfaction'.[178] Lewis says, 'All joy reminds. It is never a possession, always a desire for something longer ago or further away or still "about to be".'[179] He talks of joy as a 'stabbing' that cannot be prepared for: 'the very nature of Joy makes nonsense of our distinction between having and wanting. There, to have is to want and to want is to have. Thus, the very moment when I longed to be so stabbed again, was itself again such a stabbing.'[180] To enjoy God eternally is therefore a continual encounter that is at once both perfectly satisfying and also a dynamic movement and anticipation of still deeper satisfaction.

These reflections on the nature of joy can now be used to clarify and refine what was said towards the end of Chapter 4 about the spirituality of hoping *in* God. Specifically, borrowing insights from Rahner, it was suggested that eternal resurrection life in God will be an existence in which the dynamic of *anticipation* that characterizes the hope leading up to it will continue. While Rahner rightly emphasizes the dynamic nature of eternal life, there is an awkward, albeit very subtle, implication here that hope itself will be a feature of that life. This is problematic, because there surely is a sense in which hope *does* dissolve into possession in resurrection life, as death, pain and transience are left behind for ever. The difficulty may be overcome by identifying joy as the key dynamic of the resurrection life. That is to say, the dynamic of forever anticipating a still richer life in God in eternity does not mean that we continue to hope even after we have been raised, but that we simply *enjoy* God for ever. As Bauckham and Hart say:

> In eternity we shall no longer have goals towards which we must measure our temporal progress. In worship whose only purpose is to please God and to enjoy God, we shall eternally lose ourselves in the beauty and love of God and eternally enjoy the surprise of finding ourselves in God.[181]

Absolute hope in God for resurrection is hope that transcends all goals. But as the expectation of the ultimate promise of resurrection such absolute hope enables us to pursue goals and sustains us, in hope, on the way towards them. At the resurrection, the sense of expectation may be said to continue for all eternity, but then it will no longer be *hope* as such, but pure *joy*. In Moltmann's words: 'What is called "the end of history" is, for a Christian understanding, not an end in the sense of a goal, but release from a life subordinated by the law to goals and achievements into the joy of God.'[182] The joy that is experienced in hope is therefore that mysterious sense of expectation that anticipates but not in a way that feels shackled to specific goals. It is hope's foretaste of eternity, the 'ecstasy' of hope.[183]

We can thus affirm the theological and psychological importance of joy, laughter and humour, as vital dynamics of the experience of hoping. Our discussion must therefore turn now to the practicalities of nurturing such things, that hope itself might be cultivated. C. S. Lewis rightly points out that joy 'is never in our power'.[184] It is in the very nature of joy that it cannot be manufactured. As Moltmann says, joy, *chara*, is the spontaneous reaction to *charis*, God's gift of grace.[185] But while joy itself is something that cannot, strictly speaking, be *produced*, laughter can. Laughter is not the same thing as joy, but it is a vital part of it. As such it may help to nurture a sense of joy and in turn cultivate hope. So let us consider this in practical terms.

First, a caveat. Not all humour and laughter is healthy. In his reflection on biblical understandings of laughter Karl-Josef Kuschel distinguishes between that which is born of joy in God and that which expresses malice, cynicism and alienation.[186] Pattison says, 'Humour and laughter can be signs of callousness, cynicism, escapism and lack of involvement.'[187] In his very brief mention of humour, Rumbold highlights similar dangers, warning that cheerful, light-hearted behaviour can simply be 'a way of saying, "Let's keep this conversation light and breezy; I don't want to get serious here"'.[188] Kübler-Ross also points out that in caring for dying persons our initial reaction to their sadness is to want to 'cheer them up' and that more often than not this is simply the expression of our own struggle to tolerate that sadness.[189] But, as Pattison points out, *both* persons in a pastoral relationship can misuse humour as 'nothing more than an analgesic to take away present pain while distracting people from facing up to reality and seeking to change it'.[190] For this reason 'the pastor has to listen to her own laughter as well as that of those she offers care to', mindful of the possibility that sometimes people may attempt to 'deflect the pastor's attention from their needs by appealing to her sense of humour'. Because not all laughter is healthy, pastoral carers should always seek to discern its real meaning whenever laughter is encountered. Pattison suggests that 'sometimes it will be useful to ask a person what their laughter means to them, for they may not themselves appreciate its significance'.[191]

A brief but slightly closer look at our story of Jane may help to illustrate the need for sensitivity when laughter is encountered in pastoral care. We have already described the sense of certainty with which Jane claims that she will be miraculously cured. What has not yet been mentioned is the smile on Jane's face whenever she is in conversation about this conviction. Interestingly, she does not smile in the same way the rest of the time. Furthermore, Jane has a tendency to finish every sentence with a faint chuckle every time she talks about her condition. Is this Jane's way of masking an underlying suspicion that the miracle that she is hoping for may not be forthcoming? We do not know, and we should not make assumptions. But in this situation, where the easiest option may be to simply smile and chuckle along with Jane, a more appropriate response might be the sort of *silence* described by Campbell, which we considered earlier in this chapter as a means of confrontation in pastoral care. Meeting Jane's laughter with silence like this could be a gentle and sensitive way of putting a question mark over its real meaning. It may subsequently be appropriate for the question to be asked more directly. Here the situation is simply highlighted as an example of the ambiguous nature of laughter and the need for sensitivity in responding to it.

Accepting the need for caution, three observations can be made concerning the practical value of humour in cultivating hope. The first is that it can help to establish a sense of *humanity* in the pastoral relationship. Rumbold says, 'our sense of humour can be one of the most helpful gifts we can bring to another person, creating a real intimacy between us'.[192] In their study of the qualities most appreciated in a hospice chaplain, Paul Ballard *et al.* found that a sense of humour was one of the most valued attributes of what was considered to be a 'genuine humanity'.[193] Humour helps to create friendship. This involves building a sense of *mutuality* and, as Pattison points out, the best way of engendering humour is to encourage others to develop their own sense of humour – something that is most effectively achieved by pastoral carers who are willing to become vulnerable themselves by laughing at themselves. He writes, 'If they are willing to discover and disclose the incongruities in their own situation, this can create an environment of mutuality where those who seek care can also begin to experiment with humour and laughter.'[194] When visiting a hospital ward, especially if wearing clerical dress, a minister might be greeted with the words, 'Look out, here comes the vicar!' A response such as, 'Well, someone's got to keep you all in order' is the sort of light-hearted banter by which a minister might convey that she does not take herself too seriously.

A second observation, one that was noted in our discussion of psychology and nursing science in Chapter 2, is that humour and laughter creates a sense of *perspective*. Pattison says, 'humour requires a step back from the situation in which one is involved so that the incongruities in it are seen'.[195] For example, let us imagine that towards the end of their first meeting David and the vicar agree to get together again in two weeks' time, as we suggested above. As they write the appointment in their diaries, David, without thinking, says, 'I'll try not to die before then.' There is a pause, and then for the first time in several weeks, David smiles, before laughing out loud. Inadvertently, David has exposed himself to the irrational nature of his thought. As he laughs, he also sheds a tear, but this tear does not feel quite so bitter. For the first time since being told that no further treatment would be likely to cure him, David feels a vague sense of actually being alive again. For a few moments at least, death ceases to have the upper hand.

Maintaining a sense of perspective is highly important in the process of hope's reality surveillance. On the one hand, laughter may help create the perspective that is required if a person is to avoid being overcome by the anxieties and fears that arise as death approaches. Resurrection hope that laughs in the face of death will not allow such anxieties and fears to have the all-consuming power with which they threaten us. As Capps says, humour 'enables us to suspend the limits of everyday life, not by ignoring them, but by making ourselves invulnerable to their ability to inflict psychological pain'. On the other hand, such hope does not simply close itself off from the failures and disappointments of life. Rather, it accepts the limitations of what goals are appropriate to pursue. This is what Capps calls the *modesty* of hope. Humour is instrumental in fostering this modesty, for in being able to laugh at oneself there is 'an acceptance of one's finitude and limits'.[196] It is a modesty that helps prevent the hopeful self from becoming brittle and narrow in its expectations. If we can laugh at ourselves we can see ourselves in the right perspective, avoid attaching too much seriousness to the things we may strive to attain and let go of those past disappointments that would otherwise weigh us down. This has a special significance in the face of death, as resurrection hope is, as has been argued, in God, not the human self.

A third observation, also noted in Chapter 2 and closely related to the matter of perspective, is that humour and laughter have a deeply *empowering* quality. Pattison writes, 'For those who are suffering or involved in deeply troubling circumstances, the advent of laughter can be a sign of great hope, for it means that they are in some way transcending themselves and their circumstances.'[197] Let us, for example, imagine that Angela, who is deeply worried that she may not regain consciousness after her operation, has been talking with Sue for about half an hour. Eventually, Sue says a short prayer with Angela. Following this, the conversation begins to draw to a close. All the while, the patient in the adjacent bed is snoring at a noticeably high volume. After one exceptionally loud inhalation Sue can see a faint smile on Angela's face. She leans over and whispers in Angela's ear, 'If nothing else wakes you up from the anaesthetic, that certainly will!' As Angela bursts out laughing she seems relaxed in a way that she did not at the beginning of the conversation. Having listened to and engaged with Angela's genuine fear, Sue's quip is a way of putting the object of that fear in a certain perspective. Sue does not downplay the reality of Angela's fear, but enabling Angela to laugh in this way possibly helps to give her a sense of power over it that she did not previously have.

Laughter in the face of death does not *trivialize* the reality of human suffering, but there is a sense in which it does *relativize* it. Hope in God for resurrection places death in the light of eternal resurrection life – what might be called *God's* perspective. Thus Moltmann writes, 'by virtue of his resurrection "death has become a mockery", as Luther was able to say . . . Laughter takes away the seriousness of an attack and debases it.'[198] Cox recognizes this when he describes laughter as 'hope's last weapon'.[199] He quotes Maurice Bejart: 'If you can joke about something very important . . . you have achieved freedom'.[200] Cox talks of 'Christianity *as* comedy'.[201] His point is that seriousness is not the opposite of the comic. The comic sensibility has its own seriousness that insists that 'nothing in life should be taken too seriously'.[202] It has a rightful place in Christian faith because 'the point in Christianity is not that the world is "unreal" but that it should not be taken with ultimate or final seriousness'.[203] A practical theology of hope for the dying must, paradoxically, take laughter and humour very seriously indeed. Hope in God for resurrection can laugh in the face of death because it gives that ultimate seriousness only to that God in whom it rejoices – the God of resurrection, the Lord of life.

Nurturing Christian spirituality: autonomy, the self and hope

Our concern in this book has been for a practical theology of hope for the dying. The aim has been to bring psychology and theology together in a critical conversation in order to explore how Christian hope might inform and indeed *trans*form palliative care. The quest for the way a *Christian spiritual base* provides the foundation of hope in the face of death has therefore been the enterprise throughout. In this concluding section, Christian belief is not simply named as one 'source' of hope among others. Rather, the intention is to make more explicit the importance of the dynamic of hoping specifically *in God*. Thus we return to Sarah's longing for a deeper sense of confidence in her Christian ministry to the dying – the very concern with which we started.

We may recall that very early in his career, Moltmann argued that while a purely humanistic understanding such as Bloch's rightly takes the power of the human capacity to hope seriously, in the face of death such power 'can accomplish nothing'.[204] Only God's promised future could transcend the limits of human mortality. This is not to say that Christians are the only ones to have any hope. In this book we have affirmed hope as a naturally basic human phenomenon. But this is *God-given*, and it finds its fullness when it becomes absolute hope in God for resurrection. We name resurrection as the ultimate object of hope because it transcends all 'ordinary' objects. As such it can only be hoped *for* by hoping *in* that which is by definition the only absolute, namely, God. Towards the end of Chapter 4 reflection was given to what might be meant by the spirituality of hoping *in* God. Now as we draw this present chapter on nurturing hope to a close, let us probe further still into this spirituality. Specifically, how might a sense of personal autonomy be developed in an individual as he or she is encouraged to hope in God as the only absolute?

In Chapter 2 we noted the insights of Lynch, who suggests that it is the absolutizing instinct that threatens personal autonomy. Lynch argues that when God is recognized as the only absolute this instinct is held in check.[205] Autonomous existence is not antithetical to belief in God as absolute, but is in fact the result of such belief. Autonomy is not something that must be asserted against God's absoluteness, but is received in its very confession.

This is a vital dynamic of hoping in God. Capps says that 'autonomy and hope go together'.[206] This pertains to Capps' belief that 'images of hope originate in the capacity to be alone. They are stimulated by the felt sense that one is not in fact alone.' Capps does not refer here to the absoluteness of God, but he talks about autonomy as an internalized sense of relatedness. In other words, autonomy is not the isolation and assertion of the self against others, but the capacity to be alone and to hope as an individual self *because* that self has internalized a sense of trust that others are there. Capps comments on 'the religious implications of this phenomenon', namely that 'images of hope in God are based on our internalization of God, our felt sense that God is "within" us and is therefore always present to us'.[207] That is to say, we hope in God autonomously. Such autonomy is not set against God, but is derived from the very relatedness that is experienced with God.

The 'role of the self in the experience of hoping'[208] is an important issue facing any pastoral carer who genuinely desires to nurture hope in others, and Capps is right to give emphasis to it. In the postmodern climate that we have illustrated with Angela there is a popular suspicion that Christianity merely functions as an 'organized' religion that simply suppresses the true and authentic individuality of the believer. Pastoral carers need to be confident that this is not the case, but that the self is actually found in God as God is hoped in. At the same time, the self that Christian pastoral care would seek to nurture in hope should not be construed in narcissistic terms. Christian hope is something far more profound than a mere spiritual 'commodity', and God is more than the guarantor of whatever personal desires an individual may happen to be hoping for. So just how might the spirituality of hoping in God enable the individual to discover a real sense of personal autonomy in a way that avoids a narcissistic preoccupation with the self?

The answer lies in what we have described in this book as the kenotic spirituality of hoping in God for resurrection. Hope is not passive, but neither should it be understood in terms of mastery and control. Hope in the face of death involves the acceptance of human mortality and a process of letting go in the final stages of dying. A vital question is, *Letting go into what?* Our discussion has pointed to resurrection, and more fundamentally God as the source of that resurrection. Rumbold says that 'the prelude to resurrection is our powerlessness'.[209] But to hope in God means that such powerlessness is in fact more than just a prelude, for it is in the act of letting go itself that life in God is found. As the self is given up to God so it is actually received. Moltmann thus talks of 'the love in which we forget ourselves and at the same time find ourselves'.[210] Personal autonomy is found as the self is *emptied* (*kenosis*) into God (Philippians 2.7). As Riem says, '"Letting go", then, is the only way to find true meaning beyond the self. It leads to life because "through ego-abandonment, the person becomes what he is, he finds himself the image of the self-abandoning God".'[211]

A practical theology of hope for the dying may firmly establish this kenotic principle as its spiritual base. Further, it may be emphasized that this is a specifically Christian principle, noting that *kenosis* is set within the context of the Pauline mandate: 'Let the same mind be in you that was in Christ Jesus' (Philippians 2.5). Further still, this may be understood as *dynamically trinitarian*. We may recall from Chapter 3 that Moltmann's theology emphasizes God as *open Trinity*. In particular, we noted how this way of conceiving of God's being enables us to understand living hope as *participation in God*. Hoping in God, and seeking to nurture that same hope in others, is more than 'observation'. It is a living, dynamic and personal involvement *in* the life of God.

Fiddes makes this explicit in his book *Participating in God*. He suggests an 'epistemology of participation': we know God by experiencing life *in* God. Such experience is essentially relational – as we encounter relationship with God so we participate in the Father-Son-Spirit relational being of God.[212] Fiddes himself considers Moltmann's doctrine of the Trinity to be insufficiently radical to speak of this sort of participation in God. Fiddes suggests that instead of regarding the Father, Son and Spirit as persons *in* relationship, the strongly relational nature of the Trinity would be more adequately expressed in terms of persons *as* relationships. He argues, 'There are no persons "at each end of a relation", but the "persons" are simply the relations.' It is arguable that Fiddes somewhat over-plays his conviction that relations are 'as real and "beingful" as anything which is created or uncreated'.[213] Surely, any 'relation' is by definition something that exists between two or more subjects. If those subjects have no existence in and of themselves it is highly abstract, if not altogether nonsense to speak of any kind of relationship between them. Nevertheless, Fiddes' basic point, namely, to *know* God is to *participate in* God, is a helpful one. But Moltmann's doctrine of the Trinity, a doctrine of *perichoresis*, does not need to be rejected in order to make this point. Indeed, Moltmann's doctrine of open Trinity provides all that is required to talk of hoping in God as participating in God. This doctrine asserts that God's *perichoresis* is open to history and to creation. As we hope in God so we participate in the life of God. This is the encounter in which we let go of ourselves and so find ourselves in God. Living in God is then dying in God, and dying in God is living in God. This is *living hope*.

Of course, this kenotic principle of hope is not something to be confined to a palliative context, any more than hope itself is. To 'die daily' is vital to Christian being. But it is a spirituality that discovers a heightened relevance in the dying trajectory in which human mortality confronts us with the choice of either willingly letting go as death approaches or clinging on in desperation to the very last. It is arguable that a person whose life has been based on this kenotic spirituality will find letting go in the final stages of dying a more natural experience than one whose life has been spent in the assertion of their autonomy against or in resistance to belief in God.

In practical terms, these reflections lead pastoral care to a *God-centred* approach. This is in no way antithetical to what might be called *person-centred* care. Those who share in the pastoral care of dying persons may focus on hope in God for resurrection without the sense that in so doing they are bypassing or detracting from the personal needs and hopes of those for whom they are caring. By sharing in prayer, Bible reading, acts of worship and encouraging reflection on personal Christian experience, pastoral carers may help dying persons to focus hope in God so that they might let go into God and so find themselves there. This is a process in which personal, everyday concerns are not divorced from hope in the transcendent God. For example, a dying person who has always taken care of their household's banking and insurance matters might be worried about how their partner will manage such responsibilities alone. In pastoral conversation a carer might take these things up into a wider discussion, exploring ways in which the God who has been present through previous times of domestic struggle will continue to be there in the time ahead, committing it to God in prayer. A kenotic spiritual base is thus God-centred *and* deeply personal. It focuses on the transcendent and engages with the mundane. It looks to God in hope for resurrection and in this process discovers personal autonomy as the life of God is participated in. Living hope, that is, absolute hope in God for resurrection, can ultimately 'only be known through the mode of participation'.[214] It is the task of pastoral carers to nurture that sense of participation.

Notes

1 Moltmann, *Theology of Hope*, p. 23.
2 Marcel, *Homo Viator*, p. 30.
3 Marcel, *Homo Viator*, p. 32.
4 Moltmann, *The Crucified God*, p. 186.
5 Lester, *Hope in Pastoral Care and Counseling*, p. 72.
6 Lester, *Hope in Pastoral Care and Counseling*, chapters 5 and 6.
7 Rumbold, *Helplessness and Hope*, pp. 22–3.
8 Rumbold, *Helplessness and Hope*, p. 68.
9 Rumbold, *Helplessness and Hope*, p. 75.
10 Jürgen Moltmann, 'The Diaconal Church in the Context of the Kingdom of God', in Jürgen Moltmann *et al.*, *Hope for the Church: Moltmann in Dialogue with Practical Theology*, ET (ed. and trans. T. Runyon), Nashville: Abingdon Press, 1979, pp. 21–36, 27–8.
11 Rumbold, *Helplessness and Hope*, p. 41.
12 Rumbold, *Helplessness and Hope*, p. 51.
13 Moltmann, *Theology of Hope*, pp. 25–6.
14 Rubem Alves, *Tomorrow's Child: Imagination, Creativity, and the Rebirth of Culture*, London: SCM Press, 1972, p. 116. Here Alves is borrowing a quotation from Ernst Cassirer.
15 Alves, *Tomorrow's Child*, p. 43.
16 Alves, *Tomorrow's Child*, pp. 108, 119.
17 E.g. Jose Miguez Bonino, *Doing Theology in a Revolutionary Situation*, Philadelphia: Fortress Press, 1975, p. 151; Michel Demaison, 'The Christian Utopia', *Concilium* 9 (1970), pp. 42–58, 49. The term is derived from Bloch: see Trevor Hart, 'Imagination for the Kingdom of God?', in Richard Bauckham, ed., *God Will Be All in All: The Eschatology of Jürgen Moltmann*, Edinburgh: T & T Clark, 1999, p. 61.
18 Bonino, *Doing Theology in a Revolutionary Situation*, pp. 151–2.
19 Moltmann, *Theology of Hope*, p. 25. Italics original.
20 Moltmann, *The Experiment Hope*, p. 24.
21 The term *utopia* is used positively in Jürgen Moltmann, 'What Has Happened to our Utopias?', in Bauckham, ed. *God Will Be All in All*, pp. 115–21.
22 Moltmann, *Hope and Planning*, p. 39.

23 Lynch, *Images of Hope*, p. 138.

24 Rumbold, *Helplessness and Hope*, p. 66.

25 Rumbold, *Helplessness and Hope*, pp. 61ff.

26 Lester, *Hope in Pastoral Care and Counseling*, p. 81.

27 Lester, *Hope in Pastoral Care and Counseling*, p. 87.

28 Capps, *Agents of Hope*, pp. 154ff.

29 Capps, *Agents of Hope*, p. 158.

30 Capps, *Agents of Hope*, p. 66.

31 Lester, *Hope in Pastoral Care and Counseling*, p. 85.

32 Fiddes, *Participating in God*, p. 226.

33 Lester, *Hope in Pastoral Care and Counseling*, p. 86. Italics original.

34 Fiddes, *Participating in God*, p. 243.

35 Moltmann, *The Crucified God*, p. 243.

36 Fiddes, *Participating in God*, p. 50. Italics original.

37 Fiddes, *Participating in God*, p. 238. Italics original.

38 Roland Riem, *Stronger than Death: A Study of Love for the Dying*, London: Darton, Longman & Todd, 1993, p. 43.

39 Kübler-Ross, *On Death and Dying*, pp. 39–40.

40 Riem, *Stronger than Death*, pp. 43ff.

41 Alastair Campbell, *Rediscovering Pastoral Care* (2nd edition), London: Darton, Longman & Todd, 1986, p. 12.

42 Campbell, *Rediscovering Pastoral Care*, p. 44. Italics original.

43 Rumbold, *Helplessness and Hope*, p. 71.

44 Moltmann, *Religion, Revolution and the Future*, p. 211; cf. *The Church in the Power of the Spirit*, p. 75.

45 Rumbold, *Helplessness and Hope*, p. 65.

46 Herth, 'Fostering Hope in Terminally Ill People', p. 1255.

47 Lester, *Hope in Pastoral Care and Counseling*, p. 88.

48 Rumbold, *Helplessness and Hope*, p. 71.

49 Lester, *Hope in Pastoral Care and Counseling*, p. 33.

50 Lester, *Hope in Pastoral Care and Counseling*, pp. 87–8.

51 Moltmann, *The Spirit of Life*, p. 35.

52 Carl Braaten, *The Future of God: The Revolutionary Dynamics of Hope*, New York: Harper & Row, 1969, p. 66.

53 Martha Stoner, 'Response to "Development and refinement of an instrument to measure hope"', *Scholarly Inquiry for Nursing Practice* 5 (1991), pp. 53–6, 55.

54 Marcel, *Homo Viator*, p. 58.

55 Moltmann, *The Spirit of Life*, p. 17.

56 Moltmann, *The Spirit of Life*, p. 218.

57 Moltmann, *The Trinity and the Kingdom of God*, p. 19.

58 Moltmann, *The Spirit of Life*, p. 82.

59 Moltmann, *The Spirit of Life*, p. 219. Italics original.

60 Moltmann, *God in Creation*, p. 100.

61 Moltmann, *The Church in the Power of the Spirit*, p. 225.

62 Moltmann, *The Way of Jesus Christ*, p. 122.

63 Moltmann, *Theology of Hope*, p. 328.

64 Braaten, *The Future of God*, p. 111.

65 Braaten, *The Future of God*, p. 109.

66 Alves, *Tomorrow's Child*, p. 201.

67 Lester, *Hope in Pastoral Care and Counseling*, p. 98.

68 Moltmann, *The Church in the Power of the Spirit*, p. 121; cf. *The Spirit of Life*, pp. 255–9.

69 Moltmann, 'The Diaconal Church in the Context of the Kingdom of God', p. 25.

70 Riem, *Stronger Than Death*, p. 21.

71 Lester, *Hope in Pastoral Care and Counseling*, p. 92.

72 Moltmann, *Experiences of God*, p. 3.

73 Paul Ballard *et al.*, 'A Perception of Hospice Chaplaincy', *Contact* 130 (1999), pp. 27–34.

74 Peter Speck, *Being There: Pastoral Care in Time of Illness*, London: SPCK, 1988.

75 Rumbold, *Helplessness and Hope*, p. 11.

76 Rumbold, *Helplessness and Hope*, p. 10.

77 Riem, *Stronger than Death*, p. 37.

78 Rumbold, *Helplessness and Hope*, p. 41.

79 Rumbold, *Helplessness and Hope*, pp. 24–5.

80 Moltmann, *The Church in the Power of the Spirit*, p. 115.

81 Moltmann, *The Spirit of Life*, p. 256.

82 Moltmann, 'The Diaconal Church in the Context of the Kingdom of God', p. 25.

83 Lynch, *Images of Hope*, p. 235.

84 Michael Wilson, *A Coat of Many Colours: Pastoral Studies of the Christian Way of Life*, London: Epworth Press, 1988, p. 140.

85 Wilson, *A Coat of Many Colours*, p. 142.

86 Wilson, *A Coat of Many Colours*, p. 144.

87 Wilson, *A Coat of Many Colours*, p. 142.

88 Rumbold, *Helplessness and Hope*, pp. 10–11.

89 Moltmann, *The Church in the Power of the Spirit*, p. 116. Italics original.

90 Cited in Capps, *Agents of Hope*, p. 47.

91 Capps, *Agents of Hope*, p. 46.

92 Capps, *Agents of Hope*, p. 51.

93 Lester, *Hope in Pastoral Care and Counseling*, pp. 37–9, 99.

94 Moltmann, *The Church in the Power of the Spirit*, p. 225.

95 Rumbold, *Helplessness and Hope*, p. 90.

96 Rumbold, *Helplessness and Hope*, pp. 129ff.

97 Robert Jenson, 'Worship as Drama', in Braaten and Jenson, *The Futurist Option*, p. 160.

98 Robert Jenson, 'God, Space and Architecture', in Braaten and Jenson, *The Futurist Option*, p. 170.

99 Robert Jenson, 'Appeal to the Person of the Future', in Braaten and Jenson, *The Futurist Option*, p. 154.

100 Jürgen Moltmann, 'The Life Signs of the Spirit in the Fellowship Community of Christ', in Moltmann *et al.*, *Hope for the Church*, p. 52.

101 Moltmann, 'The Life Signs of the Spirit', p. 54.

102 Moltmann, 'The Life Signs of the Spirit', p. 55; cf. *The Church in the Power of the Spirit*, pp. 109ff.

103 Moltmann, *The Church in the Power of the Spirit*, pp. 258ff.

104 Lester, *Hope in Pastoral Care and Counseling*, p. 94.

105 Rumbold, *Helplessness and Hope*, p. 70.

106 Rumbold, *Helplessness and Hope*, p. 54.

107 Capps, *Agents of Hope*, p. 163.

108 Simon Robinson, 'Helping the Hopeless: Exploring Love as the Ground of What is Hoped For', *Contact* 127 (1998), pp. 3–20, 3–4.

109 Alves, *Tomorrow's Child*, p. 199.

110 Davie, *Religion in Britain since 1945*, p. 199.

111 Moltmann, *The Spirit of Life*, p. 263.

112 Moltmann, *The Spirit of Life*, pp. 263–7.

113 Johann Baptist Metz, *Faith in History and Society: Toward a Practical Fundamental Theology*, ET (trans. David Smith), London: Burns & Oates, 1980, p. 176.

114 Edward Schillebeeckx, *God the Future of Man*, ET (trans. N. D. Smith), London: Sheed & Ward, 1969, p. 192.

115 Bringle, *Despair*, pp. 145–53.

116 Moltmann, *Hope and Planning*, p. 173.

117 Marcel, *Homo Viator*, pp. 38, 39.

118 Lester, *Hope in Pastoral Care and Counseling*, pp. 67–8.

119 Lynch, *Images of Hope*, p. 138.

120 Lester, *Hope in Pastoral Care and Counseling*, p. 67. Italics original.

121 Dufault and Martocchio, 'Hope: Its Spheres and Dimensions', p. 380.

122 Lester, *Hope in Pastoral Care and Counseling*, p. 67.

123 Moltmann, *God in Creation*, p. 287.

124 Moltmann, *The Coming of God*, p. 138.

125 Moltmann, *The Coming of God*, p. 261.

126 Moltmann, *God in Creation*, p. 276.
127 Moltmann, *The Coming of God*, p. 138.
128 Richard Bauckham and Trevor Hart, *Hope against Hope: Christian Eschatology in Contemporary Context*, London: Darton, Longman & Todd, 1999, p. xii.
129 Bauckham and Hart, *Hope against Hope*, p. 51.
130 Bauckham and Hart, *Hope against Hope*, p. 68.
131 Bauckham and Hart, *Hope against Hope*, p. 51.
132 Bauckham and Hart, *Hope against Hope*, pp. 58–9.
133 Bauckham and Hart, *Hope against Hope*, p. 26.
134 Moltmann, *Experiences in Theology*, pp. 41–2.
135 Bauckham and Hart, *Hope against Hope*, p. 59.
136 Bauckham and Hart, *Hope against Hope*, p. 63.
137 Bauckham and Hart, *Hope against Hope*, p. 72.
138 Moltmann, *God in Creation*, p. 4.
139 Moltmann, *The Coming of God*, p. xiv. Italics original.
140 Moltmann, *The Coming of God*, p. 139.
141 Moltmann, *The Coming of God*, p. 295.
142 Moltmann, *Religion, Revolution and the Future*, p. 34.
143 Braaten, *The Future of God*, p. 26.
144 Alves, *A Theology of Human Hope*, p. 166.
145 Bauckham and Hart, *Hope against Hope*, p. 81.
146 Moltmann, *The Coming of God*, p. 29.
147 Bauckham and Hart, *Hope against Hope*, pp. 73, 74.
148 Bauckham and Hart, *Hope against Hope*, p. 95.
149 As discussed in Chapter 4, the language of heaven need not be excluded from hope that is envisioned in terms of resurrection.
150 Theo Witvliet, *The Way of the Black Messiah*, ET (trans. John Bowden), London: SCM Press, 1987, p. 203.
151 Witvliet, *The Way of the Black Messiah*, pp. 204–5.
152 Hart, 'Imagination for the Kingdom of God?', pp. 74–5.
153 Schneiders, 'The Resurrection of Jesus and Christian Spirituality', p. 102.
154 Bauckham and Hart, *Hope against Hope*, p. 122.
155 Cited in Riem, *Stronger Than Death*, pp. 47–8. Italics original.
156 Capps, *Agents of Hope*, p. 65.
157 Capps, *Agents of Hope*, p. 66.
158 Capps, *Agents of Hope*, p. 67.
159 Capps, *Agents of Hope*, pp. 68–9. Italics original.
160 Witvliet, *The Way of the Black Messiah*, p. 207.
161 Dufault and Martocchio, 'Hope: Its Spheres and Dimensions', pp. 382–4.
162 Moltmann, *Experiences of God*, pp. 19–20.

163 Moltmann, *The Coming of God*, p. 11.
164 Moltmann, 'The Liberating Feast', p. 104.
165 Moltmann, *Theology and Joy*, p. 27.
166 Moltmann, *Theology and Joy*, p. 36.
167 Harvey Cox, *The Feast of Fools: A Theological Essay on Festivity and Fantasy*, Cambridge, MA: Harvard University Press, 1969, p. 7.
168 Cox, *The Feast of Fools*, p. 11.
169 Alves, *Tomorrow's Child*, p. 93.
170 Alves, *Tomorrow's Child*, p. 97.
171 Alves, *Tomorrow's Child*, chapter 6.
172 Braaten, *The Future of God*, p. 121.
173 Moltmann, *The Church in the Power of the Spirit*, p. 261.
174 Moltmann, *The Coming of God*, p. 339.
175 Moltmann, *Experiences in Theology*, pp. 25–6.
176 Moltmann, *The Spirit of Life*, p. 153.
177 Moltmann, *The Coming of God*, pp. 337, 338.
178 C. S. Lewis, *Surprised by Joy*, London: Geoffrey Bles, 1955, pp. 23–4.
179 Lewis, *Surprised by Joy*, pp. 78–9.
180 Lewis, *Surprised by Joy*, p. 158.
181 Bauckham and Hart, *Hope against Hope*, p. 159.
182 Moltmann, 'The Liberating Feast', p. 106.
183 Moltmann, *The Spirit of Life*, p. 18.
184 Lewis, *Surprised by Joy*, p. 24.
185 Moltmann, *The Coming of God*, p. 337.
186 Karl-Josef Kuschel, *Laughter*, London: SCM Press, 1994, pp. 92–3.
187 Pattison, *A Critique of Pastoral Care*, p. 187.
188 Rumbold, *Helplessness and Hope*, p. 10.
189 Kübler-Ross, *On Death and Dying*, pp. 86–7.
190 Pattison, *A Critique of Pastoral Care*, p. 187.
191 Pattison, *A Critique of Pastoral Care*, p. 189.
192 Rumbold, *Helplessness and Hope*, p. 10.
193 Ballard *et al.*, 'A Perception of Hospice Chaplaincy', p. 29.
194 Pattison, *A Critique of Pastoral Care*, p. 190.
195 Pattison, *A Critique of Pastoral Care*, p. 184.
196 Capps, *Agents of Hope*, p. 158.
197 Pattison, *A Critique of Pastoral Care*, p. 185.
198 Moltmann, *Theology and Joy*, p. 51.
199 Cox, *The Feast of Fools*, p. 157.
200 Cox, *The Feast of Fools*, p. 145.
201 Cox, *The Feast of Fools*, p. 149. My italics.
202 Cox, *The Feast of Fools*, p. 152.
203 Cox, *The Feast of Fools*, p. 153.

204 Moltmann, *Religion, Revolution and the Future*, p. 17.
205 Lynch, *Images of Hope*, pp. 138–9.
206 Capps, *Agents of Hope*, p. 28.
207 Capps, *Agents of Hope*, pp. 45–6.
208 Capps, *Agents of Hope*, p. 6.
209 Rumbold, *Helplessness and Hope*, p. 75.
210 Moltmann, *The Spirit of Life*, p. 51.
211 Riem, *Stronger than Death*, p. 76. Here Riem borrows a quotation from Heather Ward.
212 Fiddes, *Participating in God*, p. 38.
213 Fiddes, *Participating in God*, p. 34.
214 Fiddes, *Participating in God*, p. 38.

6

Conclusion: Ministering in Hope

If for this life only we have hoped in Christ,
we are of all people most to be pitied.

1 Corinthians 15.19

So what is your hope?

This book has argued that the capacity to hope resides in us all. Hope is so basic to our humanity that without it there is no life. To hope means to look forward, to be able to identify things that are worth pursuing and living for. Hope gives us a positive outlook and enables us to cope when life is difficult. We hope when we look to the future expectantly and are motivated to move towards goals and aims. Underlying this relatively simple dynamic of expectation is a more profound form of hope that lies deep within the mystery of what it is to be human. This is a hope that looks ahead even when we are disappointed. It is a hope that does not attach itself to single objects – it is *generalized*. We have called this *the mysterious anticipation of the ultimate*. It is a fundamental human instinct that perceives a sense of possibility even in the midst of struggle. Such hope is transcendent because it enables us to envision a future beyond present circumstances and has at its core some form of personal end or purpose that we regard as ultimate. Many human beings name God as that which is ultimate.

What, then, is your hope?

Christian hope is one that does name God as the ultimate. Furthermore, it regards the basic human capacity to hope as an essential part of our God-given nature. But Christian hope is defined by something distinctive, namely the life, death and resurrection of Jesus Christ and the promises of God that Christians believe are made through that revelation. Thus we have in this book set out a practical theology of *absolute hope in God for resurrection*. We have argued that the most all-encompassing object of hope is the resurrection of the body. Indeed, it transcends all other objects and thus cannot, strictly speaking, be described as an object itself. When we look to the resurrection we envisage the ultimate transformation of individual and society – the whole cosmos – and so it is that hoping *for* resurrection is the most complete and holistic expression of human hope. It is *absolute* hope, because it is transcendent. Such absolute status can only be afforded to it because it is hope *in* God, who is the only absolute.

The pastoral context of our discussion in this book has been the care of the dying. But it has been argued that only a hope that can engage with the reality of death is robust enough to engage with any other struggle. Thus absolute hope in God for resurrection provides a basis, indeed *the* basis, for Christian pastoral care in all contexts. Arguably, such hope denotes the very core of Christian belief. That is Paul's contention in 1 Corinthians 15, so pointedly expressed in verse 19, quoted above. Paul's slight against hope that is 'for this life only' is not a bid to negate the needs of present existence for the sake of a better afterlife. After all, resurrection hope looks to the raising of the present body and so directs us to hope for and give care to precisely *this life* in *this present body*. Paul's point is that if we have no resurrection hope, then we have no hope at all. Resurrection is the basis of our belief:

> Now if Christ is proclaimed as raised from the dead, how can some of you say there is no resurrection of the dead? If there is no resurrection of the dead, then Christ has not been raised; and if Christ has not been raised, then our proclamation has been in vain and your faith has been in vain. We are even found to be misrepresenting God, because we testified of God that he raised Christ – whom he did not raise if it is true that the dead are not raised. For if the dead are not raised, then

Christ has not been raised. If Christ has not been raised, your faith is futile and you are still in your sins.[1]

And because it is the basis of our belief, resurrection is also the basis of all Christian ministry:

> And why are we putting ourselves in danger every hour? I die every day! That is as certain, brothers and sisters, as my boasting of you – a boast that I make in Christ Jesus our Lord. If with merely human hopes I fought with wild animals at Ephesus, what would be gained by it? If the dead are not raised, 'Let us eat and drink, for tomorrow we die.' . . . Therefore, my beloved, be steadfast, immovable, always excelling in the work of the Lord, because you know that in the Lord your labour is not in vain.[2]

We are thus brought back to the inseparability of *theology* and *practice*. What we *do* and what we *believe* cannot be divorced – unless, of course, integrity is to be compromised. This is true not only of Christian ministry, but of any approach to the care of people. Regardless of whether it is acknowledged, the work of every doctor, nurse, therapist or counsellor embodies a set of inherent beliefs and values of some kind or another.[3] Arguably, it is here that we arrive at the very thing that gives Christian ministry its distinctive identity. Christian pastoral carers are not simply 'baptized social workers'. Our practice is *theologically* grounded. That is why this book has not simply worked out a strategy for palliative care based on the insights of psychology and nursing science – invaluable as those insights are. Rather, our concern has been to give a considered, critical evaluation of those insights in the light of Christian theology. In short, the way we care for others may be helpfully shaped and guided by human science and the professional voices of psychology and nursing, but it is fundamentally *defined* by those theological beliefs and values that are most ultimate to Christians. Here we have identified absolute hope in God for resurrection as the very heart of such theological beliefs and values.

Another way of putting this is to say that the way we *care* is determined by the way we *hope*. That is, any set of beliefs and values with which care work is approached carries some form of hope on the part of the care worker. For Christian pastoral carers it is absolute hope in God for resurrection that determines the way we care. It is wholly appropriate to call this *practical theology*: it is practical because it is concerned with caring *actions*; it is theology because it is concerned with our hope *in God*. Thus the term *living hope* simultaneously conveys the 'work' or 'practice' of hope in pastoral care as well as the theological hope itself. Wilson writes:

> There is no special technique for giving hope to the hopeless. I know of no way of conveying hope to someone except by being hopeful. All the preparation through worship and prayer is put to the test at the moment of crisis. It is in being such a person, such a church, that pastors help most, because our hope is real: our hope is in God, not in any particular divine gifts or blessings. 'I hold and am held.'[4]

Wilson's discussion of hope in pastoral care is exceptionally brief, but for all that he captures something here that is tremendously profound: it is in *being hopeful* that pastoral carers most effectively minister in hope. While this book has not attempted to offer a 'special technique for giving hope to the hopeless', a number of practical suggestions for nurturing hope have been made. But the concern throughout the book has been for a practical theology. That means something more than a simple 'how to . . . ' formula, and here Wilson perhaps grasps what that 'something' is – namely that it is in our Christian *being* that our *doing* is grounded. In other words, it is in God, the source of our hope, that we 'live and move', because most fundamentally it is in God that we 'have our being' (Acts 17.28). Christian hope is *living hope*, for it is in the living God who promises resurrection life. We seek to nurture this hope not by means of 'strategy' or 'formula' but by expressing it in and through the way we live. To minister in hope then, in any context, can thus be understood as living hope. In the rest of this concluding chapter let us highlight some of the wider implications of this practical theology of living hope for Christian ministry.

Hopeful pastoral relationships

In this book it has been suggested that pastoral relationships based upon *friendship* are more likely to be conducive for the nurturing of hope. Such a model emphasizes *mutuality* as a core value, advocating an approach of caring *with* rather than *for* others. We may expand on this here because of the challenge it presents to all pastoral care contexts.

Eric Berne's *Transactional Analysis* provides a useful tool for describing the difference between caring for and caring with. According to this theory, in every person there exists three categories of 'ego states', namely the figures of *parent*, *adult* and *child*. In any social interaction between persons, each individual involved will tend to implement one of these figures within him- or herself.[5] Thus if a transaction involves the parent in one person addressing the child in the other, the dynamics are as a parent would condescend to a child. This helps to illustrate the nature of a *caring for* approach to pastoral relationships. Diagrammatically, it could be set out in this way:

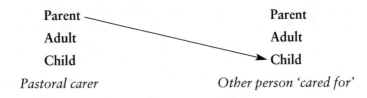

If a *caring for* approach can be represented in terms of a *parent–child* model of intercourse, then an *adult–adult* model appropriately depicts the dynamics of a *caring with* approach. Here there is recognition of a sense of commonality of condition and care is mutually shared rather than simply given by one and received by the other:

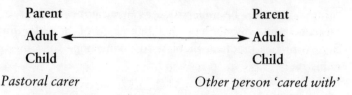

Parent	Parent
Adult ←————————————→	Adult
Child	Child
Pastoral carer	*Other person 'cared with'*

Approaching pastoral relationships with this sort of *caring with* model of friendship would seem to be especially appropriate in our contemporary postmodern context, in which Christian pastoral carers may often be regarded as simply the representatives of the Church as an 'institution' – custodians of 'religious hierarchy'. In the interaction between Angela and Sue, which we have used to illustrate this postmodern climate, Angela clearly detects that there is something about Sue that makes her approachable, for all her suspicion of organized religion – so much so that Angela feels able to share her feelings so openly. Now, there may be no formula as such for simply 'being approachable'. But it is arguable that a natural readiness to affirm our shared common humanity is a good basis for pastoral care if our desire is break down barriers of suspicion and enable others to feel confident that they can be open with us.

The model of friendship as *caring with* others should not be taken to undermine the genuinely helping and supportive role that pastoral carers provide. As David Deeks points out, in friendship two people may not necessarily experience mutuality every time they meet; of course there are times when one friend will be supported by the other.[6] Nevertheless, 'by offering himself or herself as a friend, the carer can prevent any help offered leading to the recipient becoming unhealthily dependent on the pastor'.[7]

In this respect friendship helps to prevent pastoral care from slipping into a form of paternalism. Over recent years the traditional image of *shepherding* from which the term *pastoral* derives has received criticism for its implication of a mindless dependency of the flock upon the pastor.[8] Campbell argues that such concerns should lead not to the dismissal of the shepherding image but the rediscovery of its authentically biblical meaning, namely courage.[9] Derek Tidball, endorsing Seward Hiltner's notion of the 'shepherding perspective' as the paradigm for practical theology,[10] also defends the image, appealing to its references to 'authority, tender care, specific tasks, courage and sacrifice'.[11] Rumbold affirms these things, emphasizing that 'shepherding care for individuals also has a corporate intention'.[12] He argues that it should be complemented with the image of *servant* and used to emphasize the 'mutual care of the fellowship'.[13] Thus it may not suffice to simply dismiss the image of shepherding through a suspicion that it must exclude the sort of mutuality that has been advocated in this book. But stressing the image of friend alongside shepherd, and also servant, reinforces the importance of *mutuality* in the pastoral relationship.

Another closely related concern is *professionalism*. Campbell's lucid discussion of this issue in his book *Paid to Care?* details how pastoral care has in recent years become increasingly motivated to embrace counselling skills and stress the importance of training practitioners. Good pastoral practice recognizes its responsibility to be well informed. At the same time Campbell highlights the dangers of allowing specialized skills and formal training to become normative for pastoral care. That devalues mutuality, making care the domain of the clergy as a group of paid professionals. Campbell asks, 'Can we translate the command of Jesus to love thy neighbour simply into the instruction to become a trained counsellor?'[14]

Friendship as a model for pastoral relationships counteracts the dangers of both paternalism and professionalism by emphasizing mutuality. This does not deny the importance of specialist skills such as counselling or the value of formal training. But such things should not obscure the fundamental recognition of a shared humanity that underlies any pastoral relationship. In a palliative context the mortality that is part of our common humanity is more difficult to ignore. Perhaps one of the most valuable ways in which such a context can inform the wider practice of pastoral care is to enable the rediscovery of this shared humanity.

A remaining question, however, relates to how care for the dying might be sustained in the context of friendship and the personal involvement that friendship denotes, without being personally consumed by that involvement. It is worth pointing out that the importance of this question is not confined to the palliative context. Pastoral carers in all sorts of situations face the challenge of bearing the tension of sustaining compassion for others without being personally overpowered by disappointment and tragedy. It is here that the need for some kind of *detachment* seems quite plausible. Wesley Carr warns of 'the seduction of "Incarnational Ministry"', by which he refers to the urge towards 'being at one with everyone'. He argues that incarnation in fact denotes the fundamental difference between God and humanity that is united in Christ. Pastoral ministry should emphasize the role of the pastor: '*Who* we are as persons does matter, but for pastoral ministry in human relationships we need a strong sense of *what* we are, our role.'[15] Riem suggests that Carr 'comes perilously close' to a 'neat professionalism' here.[16] A more satisfactory understanding of detachment, says Riem, is described by Rowan Williams, who distinguishes between *emotion* and *feeling*. Williams argues that with emotion the subject is absorbed with his or her own self, not the other person who has created that emotion. By contrast, feeling focuses on the person that the subject stands in relation to. Williams thus advocates an ideal of detachment that is characterized by *dispassionate feeling*.[17] It is not easy to make sense of this apparent paradox, and tension seems to exist with Moltmann's emphasis on pathos. Clarification of just how pastoral care might be grounded in friendship in a way that avoids being consumed by personal emotional involvement is required.

The most productive response to this dilemma may well lie in what we have described as the kenotic spirituality of *letting go*. Such a spirituality embraces friendship wholeheartedly but with a readiness to 'empty the self' to God. Emotion is a live part of this process, and thus it is not really a form of 'detachment' as such. And yet neither does it involve 'attachment', because the emotions are freely and unreservedly 'emptied' – that is, 'poured out' from the self into God. Thus the subject is not absorbed by his or her own self, because God is the focus – the one in whom resurrection is hoped for. Pastoral relationships – friendships – that are formed on the basis of this kind of spirituality are relationships that are willing to risk the personal involvement of hoping and caring with others in the midst of tragedy and pain, and which at the same time are free to let go of them as they are hoped for in God. Such an approach denotes a healthy perspective on the reality of death and dying, and indeed all experiences of suffering and disappointment, without implying the distance of detachment that is difficult to reconcile with friendship.

The perspective sustained by humour may well play a vital part in this. Pattison writes:

> Christian pastoral care badly needs to rediscover the possibility of involved detachment based on the perspective gained by trying to see the world through God's eyes and so seeing reality as it is. The outward sacrament of this rediscovery will be the sound of laughter.[18]

There is a sense in which such paradoxical 'involved detachment' in pastoral care embodies the characteristics of the clown, jester or fool. Heije Faber's classic discussion of the image of the clown as a model for pastoral care in the hospital expresses this. He describes how both the clown and the hospital chaplain experience a tension between being part of a team and being in isolation.[19] In the model of pastoral friendship that we have discussed here, the pastoral carer seeks to establish a shared sense of humanity yet also maintains a sense of perspective with the use of humour, for the sake of both parties in the pastoral relationship. Clowning is thus a part of pastoral befriending. Such humour enables a stepping back, not from the other person but from the circumstances that could otherwise overpower the possibilities of sustained care.

Living hope – living imaginatively

A second important theme in this book that has wider implications for Christian ministry in other contexts is the use of the
imagination. It has been argued that a hopeful perspective is
sustained when we imagine how things can and will be different. This adds to a growing recognition of the importance of the
imagination within practical theology. Two particular examples are worth citing here, for reasons that will subsequently
become apparent. First, it is increasingly acknowledged that
theological education would be deeply enriched were a more
serious focus given to the nurturing of the imagination. Anne
Tomlinson sets out some of the mounting concerns that exist
among theological tutors. She describes a 'dumbing down of
creativity' as ministerial students, often under pressure to complete written assignments, have a tendency to eschew the arts:

> Ceasing to be fed by music, film and literature, their imagina-
> tions become dessicated. Sermons which once had been
> sparked by scenes from films become more intellectual and
> cerebral, pastoral encounters more ponderous and laboured,
> prayer more full of Edwin Muir's 'fleshless word'. In short,
> there is a deskilling of intuition.

Tomlinson calls for a rediscovery of the imagination as a vital
part of the process of formation in ministry. As long as we
confine the imagination to the enjoyment of aesthetics and
compartmentalize such things as 'leisure activities' – pursuits
that ministerial students find themselves having to put on hold
until they 'finish the course' – the formation process is impover-
ished of a true sense of theological 'vision'. If ministers are to be
really effective in discerning God in the aesthetics of everyday
life, and in helping others so to discern, a more holistic theological education is called for – one that actively seeks to cultivate the imagination. In Tomlinson's words, ministers should
be trained to 'stand and stare'.[20]

A second example of the growing recognition given by

practical theology to the importance of the imagination has to do with *preaching*. Thomas Troeger's *Imagining a Sermon* may be highlighted here. Troeger challenges the popular notion that the imagination and reality are opposites and expounds the 'constructive role of the imagination in defining what is real and unreal'.[21] Imaginative preaching is that which enables congregations to engage with the images set before them by the preacher and so imagine for themselves. Then listeners do not simply 'hear sermons' – they personally encounter the reality that is being presented. Troeger writes, 'I will not cheat the congregation by handing them a souvenir from my trip on the river when I can take them along on the voyage and let them feel the current and the water for themselves.'[22] But just how might a preacher become more imaginative? Troeger suggests:

> The imaginative process can be compared to the art of sailing a boat: We cannot make the wind blow, but we can trim the sails and tend the helm. We cannot compel the Spirit to fill our imaginations with wind and fire, but we can practice those disciplines of prayer and thought that will open us to God's revelations . . . The primary principle from which all the others are derived is that we are attentive to what is.[23]

One thing in particular unites Tomlinson and Troeger in the importance they give to the use of the imagination. In both theological formation and in preaching, imagining is not to be simply regarded as a useful appendix that would enhance and enrich ministry in different ways. Rather, the imagination is really at the very core of Christian being. Only when we can 'stand and stare' and 'be attentive to what is', are we likely to grow as Christians and become more deeply rooted in an authentically Christian spirituality. In her discussion of the imagination in Christian spirituality, morality and ministry, Kathleen Fischer describes the imagination as the 'inner rainbow' – the bow of prismatic colours that is produced as the human imaginative capacity reflects and refracts the light of the sacred in the midst of the secular. She suggests, 'As ministers, we preach, teach, counsel, and celebrate', and through these things 'Every minister must be a tender of the inner rainbow'.[24]

In this book it has been argued that the cultivation of the imagination lies at the heart of the process of hoping. As Lynch says, 'Hope imagines . . . it is always imagining what is not yet seen, or a way out of difficulty, or a wider perspective of life or thought.'[25] Now we can take this further and affirm the foundational status of the hopeful imagination for all Christian ministry in the very widest sense. In response to Tomlinson we may suggest that those who are trained to minister imaginatively are also likely to be better placed to minister in hope. In response to Troeger we may suggest that those who preach imaginatively are also better placed to preach hope more effectively. And in response to Fischer, as well as Tomlinson and Troeger, we may suggest that those who recognize the centrality of the imagination in Christian spirituality and who thus tend to the imagination in order to grow spiritually are better placed to become more essentially hopeful in their very being. In short, living hope is about *living imaginatively*.

Worship is especially pertinent to the cultivation of the imagination. It should be emphasized that while we may need to 'stand and stare', 'be attentive to what is' and tend to 'the inner rainbow' as individuals, Christians are also called to imagine *collectively* in corporate worship, coming together as the 'gathered community of hope'. Apart from anything else, an individual imagination that develops in isolation from the wider Christian fellowship is in danger of assuming an unbridled authority of its own, drifting away from the narrative of cross and resurrection that is the very basis of Christian hope. An imagination that takes leave of the collective Christian story of salvation may be a hopeful one, but it cannot claim to be Christian. And when God is no longer afforded absolute status as the one who is truly and ultimately hoped *in*, hope risks forfeiting its imaginative nature only to become *imaginary*.

As Christians worship together imaginatively, the resurrection future promised by God is envisioned collectively. It is a corporate act of the imagination because it is rooted in the one unifying cross and resurrection dialectic of Christ. This is the cross that engages with our present suffering and the resurrection that points us to the future transformation of the body, enabling us to live in hopeful anticipation of it now as we 'body forth' in hope. But how might worship be truly imaginative? Furthermore, how might we strive to imagine the resurrection future in worship in a way that affirms the presence of God *now*? We may recall from Chapter 3 the charge levied against Moltmann that he polemically champions a 'God of tomorrow', but in so doing downplays the reality of the 'God of today'. How might the God who promises the future resurrection that we imagine in hope be worshipped as the God who is encountered here and now?

We may respond to these questions by simply clarifying what it actually means to hope imaginatively in God. In many ways, the imagination is no stranger in our contemporary cultural climate. The tragedy is that its use is generally confined to the *simulation* of experience as personal fulfilment is pursued through private consumption of media such as the internet, satellite television and computer games. We may recall Bauckham and Hart's analysis, considered in Chapter 5: this is a culture that has sold out to the escapism of virtual reality. Opium is the religion of postmodernity. Children are deprived of imaginative play as they are given electronic toys that do the imagining for them, while teenagers assume false identities in internet chat rooms, entering a world of artificial social interaction in which personal and genuine human encounters never really take place. The imagination has a major part to play in this, but only in a contrived, manipulated way that immerses the individual in their private fantasy and disengages them from the challenge of real life in the real world. In short, there is plenty of simulation to hand, bidding the imagination to indulge itself and so forget about the realities of life and death for a while. The truly hopeful imagination, on the other hand, cares not for simulation but engages in *stimulation*. The one who imagines in hope is the one who dares to stare reality in the face and envisage how it might be different.

To hope imaginatively in God means not only to imagine how things might be *different*, but how they may be *transformed*. To hope in God for resurrection means to allow the imagination to envision this bodily life healed and made whole to perfection. Such a transformation can only be imagined in this present life, for it has not grasped perfection yet. But in daring to hope in this way, the imagination will not content itself with the self-indulgent distractions of simulation. Instead, it is characterized by a profound stimulation, a sense of vision that urges life to be lived in anticipation of the transformation that is hoped for. Christian worship that is truly imaginative in this way, and that unreservedly affirms the 'God of today' as much as the 'God of tomorrow', is worship that is noticeably stimulating. Such worship envisions the resurrection future in God, and as that future is hoped *for* and striven *towards*, so God is encountered in the here and now as the one who is hoped *in*. But what might some of the features of such worship be?

First, worship becomes stimulating when it bears *variety*. A fixed diet breeds familiarity and predictability. Worship that follows unchanging forms and patterns can easily be reduced to a matter of routine. Now, there is arguably a rightful place for a degree of 'ritual' in Christian worship, as it provides a sense of continuity, and indeed identity, in the midst of the change and flux of life. However, the imagination can be inhibited if we become rigidly fixed on a particular set form of worship. Then not only do we cheat ourselves of the rich diversity that exists within the world Church, but we disallow our imaginations to venture into new areas. Worship that embraces a variety of music styles and that is open to experiencing diverse ways of praying is worship that is willing to expose the imagination to a sense of adventure. Of course, every individual and every local church is likely to have some form of preferred tradition, but such preference need not exclude a willingness to explore alternative ways of worshipping God. When the imagination is exposed to the unfamiliar in worship, it has opportunity to envision the future in God in new and different ways, stimulating worshippers to live hope afresh.

Second, truly imaginative worship is stimulating when it is *sensual*. Worship that incorporates a range of aesthetic experience such as art, dance, drama, film and poetry as well as a variety of music, and that gives expression through the use of symbols as well as words, is better placed to engage the senses more fully. Such worship has the power to stimulate because it can enable us to discover fresh ways of imagining the future in God. In symbols and through the use of the arts we may simultaneously depict that future, which can only be imagined, and present experience, which we actually know and relate to in the here and now. Holding the imagined future together with present experience in this way earths the resurrection promise that is hoped for in the life that is to be lived now. Such worship does not simply dream of 'pie in the sky when you die', but imagines the resurrection future so as to mobilize us in the task of daily living. Thus the 'God of tomorrow' is indeed the 'God of today', and the tension that is generated between present experience and the imagined future stimulates us to *live hope*.

Sustaining hope in ministry – rediscovering a hopeful perspective in pastoral care

In summary, the challenge of ministering in hope can be understood in terms of the calling to *live* hope. We have highlighted two things in particular as basic to this task: *friendship* as a model for pastoral relationships, and the cultivation of an essentially *imaginative* Christian spirituality. But how might we sustain this hopeful living? This book has focused on the palliative context, and as such the emphasis has been care rather than cure. Arguably, if pastoral ministry in any context is to really sustain hope, the very same emphasis is called for. After all, wherever we seek to nurture hope in life, there will be tragedy, suffering, struggle and disappointment in various forms. Ministry driven by the pursuit of quick-fixes, problem-shooting and solution-finding may yield a temporary surge of expectant anticipation, but disillusionment and despair will never be that far away when pastoral work lacks an ongoing commitment to

sustained care in the midst of life's messiness. The question is –
how might pastoral carers themselves sustain hope when
immersed in suffering and sadness? We have already given some
consideration to this concern above. It was suggested that a
kenotic readiness to 'let go', combined with a sense of perspective created by humour, may help to enable us to 'step back'
from the consuming potential of pastoral pain while staying
close in pastoral friendship to people who bear that pain first
hand. Now let us give reflection to the more general question of
how pastoral carers might sustain hope personally, faced not
only with the demands of 'letting go' in individual relationships,
but also the wider challenge of carrying the burden of ministry
year in, year out.

It may be helpful to elaborate on why pastoral ministry might
be considered burdensome. It should, of course, be pointed out
that before anything else, ministry is a tremendous privilege,
and the challenge of nurturing hope in others is a most fulfilling
and deeply satisfying prospect. But we cannot deny the reality
of stress and burnout among ministers today, which accounts
for the growing recognition given to the need for ongoing support in ministry such as spiritual direction, counselling, retreats
and mentoring.[26] Casualties perhaps occur most frequently
where ministers feel that they cannot keep up with the demands
and expectations that only seem to increase. Furthermore, the
'shepherding perspective' identified by Hiltner as the vantage
point of pastoral care[27] can actually denote a very lonely,
isolated position. That is because such a vantage point may
often also become something of a *focal* point whenever there is
conflict, frustration or pain within a local church or community. It is sometimes remarked that 'a week is a long time in
politics', such is the vast range of issues that politicians can
expect to engage with in a relatively short amount of time,
together with the roller coaster of circumstantial change and
emotional flux that may be encountered. Something similar
might be said of ministry. All manner of joys, pains, struggles,
conflicts, frustrations, acts of sin and estrangement, as well
as movements of repentance and reconciliation, can all be

experienced in a very short amount of time. As such, the 'shepherding perspective' can be the point where an enormous quantity and diversity of emotional experience is compressed.

So how might the practical theology developed in this book enable men and women to sustain hope personally when ministry becomes burdensome? Any attempt to answer this question with an easy formula would probably lack credibility. Nevertheless, our practical theology of absolute hope in God for resurrection offers three themes in particular that are worth highlighting.

First, hoping in God for resurrection acknowledges *God alone* as absolute and looks to the future resurrection life *in* God and promised *by* God as ultimate. That is especially pertinent when the pastoral heaviness and intensity of the 'shepherding perspective' threatens to overpower and consume us, for then we may be tempted to afford ultimate status to the present moment. When we feel engulfed by the immediacy of current circumstances we may be lured into believing that the 'now' is all there is. But daring to hope in God for resurrection means refusing to see the present as ultimate, despite all its intensity. Though we remain in the present and must face the challenges that we encounter here and now, as we hope in God we set our sights on the future promise that is truly ultimate, and present burdens, in all their weight, are put in perspective. Confessing God as the only absolute and hoping in God for the resurrection promised through the cross and resurrection dialectic of Jesus thus relativizes the power with which the present can threaten us. This relativizing force of the Christian vision is expressed in Charles' Wesley's hymn:

> Jesus – the name high over all,
> In hell, or earth, or sky!
> Angels and men before it fall,
> And devils fear and fly.

Second, hoping in God for resurrection enables us to be-hold present circumstance in all its brokenness, mess, chaos, confusion and devastation, and yet see beyond those things. The resurrection vision depicts present reality in its future state, raised and transformed. Through the lens of such hope we encounter things not simply as they presently appear – rather we discern what they may become. Like Ezekiel, hope empowers us to look upon a valley of dry bones and see a living people. That does not simply mean the recognition of the potential that resides in people and in situations. Hope in God is more profound than optimism, which merely stresses whatever positives might be found in the midst of negativity. Ezekiel's prophetic vision was a gift of God's grace, by which he was enabled to discern, in hope, God's future transformation of an otherwise hopeless present reality.[28] Hope in God is not depleted of its power even when the last remaining inherent possibilities lying dormant in the present cease to exist. Resurrection hope may be found even in the midst of crucifixion, for it is precisely in and through that dialectic that God's promise to us has been made.

Third, because it is God in whom we hope for resurrection, a key principle for sustaining hope in ministry is to *let God be God*. In this book it has been argued that hoping in God is not passive – indeed there is a rightful place for the fighting spirit of protest and resistance in Christian hope. But these active dynamics are located within and defined by a spirituality that is essentially kenotic. We are mobilized into action because of a deeper courage to accept the reality of death and to 'let go', for our hope is in the coming God (*adventus*). We do not hope to 'arise' from death but to be raised by God in the resurrection – it is by the power of God's promise alone that resurrection hope is brought into being. Thus if we are to really *live* hope, we must let God be God, and accept our human limitations. When we do, the intensity of present circumstance is stripped of its all-consuming power over us as our vision is extended beyond our human emotions to the God in whom we hope.

The struggle to sustain hope in ministry could be described in terms of the experience of tears. While the shedding of tears has a certain cathartic value and can play an important part in the process of emotional healing, tears themselves distort, blur and obscure our vision. When ministry becomes burdensome, the 'shepherding perspective' can be limited in just this sort of way. As with tears, our eyes are flooded and we cannot see beyond that which is absorbing and consuming us. In the Bible there is no shortage of tears, but it is the eschatological vision of the Revelation to John that has the last word:

> And I heard a loud voice from the throne saying, 'See, the home of God is among mortals. He will dwell with them; they will be his peoples, and God himself will be with them; he will wipe every tear from their eyes. Death will be no more; . . . for the first things have passed away.' And the one who was seated on the throne said, 'See, I am making all things new.'[29]

Our hope is in the coming God who wipes away tears. Only at the resurrection will every last one be wiped away, and then shall our vision be made perfect as our life is transformed in God for all eternity. For now, we lay hold of that promise in hope. The tears have not yet stopped flowing, and if we are to minister in hope we must be ready to shed them. But as we *live* hope so we are sustained and empowered by the God whose transcendence enables us to look beyond the tears and see the resurrection promise.

Notes

1 1 Corinthians 15.12–17.
2 1 Corinthians 15.30–32, 58.
3 See Paul Halmos, *Faith of the Counsellors*, London: Constable, 1965.
4 Wilson, *A Coat of Many Colours*, p. 150.
5 Eric Berne, *Games People Play*, Middlesex: Penguin, 1964.
6 David Deeks, *Pastoral Theology: An Inquiry*, London: Epworth Press, 1987, pp. 172–3.
7 Deeks, *Pastoral Theology: An Inquiry*, p. 180.
8 E.g. Pattison, *A Critique of Pastoral Care*, pp. 8–9; Wilson, *A Coat of Many Colours*, p. 10; Deeks, *Pastoral Theology: An Inquiry*, pp. 252–3.

9 Campbell, *Rediscovering Pastoral Care*, chapter 3.

10 Seward Hiltner, *Preface to Pastoral Theology*, Nashville: Abingdon Press, 1958, p. 20.

11 Derek Tidball, *Skilful Shepherds* (2nd edition), Leicester: IVP, 1997, p. 54.

12 Rumbold, *Helplessness and Hope*, p. 45.

13 Rumbold, *Helplessness and Hope*, pp. 46–7ff.

14 Alastair Campbell, *Paid to Care? The Limits of Professionalism in Pastoral Care*, London: SPCK, 1985, p. 4.

15 Wesley Carr, *The Pastor as Theologian: The Integration of Pastoral Ministry, Theology and Discipleship*, London: SPCK, 1989, pp. 85–8. Italics original.

16 Riem, *Stronger Than Death*, p. 26.

17 Rowan Williams, *Christianity and the Ideal of Detachment – 1988 Frank Lake Memorial Lecture*, Oxford: Clinical Theology Association Lingdale Papers, 1989, pp. 10f.

18 Pattison, *A Critique of Pastoral Care*, pp. 191–2.

19 Heije Faber, *Pastoral Care in the Modern Hospital*, ET (trans. Hugo de Waal), London: SCM Press, 1971, pp. 81ff.

20 Anne Tomlinson, 'Training God's Spies: Developing the imagination in theological formation', *Contact Monograph 11*, 2001, pp. 4, 3.

21 Thomas Troeger, *Imagining a Sermon*, Nashville: Abingdon Press, 1990, p. 100.

22 Troeger, *Imagining a Sermon*, p. 26.

23 Troeger, *Imagining a Sermon*, p. 15.

24 Kathleen Fischer, *The Inner Rainbow: The Imagination in Christian Life*, New York: Paulist Press, 1983, p. 153.

25 Lynch, *Images of Hope*, p. 23.

26 Nick Helm and Philip Allin, eds., *Finding Support in Ministry*, Grove Pastoral Series 90, 2002.

27 Hiltner, *Preface to Pastoral Theology*, p. 20.

28 Ezekiel 37.1–14.

29 Revelation 21.3–5a.

Index